FUNDAMENTAL OF POLITICAL SOCIOLOGY

FUNDAMENTAL OF POLITICAL SOCIOLOGY

Balwant Mehta

CYBER TECH PUBLICATIONS
4264/3, Ansari Road, Daryaganj, New Delhi-110002 (India)
Ph.: 011-23244078, 011-43559448 Fax: 011-23280028
E-Mail: cyberpublicationsdelhi@yahoo.com
Website: www.cybertechpublications.com

FUNDAMENTAL OF POLITICAL SOCIOLOGY

Balwant Mehta

First Edition 2010

Published by :

G.S. Rawat for **Cyber Tech Publications**

4264/3, Ansari Road, Daryaganj, New Delhi-110002 (India)

Ph.: 011-23244078, 011-43559448 Fax: 011-23280028

E-Mail: cyberpublicationsdelhi@yahoo.com

Website: www.cybertechpublications.com

Printed at: Asian Offset Printers, Delhi-53

Preface

This is an introductory book to the major themes and debates in political sociology—an incredibly diverse field. In this book, we will explore political sociology as the study of the nexus of power relations between state and society. In examining the constellation of actors and institutions within which these relations reside, we will ask some fundamental questions such as what is power? Where does it exist? What change, if any, can it generate? For whom or what does it serve? For what purpose or goals? We will investigate these questions as we critically engage both theoretical and empirical works. Given limited time and wide breadth of the field, the goal of the course is not to make you experts in any given subfield. Rather, my expectation is that you will develop a critical understanding of the theoretical underpinnings of power relations between state and society. In particular, my hope is that you will gain insight into how to ask incisive questions in political sociology. Towards that purpose, we will spend the most time examining "the state" – by which I mean we will consider what the state is, how it developed, and critical challenges to these interpretations – particularly from gender and race and ethnicity scholars. We will then follow with important subfields, including studies of nationalism, democracy, revolutions, social movements, political organization, and civic participation.

The conservative approach to the study of political science with the main focus of state government legal institutions and structures has undergone a tremendous change. Political science has become more akin to sociology psychology economics geography history women studies anthropology and other social sciences. The writings of Karl Marx Max Weber have contributed to the development of the political sociology. The inter change and interaction between political science and sociology has resulted in the development of a new term called political sociology. Attempts have been made in this book to make a lucid presentation of very complicated aspects political system political development political socialisation structural functional approach political modernisation evolution of political sociology relationship between political system and other systems and many other concepts in a simple and lucid style. Besides discussing the subject in its general and wider perspective the author have laid particular emphasis upon the Indian situations concerning these concepts. While the theoretical discussion is based upon matter drawn from standard reference books details have been worked out with the help of research journals and data available in magazines and newspapers.

—Author

Contents

1

The Study of Society

Perhaps the great question which sociology seeks to answer is this question which we have put at the beginning. Just as biology seeks to answer the question "What is life?"; zoology, "What is an animal?"; botany, "What is a plant?"; so sociology seeks to answer the question "What is society?" or perhaps better, "What is association?" Just as biology, zoology, and botany cannot answer their questions until those sciences have reached their full and complete development, so also sociology cannot answer the question "What is society?" until it reaches its final development.

Nevertheless, some conception or definition of society is necessary for the beginner, for in the scientific discussion of social problems we must know first of all what we are talking about. We must understand in a general way what society is, what sociology is, what the relations are between sociology and other sciences, before we can study the social problems of to-day from a sociological point of view. The word "society" is used scientifically to designate the reciprocal relations between individuals. More exactly, and using the term in a concrete sense, a society is any group of individuals who have more or less conscious relations to each other. We say conscious relations because it is not necessary that these relations be specialized into industrial, political, or ecclesiastical relations. Society is constituted by the mental interaction of individuals and exists wherever two or three individuals have reciprocal conscious relations to each other. Dependence upon a common economic environment, or the mere contiguity in space is not sufficient to constitute a society. It is the interdependence in function on the mental side, the contact and overlapping of our inner selves, which makes possible that form of collective life which we call society. Plants and lowly types of organisms do not constitute true societies, unless it can be shown that they have some degree of mentality.

On the other hand, there is no reason for withholding the term "society" from many animal groups. These animal societies, however, are very different in many respects from human society, and are of interest to us only as certain of their forms throw light upon human society. We may dismiss with a word certain faulty conceptions of society. In some of the older sociological writings the word society is often used as nearly synonymous with the word nation. Now, a nation is a body of people politically organized into an independent government, and it is manifest that it is only one of many forms of human society. Another conception of society, which some have advocated, is that it is synonymous with the cultural group. That is, a society is any group of people that have a common civilization, or that are bearers of a certain type of culture. In this case Christendom, for example, would constitute a single society. Cultural groups no doubt are, again, one of the forms of human society, but only one among many. Both the cultural group and the nation are very imposing forms of society and hence have attracted the attention of social thinkers very often in the past to the neglect of the more humble forms. But it is evident that all forms of association are of equal interest to the sociologist, though, of course, this is not saying that all forms are of equal practical importance.

Any form of association, or social group, which may be studied, if studied from the point of view of origin and development, whether it be a family, a neighborhood group, a city, a state, a trade union, or a party, will serve to reveal many of the problems of sociology. The natural or genetic social groups, however, such as the family, the community, and the nation, serve best to exhibit sociological problems. In this text we shall make particular use of the family, as the simplest and, in many ways, the most typical of all the forms of human association, to illustrate concretely the laws and principles of social development. Through the study of the simple and primary forms of association the problems of sociology can be much better attacked than through the study of society at large, or association in general. From what has been said it may be inferred that society as a scientific term means scarcely more than the abstract term association, and this is correct. Association, indeed, may be regarded as the more scientific term of the two; at any rate it indicates more exactly what the sociologist deals with. A word may be said also as to the meaning of the word social. The sense in which this word will generally be used in this text is that of a collective adjective, referring to all that pertains to or relates to society in any way. The word social, then, is much broader than the words industrial, political, moral, religious, and embraces them all; that is, social phenomena are all phenomena which involve the interaction of two or more individuals. The word social, then, includes the economic, political, moral, religious, etc., and must not be thought of as something set in opposition to, for instance, the industrial or the political.

SOCIETY AND ITS PRODUCTS

Beneath all the forms and processes of human society lies the fact of association itself. Industry, government, and civilization itself must be regarded as expressions of collective human life rather than vice versa. Industry, for example, is one side or aspect of man's social life, and must not be mistaken for society itself. Industry, government, religion, education, art, and the like, are all products of the social life of man. Among these coordinate expressions of collective human life, industry, being concerned with the satisfying of the material needs of men, is perhaps fundamental to the rest. But this must not lead to the mistaken view that the social life of man can be interpreted completely through his industrial life; for, as has just been said, beneath industry and all other aspects of man's collective life lies the biological and psychological fact of association. This is equivalent to saying that industry itself must be interpreted in terms of the biology and psychology of human association. In other words, industrial problems, political problems, educational problems, and the like must be viewed from the collective or social standpoint rather than simply as detached problems by themselves. We must understand the biological and psychological aspects of man's social life before we can understand its special phases.

THE ORIGIN OF SOCIETY

From the definition of society that we have given it is evident that society is something which springs from the very processes of life itself. It is not something which has been invented or planned by individuals. Life, in its higher forms at least, could not exist without association. From the very beginning the association of the sexes has been necessary for reproduction and for the care and rearing of offspring, and it has been not less necessary for the procuring of an adequate food supply and for protection against enemies. From the association necessary for reproduction has sprung family life and all the altruistic institutions of human society, while from the association for providing food supply have sprung society's industrial institutions. Neither society nor industry, therefore, has had a premeditated, reflective origin, but both have sprung up spontaneously from the needs of life and both have developed down to the present time at least with but little premeditated guidance. It is necessary that the student should understand at the outset that social organization is not a fabrication of the human intellect to any great degree, and the old idea that individuals who existed independently of society came together and deliberately planned a certain type of social organization is utterly without scientific validity. The individual and society are correlatives. We have no knowledge of individuals apart from society or society apart from individuals. What we do know is that human life everywhere is a collective or associated life, the individual being on the one hand largely an expression of the social life surrounding him and on the other hand society being largely an expression of individual character. The reasons for these assertions will appear later as we develop our subject.

What is Sociology?

The science which deals with human association, its origin, development, forms, and functions, is sociology. Briefly, sociology is a science which deals with society as a whole and not with its separate aspects or phases. It attempts to formulate the laws or principles which govern social organization and social evolution. This means that the main problems of sociology are those of the organization of society on the one hand and the evolution of society on the other. These words, organization and evolution, however, are used in a broader sense in sociology than they are generally used. By organization we mean any relation of the parts of society to each other. By evolution we mean, not necessarily change for the better, but orderly change of any sort. Sociology is, therefore, a science which deals with the laws or principles of social organization and of social change. Put in more exact terms this makes sociology, as we said at the beginning, the science of the origin, development, structure, and function of the forms of association. We may pass over very rapidly certain faulty conceptions of sociology.

The first of these is that it is the study of social evils and their remedies. This conception is faulty because it makes sociology deal primarily with the abnormal rather than the normal conditions in society, and secondly, it is to be criticized because it makes sociology synonymous with scientific philanthropy. It is rather the science of philanthropy, which is an applied science resting upon sociology, that studies social evils and their remedies. This is not saying, of course, that sociology does not consider social evils, but that it considers them as incidents in the normal processes of social evolution rather than as its special matter.

A second conception of sociology which is to be dismissed as inadequate is the conception that it is the science of social phenomena. This conception is not incorrect, but is somewhat vague, as there are manifestly other sciences of social phenomena, such as economics and political science. Such a conception of sociology would make it include everything in human society. A third faulty conception is that it is the science of human institutions.

This is faulty because it again is too narrow. An institution is a sanctioned form of human association, while sociology deals with the ephemeral and unsanctioned forms, such as we see in the phenomena of mobs, crazes, fads, fashions, and crimes, as well as with the sanctioned forms. A fourth conception which might be criticized is that sociology is the science of social organization. This makes sociology deal with the laws or principles of the relations of individuals to one another, and of institutions to one another. It is to be criticized as faulty because it fails to emphasize the evolution of those relations.

All science is now evolutionary in spirit and in method and believes that things cannot be understood except as they are understood in their genesis and development. It would, therefore, perhaps be more correct to define sociology as the science of the evolution of human interrelations than to define it simply as the science of social organization.

The Problems of Sociology

The problems of sociology fall into two great classes; first, problems of the organization of society, and second, problems of the evolution of society. The problems of the organization of society are problems of the relations of individuals to one another and to institutions. Such problems are, for example, the influence of various elements in the physical environment upon the social organization; or, again, the influence of various elements in human nature upon the social order. These problems are, then, problems of society in a hypothetically stationary condition or at rest. For this reason Comte, the founder of modern sociology, called the division of sociology which deals with such problems Social Statics.

But the problems which are of most interest and importance in sociology are those of social evolution. Under this head we have the problem of the origin of society in general and also of various forms of association. More important still are the problems of social progress and social retrogression; that is, the causes of the advancement of society to higher and more complex types of social organization and the causes of social decline.

The former problem, social progress, is in a peculiar sense the central problem of sociology. The effort of theoretical sociology is to develop a scientific theory of social progress. The study of social evolution, then, that is, social changes of all sorts, as we have emphasized above, is the vital part of sociology; and it is manifest that only a general science of society like sociology is competent to deal with such a problem. Inasmuch as the problems of social evolution are problems of change, development, or movement in society, Comte proposed that this division of sociology be called Social Dynamics.

THE RELATIONS OF SOCIOLOGY TO OTHER SCIENCES

Relations to Biology and Psychology

In attempting to give a scientific view of social organization and social evolution, sociology has to depend upon the other natural sciences, particularly upon biology and psychology. It is manifest that sociology must depend upon biology, since biology is the general science of life, and human society is but part of the world of life in general.

It is manifest also that sociology must depend upon psychology to explain the interactions between individuals because these interactions are for the most part interactions between their minds. Thus on the one hand all social phenomena are vital phenomena and on the other hand nearly all social phenomena are mental phenomena. Every social problem has, in other words, its psychological and its biological sides, and sociology is distinguished from biology and psychology only as a matter of convenience.

The scientific division of labor necessitates that certain scientific workers concern themselves with certain problems. Now, the problems with which the biologist and the psychologist deal are not the problems of the organization and evolution of society. Hence, while the sociologist borrows his principles of interpretation from biology and psychology, he has his own distinctive problems, and it is this fact which makes sociology a distinct science.

Sociology is not so easily distinguished from the special social sciences like politics, economics, and others, as it is from the other general sciences. These sciences occupy the same field as sociology, that is, they have to do with social phenomena. But in general, as has already been pointed out, they are concerned chiefly with certain very special aspects or phases of the social life and not with its most general problems. If sociology, then, is dependent upon the other general sciences, particularly upon biology and psychology, it is obvious that its relation to the special sciences is the reverse, namely, these sciences are dependent upon sociology. This is only saying practically the same thing as was said above when we pointed out that industry, government, and religion are but expressions of human social life. In other words, sociology deals with the more general biological and psychological aspects of human association, while the special sciences of economics, politics, and the like, generally deal with certain products or highly specialized phases of society.

Relations to History

A word may be said about the relation of sociology to another science which also deals with human society in a general way, and that is history. History is a concrete, descriptive science of society which attempts to construct a picture of the social past. Sociology, however, is an abstract, theoretical science of society concerned with the laws and principles which govern social organization and social change.

In a sense, sociology is narrower than history inasmuch as it is an abstract science, and in another sense it is wider than history because it concerns itself not only with the social past but also with the social present. The facts of contemporary social life are indeed even more important to the sociologist than the facts of history, although it is impossible to construct a theory of social evolution without taking into full account all the facts available in human history, and in this sense history becomes one of the very important methods of sociology. Upon its evolutionary or dynamic side sociology may be considered a sort of philosophy of history; at least it attempts to give a scientific theory which will explain the social changes which history describes concretely.

Relations to Economics

Economics is that special social science which deals with the wealth-getting and wealth-using activities of man. In other words, it is concerned with the commercial and industrial activities of man. As has already been implied, economics must be considered one of the most important of the special social sciences, if not the most important. Yet it is evident that the wealth-getting and wealth-using activities of man are strictly an outgrowth of his social life, and that economics as a science of human industry must rest upon sociology.

Sometimes in the past the mistake has been made of supposing that economics dealt with the most fundamental social phenomena, and even at times economists have spoken of their science as alone sufficient to explain all social phenomena. It cannot be admitted, however, that we can explain social organization in general or social progress in terms of economic development. A theory of progress, for example, in which the sole causes of human progress were found in economic conditions would neglect political, religious, educational, and many other conditions.

Only a very one-sided theory of society can be built upon such a basis. Economics should keep to its own sphere of explaining the commercial and industrial activities of man and not attempt to become a general science dealing with social evolution. This is now recognized by practically all economists of standing, and the only question which remains is whether economics is independent of sociology or whether it rests upon sociology.

The view which has been presented thus far and which will be adhered to is that economics should rest upon sociology. That economics does rest upon sociology is shown by many considerations. The chief problem of theoretical economics is the problem of economic value. But economic value is but one sort of value which is recognized in society, moral and aesthetic values being other examples of the valuing process, and all values must express the collective judgment of some human group or other.

The problem of economic value, in other words, reduces itself to a problem in social psychology, and when this is said it is equivalent to making economics dependent upon sociology, for social psychology is simply the psychological aspect of sociology. Again, industrial organization and industrial evolution are but parts or phases of social evolution in general, and it is safe to say that industry, both in its organization and evolution, cannot be understood apart from the general conditions, psychological and biological, which surround society. Again, many non-economic forces continually obtrude themselves upon the student of industrial conditions, such as custom, invention, imitation, standards, ideals, and the like.

These are general social forces which play throughout all phases of human social life and so show the dependence of industry upon society in general, and, therefore, of economics upon sociology. Much more might be said in the way of concretely illustrating these statements, but the purpose of this text precludes anything but the briefest and most elementary statement of these theoretical facts.

Relations to Politics

We have already said that the state is one of the chief forms of human association. The science which treats of the state or of government is known as political science or politics. It is one of the oldest of the social sciences, having been more or less systematized by Aristotle. The problems of politics are those of the origin, nature, function, and development of government. It is manifest that politics, both on its practical and theoretical sides, has many close relations to sociology.

While the state or nation must not be confused with society in general, yet because the state is the most imposing, if not the most important, form of human association, the relations of politics and sociology must be very intimate. On the one hand, political scientists can scarcely understand the origin, nature, and proper functions of government without understanding more or less about the social life generally; and, on the other hand, the sociologist finds that one of the most important facts of human society is that of social control, or of authority. While political science deals only with the organized authority manifested in the state, which we call government, yet inasmuch as this is the most important form of social control, and inasmuch as political organization is one of the chief manifestations of social organization, the sociologist can scarcely deal adequately with the great problems of social organization and evolution without constant reference to political science.

An important branch of political science is jurisprudence, or the science of law. This, again, is closely related with sociology, on both its theoretical and practical sides. Law is, perhaps, the most important means of social control made use of by society, and the sociologist needs to understand something of the principles of law in order to understand the nature of the existing social order. On the other hand, the jurist needs to know the principles of social organization and evolution in general before he can understand the nature and purpose of law.

Relations to Ethics

Ethics is the science which deals with the right or wrong of human conduct. Its problems are the nature of morality and of moral obligation, the validity of moral ideals, the norms by which conduct is to be judged, and the like. While ethics was once considered to be a science of individual conduct it is now generally conceived as being essentially a social science. The moral and the social are indeed not clearly separable, but we may consider the moral to be the ideal aspect of the social.

This view of morality, which, for the most part, is indorsed by modern thought, makes ethics dependent upon sociology for its criteria of rightness or wrongness. Indeed, we cannot argue any moral question nowadays unless we argue it in social terms. If we discuss the rightness or wrongness of the drink habit we try to show its social consequences. So, too, if we discuss the rightness or wrongness of such an institution as polygamy we find ourselves forced to do so mainly in social terms.

This is not denying, of course, that there are religious and metaphysical aspects to morality,—these are not necessarily in conflict with the social aspects,—but it is saying that modern ethical theory is coming more and more to base itself upon the study of the remote social consequences of conduct, and that we cannot judge what is right or wrong in our complex society unless we know something of the social consequences. Ethics must be regarded, therefore, as a normative science to which sociology and the other social sciences lead up. It is, indeed, very difficult to separate ethics from sociology. It is the business of sociology to furnish norms and standards to ethics, and it is the business of ethics as a science to take the norms and standards furnished by the social sciences, to develop them, and to criticize them. This text therefore, will not attempt to exclude ethical implications and judgments from sociological discussions, because that would be futile and childish.

Relations to Education

Among the applied sciences, sociology is especially closely related to education, for education is not simply the art of developing the powers and capacities of the individual; it is rather the fitting of individuals for efficient membership, for proper functioning, in social life. On its individual side, education should initiate the individual into the social life and fit him for social service.

It should create the good citizen. On the social or public side, education should be the chief means of social progress. It should regenerate society, by fitting the individual for a higher type of social life than at present achieved. We must have a socialized education if our present complex civilization is to endure. Social problems touch education on every side, and, on the other hand, education must bear upon every social problem. It is evident, therefore, that sociology has a very great bearing upon the problems of education; and the teacher who comes to his task equipped with a knowledge of social conditions and of the laws and principles of social organization and evolution will find a significance and meaning in his work which he could hardly otherwise find.

Relations to Philanthropy

The great science which deals directly with the depressed classes in society and with their uplift may be called the science of philanthropy. It may be regarded as an applied department of sociology. The science of philanthropy is especially concerned with the prevention, as well as with the curative treatment, of dependency, defectiveness, and delinquency. That part which deals with the social treatment of the criminal class is generally called penology, while the subdivision which treats of dependents and defectives is generally known as "charities" or "charitology."

It is evident that there are very close relations between the science of philanthropy and sociology. The elimination of hereditary defects, the overcoming of the social maladjustment of individuals, and the correction of defective social conditions, the three great tasks of scientific philanthropy, all require great knowledge of human society. The social or philanthropic worker, therefore, requires thorough equipment in sociology that he may approach his tasks aright.

The Relation of Sociology to Socialism

Curiously enough sociology is often confused with socialism by those who pay but little attention to scientific matters. This comes from the fact that some of the adherents of socialism claim that socialism is a science. As a matter of fact, socialism is primarily a party program. It is the platform of a social and political party that has as the main tenet of its creed the abolition of private property in the means of production. Socialism, in other words, is a scheme to revolutionize the present order of society. It cannot claim to be a science in any sense, though it may rest upon theories which its adherents believe to be scientific. Sociology, on the other hand, is a science, and is concerned not with revolutionizing the social order, but with studying and understanding social conditions, especially the more fundamental conditions upon which social organization and social changes depend. As a science it aims simply at understanding society, at getting at the truth. It is no more related logically to socialism than to the platform of the Republican or the Democratic party.

The theories upon which revolutionary socialism rest may be proved or disproved by scientific sociology. It is perhaps too early to say finally whether sociology will pronounce the theoretical assumptions of socialism correct or incorrect; but so far as we can see it seems probable that the theories of social evolution advocated by the Marxian socialists at least will be pronounced erroneous.

In any case, there is no logical connection between sociology as a science and socialism as a program for social reconstruction. Nevertheless, there has been a close connection between sociology and socialism historically. It has been largely the agitations of the socialists and other radical social reformers which have called attention to the need of a scientific understanding of human society.

The socialists and other radical reformers, in other words, have very largely set the problem which sociology attempts to solve. Practically, moreover, the indictments and charges of the socialists and anarchists against the present social order have made necessary some study of that order to see whether these charges were well founded or not. In this sense sociology may be said to be a scientific answer to socialism, not in the sense that sociology is devoted to refuting socialism, but in the sense that sociology has been devoted very largely to inquiring into many of the theoretical assumptions which revolutionary socialism makes. The further relations of sociology to socialism will be taken up later.

Here we are only concerned to have the reader see that there is a sharp distinction between the sociological movement on the one hand, that is, the movement to obtain fuller and more accurate knowledge concerning human social life, and the socialist movement, the movement to revolutionize the present social and economic order.

Moreover, it may be remarked that while socialism seems to be mainly an economic program, it involves such total and radical reconstruction of social organization that in the long run the claims of socialism to a scientific validity must be passed upon by sociology rather than by economics.

THE RELATION OF SOCIOLOGY TO SOCIAL REFORM

From what has been said it is also evident that sociology must not be confused with any particular social reform movement or with the movement for social reform in general. Sociology, as a science, cannot afford to be developed in the interest of any social reform. Certain social reforms, sociology may give its approval to; others it may designate as unwise; but this approval or disapproval will be simply incidental to its discovery of the full truth about human social relations. This is not saying, of course, that social theory should be divorced from social practice, or that the knowledge which sociology and the other social sciences offer concerning human society has no practical bearing upon present social conditions.

On the contrary, while all science aims abstractly at the truth, all science is practical also in a deeper sense. No science would ever have been developed if it were not conceived that the knowledge which it discovers will ultimately be of benefit to man. All science exists, therefore, to benefit man, to enable him to master his environment, and the social sciences not less than the other sciences. The physical sciences have already enabled man to attain to a considerable mastery over his physical environment. When the social sciences have been developed it is safe to say that they will enable man not less to master his social environment. Therefore, while sociology and the special social sciences present as yet no program for action, aiming simply at the discovery of the abstract truth, they will undoubtedly in time bring about vast changes for the betterment of social conditions.

2

The Bearing of the Theory of Evolution Upon Social Problems

Since Darwin wrote his Origin of Species all the sciences in any way connected with biology have been profoundly influenced by his theory of evolution. It is important that the student of sociology, therefore, should understand at the outset something of the bearing of Darwin's theory upon social problems. We may note at the beginning, however, that the word evolution has two distinct, though related, meanings. First, it usually means Darwin's doctrine of descent; secondly, it is used to designate Spencer's theory of universal evolution. Let us note somewhat in detail what evolution means in the first of these senses.

THE DARWINIAN THEORY OF DESCENT

Darwin's theory of descent is the doctrine that all forms of life now existing or that have existed upon the earth have sprung from a few simple primitive types. According to this theory all forms of animals and plants have sprung from a few primitive stocks, though not necessarily one, because even in the beginning there may have existed a distinction at least between the plant and the animal types.

So far as the animal world is concerned, then, this theory amounts to the assertion of the kinship of all life. From one or more simple primitive unicellular forms have arisen the great multitude of multicellular forms that now exist. Popularly, Darwin's theory is supposed to be that man sprang from the apes, but this, strictly speaking, is a misconception. Darwin's theory necessitates the belief, not that man sprang from any existing species of ape, but rather that the apes and man have sprung from some common stock. It is equally true, however, that man and many other of the lower animals, according to this theory, have come from a common stock.

As was said above, the theory is not a theory of the descent of man from any particular animal type, but rather the theory of the kinship, the genetic relationship, of all animal species. It is evident that if we assume Darwin's theory of descent in sociology we must look for the beginnings of many peculiarly human things in the animal world below man. Human institutions, according to this theory, could not be supposed to have an independent origin, or human society in any of its forms to be a fact by itself, but rather all human things are connected with the whole world of animal life below man. Thus if we are, according to this theory, to look for the origin of the family, we should have to turn first of all to the habits of animals nearest man. This is only one of the many bearings which Darwin's theory has upon the study of social problems; but it is evident even from this that it revolutionizes sociology. So long as it was possible to look upon human society as a distinct creation, as something isolated, by itself in nature, it was possible to hold to intellectualistic views of the origin of human institutions.

But some one may ask: Why should the sociologist accept Darwin's theory? What proofs does it rest upon? What warrant has a student of sociology for accepting a doctrine of such far-reaching consequences? The reply is, that biologists, generally, during the last fifty years, after a careful study of Darwin's arguments and after a careful examination of all other evidence, have come substantially to agree with him. There is no great biologist now living who does not accept the essentials of the doctrine of descent. Five lines of proof may be offered in support of Darwin's theories, and it may be well for us, as students of sociology, briefly to review these.

(1) The homologies or similarities of structure of different animals. There are very striking similarities of structure between all the higher animals. Between the ape and man, for example, there are over one hundred and fifty such anatomical homologies; that is, in the ape we find bone for bone, and muscle for muscle, corresponding to the structure of the human body. Even an animal so remotely related to man as the cat has many more resemblances to man in anatomical structure than dissimilarities. Now, the meaning of these anatomical homologies, biologists say, is that these animals are genetically related, that is, they had a common ancestry at some remote period in the past.

(2) The presence of vestigial organs in the higher animals supplies another argument for the belief in common descent. In man, for example, there exist over one hundred of these vestigial or rudimentary organs, as the vermiform appendix, the pineal gland, and the like. Many of these vestigal organs, which are now functionless in man, perform functions in lower animals, and this is held to show that at some remote period in the past they also functioned in man's ancestors.

(3) The facts of embryology seem to point to the descent of the higher types of animals from the lower types. The embryo or fetus in its development seems to recapitulate the various stages through which the species has passed. Thus the human embryo at one stage of its development resembles the fish; at another stage, the embryo of a dog; and for

a long time it is impossible to distinguish between the human embryo and that of one of the larger apes. These embryological facts, biologists say, indicate genetic relation between the various animal forms which the embryo in its different stages simulates.

(4) The fossil remains of extinct species of 'animals are found in the earth's crust which are evidently ancestors of existing species. Until the doctrine of descent was accepted there was no way of explaining the presence of these fossil remains of extinct animals in the earth's crust. It was supposed by some that the earth had passed through a series of cataclysms in which all forms of life upon the earth had been many times destroyed and many times re-created. It is now demonstrated, however, that these fossils are related to existing species, and sometimes it is possible to trace back the evolution of existing forms to very primitive forms in this way. For example, it is possible to trace the horse, which is now an animal with a single hoof, walking on a single toe, back to an animal that walked upon four toes and had four hoofs and was not much larger than a fox. It is not so generally known that it is also possible to trace man back through fossil human remains that have been discovered in the earth's crust to the time when he is apparently just emerging from some apelike form. The latest discovery of the fossil remains of man made by Dr. Dubois in Java in 1894 shows a creature with about half the brain capacity of the existing civilized man and with many apelike characteristics. Thus we cannot except even man from the theory of evolution and suppose that he was especially created, as Alfred Russel Wallace, Darwin's contemporary and colaborer, and others, have supposed.

(5) The last line of argument in favor of the belief that all existing species have descended from a few simple primitive forms is found in the fact of the variation of animals through artificial selection under domestication. For generations breeders have known that by carefully selecting the type of animal or plant which they have desired, it is possible to produce approximately that type. Thus have originated all the breeds or varieties of domestic plants and animals. Now, Darwin conceived that nature also exercises a selection by weeding out those individuals that are not adapted to their environment. In other words, nature, though unconscious, selects in a negative way the stronger and the better adapted. Animals vary in nature as well as under domestication from causes not yet well understood. The variations that were favorable to survival, Darwin argued, would secure the survival, through the passing on of these variations by heredity of the better adapted types of plants and animals. The natural process of weeding out the inferior or least adapted through early death, or through failure to reproduce, Darwin called "natural selection", and likened it in its effect upon organisms to the artificial selection which breeders consciously use to secure types of plants or animals that they desire. The only great addition to Darwin's theories which has been made since he wrote is that of the Dutch botanist, Hugo de Vries, who has shown that the variations which are fruitful for the production of new species are probably great or discontinuous variations, which he terms

"mutations," instead of the small fluctuating variations which Darwin thought were probably most important in the production of new species. De Vries' theory in no way affects the doctrine of descent, nor does it take away from the importance of natural selection in fixing the variations. Darwin's theory, therefore, stands in all of its essentials to-day unquestioned by men of science, and it must be assumed by the student of sociology in any attempt to explain social evolution.

SPENCER'S THEORY OF UNIVERSAL EVOLUTION

A second meaning given to the word evolution is that which Spencer popularized in his First Principles. This is a philosophical theory of the universe which asserts that not only have species of animals come to be what they are through a process of development, but everything whatsoever that exists, from molecules of matter to stars and planets. It is the view that the universe is in a process of development. Evolution in this wider sense includes all existing things whatsoever, while evolution in the sense of Darwin's theory is confined to the organic world. While the theory that all things existing have through a process of orderly change come to be what they are, is a very old one, yet it was undoubtedly Spencer's writings which popularized the theory, and to Spencer we also owe the attempt in his Synthetic Philosophy to trace the working of evolution in all the different realms of phenomena. The belief in universal evolution which Spencer popularized has also come to be generally accepted by scientific and philosophical thinkers. While Spencer's particular theories of evolution may not be accepted, some form of universal evolution is very generally believed in. The thought of evolution now dominates all the sciences,—physical, biological, psychological, and sociological. It is evident that the student of society, if he accepts fully the modern scientific spirit, must also assume evolution in this second or universal sense.

The Different Phases of Universal Evolution

It may be well, in order to correlate our knowledge of social evolution with knowledge in general, to note the different well-marked phases of universal evolution.

(1) *Cosmic Evolution.* This is the phase the astronomer and the geologist are particularly interested in. It deals with the evolution of worlds. In this phase we are dealing merely with physical matter, and it is supposed that the active principle which works in this phase of evolution is the attraction of particles of matter for one another. This leads to the condensation of matter into suns and their planets, and the geological evolution of the earth, for example. Laplace's nebular hypothesis is an attempt to give an adequate statement of the cosmic phase of evolution. While this hypothesis has been much criticized of late, in its essentials it seems to stand. We are not, however, as students of society, concerned with this phase of evolution.

(2) *Organic Evolution.* This is the phase of evolution with which Darwin dealt and which biology, as a science of evolution of living forms, deals with. The great merit of Darwin's

work was that he showed that the active principle in this phase of evolution is natural selection; that is, the extermination of the unadapted through death or through failure to reproduce. Types unsuited to their environment thus die before reproduction. The stronger and better fitted survive, and thus the type is raised. Natural selection may be regarded, then, as essentially the creative force in this phase of evolution.

(3) *The Evolution of Mind.* This might be included in organic evolution, but all organisms do not apparently have minds. It is evident that among animals those that would stand the best chance of surviving would not be simply those that have the strongest brute strength, but rather those that have the keenest intelligence and that could adapt themselves quickly to their environment, that could see approaching danger and escape it. Natural selection has, therefore, favored in the animal world the survival of those animals with the highest type of intelligence. It cannot be said, however, that natural selection is the only force which has created the mind in all its various expressions.

(4) *Social Evolution.* By social evolution we mean the evolution of groups, or, in strict accordance with our definition of society, groups of psychically interconnected individuals. Groups are to be found throughout the animal world, and it is in the human species, as we have already seen, that the highest types of association are found. This is not an accident. Association, or living together in groups, has been one of the devices by which animal species have been enabled to survive. It is evident that not only would intelligence help an animal to survive more than brute strength, but that ability to cooperate with one's fellows would also help in the same way. Consequently we find a degree of combination or cooperation almost at the very beginning of life, and it is without doubt through cooperation that man has become the dominant and supreme species upon the planet. Man's social instincts, in other words, have been perhaps even more important for his survival than his intelligence. The man who lies, cheats, and steals, or who indulges in other unsocial conduct sets himself against his group and places his group at a disadvantage as compared with other groups. Now, natural selection is continually operating upon groups as well as upon individuals, and the group which can command the most loyal, most efficient membership, and has the best organization, is, other things being equal, the group which survives. Natural selection is, then, active in social evolution as well as in general organic evolution. But the distinctive principle of social evolution is cooperation. In other words, it is sympathetic feeling, altruism, which has made the higher types of social evolution possible.

While the same factors are at work in the higher phases of evolution which are at work in the lower phases, yet it is evident that the higher phases have new and distinct factors. Sociology, being especially concerned with social evolution, has a new and distinct factor at work which we may call association, cooperation, or combination, and this it is which gives sociology its distinct place in the list of general sciences. Factors In Organic Evolution.—As has already been said, the factors which are at work in organic evolution generally are also at work in social evolution. We need, therefore, to note these factors carefully and to see how they are at work in human society as well as in the animal world below man. While these factors are not all of the factors which are at work in social evolution, still they are the primitive factors, and are, therefore, of fundamental importance. Let us see what these factors are.

(1) *The Multiplication of Organisms in Some Geometric Ratio through Reproduction.* It is a law of life that every species must increase so that the number of offspring exceeds the number of parents if the species is to survive. If the offspring only equal in number the parents, some of them will die before maturity is reached or will fail to reproduce, and so the species will gradually become extinct. Every species normally increases, therefore, in some geometric ratio. Now, this tendency to reproduce in some geometric ratio, which characterizes all living organisms, means that any species, if left to itself, would soon reach such numbers as to occupy the whole earth. Darwin showed, for example, that though the elephant is the slowest breeding of all animals, if every elephant lived its normal length of life (one hundred years) and to every pair were born six offspring, then, at the end of seven hundred years there would be nineteen million living elephants descended from a single pair. This illustration shows the enormous possibilities of any species reproducing in geometric ratio, as all species in order to survive must do. That this tendency to increase in some geometric ratio applies also to man is evident from all of the facts which we know concerning human populations. It is not infrequent for a people to double its numbers every twenty-five years. If this were continued for any length of time, it is evident that a single nation could soon populate the whole earth.

(2) *Heredity.* Heredity in organic evolution secures a continuity of the species or racial type. By heredity is meant the resemblance between parent and offspring. It is the law that like begets like. Offspring born of a species belong to that species, and usually resemble their parents more closely even than other members of the species. It is evident that heredity is at work also in human society as well as in the animal world. We do not expect that the children born of parents of one race, for example, will belong to another race. Racial heredity is one of the most significant facts of human society, and even family heredity counts in its influence far more than some have supposed.

(3) *Variation.* This factor in organic evolution means that no two individuals, even though born of the same parents, are exactly like each other. Neither are they of a type exactly between their two parents, as theoretically they should be, since inheritance is equal from both parents. Every new individual born in the organic world, while it resembles its parents and belongs to its species or race, varies within certain limits. This variation so runs through organic nature that we are told that there are no two leaves on a single tree exactly alike. The result of this variation, the causes of which are not yet well understood, is that some individuals vary in favorable directions, others in unfavorable directions. Some

are born strong, some weak; some inferior, some superior. It is evident that variation characterizes the human species quite as much as other species, and indeed the limits of variation are wider, probably, in the human species than in any other species. Man is the most variable of all animals, and human individuality and personality owe not a little of their distinctiveness to this fact.

(4) *The Struggle for Existence. Individuals in all species, as we have seen, are born in larger numbers than is necessary.* The result is that a competition is entered into between species and individuals within the species for place and for existence. This competition or struggle results in the dying out of the inferior, that is, of those who are not adapted to their environment. The gradual dying out of the inferior or unadapted through competition results in the survival of the superior or better adapted, and ultimately in the survival of the fittest or those most adapted. Thus the type is raised, and we have evolution through natural selection, that is, through the elimination of the unfit. Some have thought that this struggle for existence which is so evident in the animal world does not take place in human society. This, however, is a mistake. The struggle for existence in human society is not an unmitigated one, as it seems to be very often in the animal world, but it is nevertheless a struggle which has the same consequences. In the human world the competition, except in the lower classes, is not so much for food, as it is for position and for supremacy. But this struggle for place and power results in human society in the weak and inferior going to the wall, and therefore ultimately in their elimination. In all essential respects, then, the struggle for existence goes on in human society as it does in the animal world. This means that in society, as in the animal world, progress comes primarily through the elimination of unfit individuals. The unfit in human society, as we shall see, are especially those who cannot adapt themselves to their social environment. Progress in society, in a certain sense, waits upon death, as it does in all the rest of the animal world. Death is the means by which the stream of life is purged from its inferior and unfit elements.

(5) *Another Factor in Organic Evolution is Cooperation, or altruism, as we have already called it.* As Henry Drummond has said, this is the struggle not for one's own life but for the lives of others. Really, however, it is a device which enables a group of individuals to struggle more successfully with the adverse factors in their environment. Something of cooperation,—that is, a group of individuals carrying on a common life,—is found almost at the beginning of life, and, as we rise in the scale of animal creation, the amount of cooperation and of altruistic feelings which accompany it very greatly increases. Perhaps the chief source of this cooperation is to be found in the rearing of offspring. The family group, even in the lower animals, seems to be the chief source of altruism. At any rate, sympathetic or altruistic instincts grow up in all animals, probably chiefly through the necessities of reproduction. It is only in human social life that cooperation, or altruism, attains its full development. Human society is characterized by the protection it affords

to its weaker members, and in human society the natural process of eliminating the inferior often seems reversed. As Huxley has pointed out, human society tries to fit as many as possible to survive, and we may add, not only to survive, but to live well. Altruism and its resulting cooperation have come especially to characterize human social evolution.

To some extent this is due, no doubt, to the necessities of group survival; for only that nation, for example, can survive that can maintain the most loyal citizenship, the best institutions, and the largest spirit of self-sacrifice in its members. Human social groups, therefore, try to fit as many individuals as possible for the most efficient membership, and this necessitates caring for the temporarily weak, and also for the permanently incapacitated, in order that the sentiments of social solidarity may be strengthened to their utmost. It is evident, then, that all the factors at work in organic evolution are at work also in social evolution, though in some part modified and varying in degree. The struggle for existence in human society, for example, has been greatly modified from the condition in the early animal world, while cooperation, or altruism, is much more highly developed. Nevertheless, these factors of organic evolution are at work in social evolution and must be taken into full account by the student of social problems. Social evolution rests upon organic evolution.

SOME EFFECTS UPON INDUSTRY

These factors in organic evolution express themselves more or less in the industrial phase of human society. Thus, the first factor, the multiplication of organisms through reproduction in some geometric ratio, was first studied by Malthus, an economist in the beginning of the nineteenth century, and exclusively with reference to its effect upon economic conditions. Malthus perceived the tendency for human beings to multiply in some geometric ratio where food supply was sufficiently abundant, and argued from this that if better wages, and so a larger food supply, were given the lower classes, they would multiply so much more rapidly that worse poverty would result than before. There is no doubt that in certain classes of human society there is a tendency for population to press against food supply, and it is in these classes that the struggle for existence takes on its most animal-like forms. Again, the struggle for existence is continually illustrated in the world of human industry. Not only do individuals lose place and power because they are unadapted to their environment, but also economic groups, such as corporations, show the natural competition or struggle for existence sometimes in its most intense form.

The result in all cases is the dying out of the least adapted and the survival of the better adapted. Thus, through competition and the survival of the better adapted we secure in industry the evolution of higher types of industrial organization, industrial methods, and the like, just as higher types are secured in the same way in the animal world. Again, in economic matters, as in other social affairs, cooperation continually comes in to modify competition and to lift it to a higher plane. Just as the higher type of societies has been characterized by higher types of cooperation, so it is safe to say that the higher types of industry are characterized by higher types of cooperation. And while, as we shall see later, cooperation can never displace competition in industry any more than elsewhere in life, yet increasing cooperation characterizes the higher types of industry as well as the higher types of society. A word of caution is perhaps necessary against confusing the economic struggle as it exists in modern society with the natural struggle under primitive conditions. It is evident that in present society the economic struggle has been greatly changed in character from the primitive struggle, and therefore can no longer have the same results. Laws of inheritance, of taxation, and many other artificial economic conditions, have greatly interfered with the natural struggle. The rich and economically successful are therefore by no means to be confused with the biologically fit. On the contrary, many of the economically successful are such simply through artificial advantageous circumstances, and from the standpoint of biology and sociology they are often among the less fit, rather than the more fit, elements of society.

A BRIEF SURVEY OF SOCIAL EVOLUTION FROM THE BIOLOGICAL STANDPOINT

In order to sum up and make clear some of the principal applications to social evolution of the biological principles just stated we shall endeavor to state in a brief way some of the salient features of social evolution from the biological standpoint. From the very beginning there has been no such thing as unmitigated individual struggle among animals. Nowhere in nature does pure individualism exist in the sense that the individual animal struggles alone, except perhaps in a few solitary species which are apparently on the way to extinction.

The assumption of such a primitive individual struggle has been at the bottom of many erroneous views of human society. The primary conflict is between species. A secondary conflict, however, is always found between the members of the same species. Usually this conflict within the species is a competition between groups. The human species exactly illustrates these statements. Primitively its great conflict was with other species of animals. The supremacy of man over the rest of the animal world was won only after an age-long conflict between man and his animal rivals. While this conflict went on there was apparently but little struggle within the species itself.

The lowest groups of which we have knowledge, while continually struggling against nature, are rarely at war with one another. But after man had won his supremacy and the population of groups came to increase so as to encroach seriously upon food supply, and even on territorial limits of space, then a conflict between human groups, which we call war, broke out and became almost second nature to man.

It needs to be emphasized, however, that the most primitive groups are not warlike, but only those that have achieved their supremacy over nature and attained considerable size. In other words, the struggle between groups which we call war was occasioned very largely by numbers and food supply. To this extent at least war primitively arose from economic conditions, and it is remarkable how economic conditions have been instrumental in bringing about all the great wars of recorded human history. The conflict among human groups, which we call war, has had an immense effect upon human social evolution. Five chief effects must be noted.

(1) Intergroup struggle gave rise to higher forms of social organization, because only those groups could succeed in competition with other groups that were well organized, and especially only those that had competent leadership.

(2) Government, as we understand the word, was very largely an outcome of the necessities of this intergroup struggle, or war. As we have already seen, the groups that were best organized, that had the most competent leadership, would stand the best chance of surviving. Consequently the war leader or chief soon came, through habit, to be looked upon as the head of the group in all matters. Moreover, the exigencies and stresses of war frequently necessitated giving the war chief supreme authority in times of danger, and from this, without doubt, arose despotism in all of its forms. The most primitive tribes are republican or democratic in their form of government, but it has been found that despotic forms of government rapidly take the place of the primitive democratic type, where a people are continually at war with other peoples.

(3) A third result of war in primitive times was the creation of social classes. After a certain stage was reached groups tried not so much to exterminate one another as to conquer and absorb one another. This was, of course, after agriculture had been developed and slave labor had reached a considerable value. Under such circumstances a conquered group would be incorporated by the conquerors as a slave or subject class. Later, this enslaved class may have become partially free as compared with some more recently subjugated or enslaved classes, and several classes in this way could emerge in a group through war or conquest. Moreover, the presence of these alien and subject elements in a group necessitated a stronger and more centralized government to keep them in control, and this was again one way in which war favored a development of despotic governments. Later, of course, economic conditions gave rise to classes, and to certain struggles between the classes composing a people.

(4) Not only was social and political organization and the evolution of classes favored by intergroup struggle, but also the evolution of morality. The group that could be most efficiently organized would be, other things being equal, the group which had the most loyal and most self-sacrificing membership. The group that lacked a group spirit, that is, strong sentiments of solidarity and harmonious relations between its members, would be the group that would be apt to lose in conflict with other groups, and so its type would tend to be eliminated. Consequently in all human groups we find recognition of certain standards of conduct which are binding as between members of the same group. For example, while a savage might incur no odium through killing a member of another group, he was almost always certain to incur either death or exile through killing a member of his own group. Hence arose a group code of ethics founded very largely upon the

conceptions of kinship or blood relationship, which bound all members of a primitive group to one another.

(5) A final consequence of war among human groups has been the absorption of weaker groups and the growth of larger and larger political groups, until in modern times a few great nations dominate the population of the whole world. That this was not the primitive condition, we know from human history and from other facts which indicate the disappearance of a vast number of human groups in the past. The earth is a burial ground of tribes and natrons as well as of individuals. In the competition between human groups, only a few that have had efficient organization and government, loyal membership and high standards of conduct within the group, have survived. The number of peoples that have perished in the past is impossible to estimate. But we can get some inkling of the number by the fact that philologists estimate that for every living language there are twenty dead languages.

When we remember that a language not infrequently stands for several groups with related cultures, we can guess the immense number of human societies that have perished in the past in this intergroup competition. Even though war passes away entirely, nations can never escape this competition with one another. While the competition may not be upon the low and brutal plane of war, it will certainly go on upon the higher plane of commerce and industry, and will probably be on this higher plane quite as decisive in the life of peoples in future as war was in the past. While the primary struggle within the human species has been in the historic period between nations and races, this is not saying, of course, that struggle and competition have not gone on within these larger groups.

On the contrary, as has already been implied, a continual struggle has gone on between classes, first perhaps of racial origin, and later of economic origin. Also there is within the nation a struggle between parties and sects, and sometimes between "sections" and communities. Usually, however, the struggle within the nation is a peaceful one and does not come to bloodshed. Again, within each of these minor groups that we have mentioned struggle and competition in some modified form goes on between its members. Thus within a party or class there is apt to be a struggle or competition between factions. There is, indeed, no human group that is free from struggle or competition between its members, unless it be the family. The family seems to be so constituted that normally there is no competition between its members,—at least, there is good ground tor believing that competition between the members of a family is to be considered exceptional, or even abnormal. From what has been said it is evident that competition and cooperation are twin principles in the evolution of social groups. While competition characterizes in the main the relation between groups, especially independent political groups, and while cooperation characterizes in the main the relation of the members of a given group to one another, still competition and cooperation are correlatives in practically every phase of the social life. Some degree of competition, for example, has to be maintained by every group between its members if it is going to maintain high standards of efficiency or of loyalty. If there were no competition with respect to the matters that concern the inner life of groups, it is evident that the groups would soon lose efficiency in leadership and in membership and would sooner or later be eliminated. Consequently society, from certain points of view, presents itself to the student at the present time as a vast competition, while from other standpoints it presents itself as a vast cooperation. It follows from this that competition and cooperation are both equally important in the life of society. It has been a favorite idea that competition among human beings should be done away with, and that cooperation should be substituted to take its place entirely. It is evident, however, that this idea is impossible of realization. If a social group were to check all competition between its members, it would stop thereby the process of natural selection or of the elimination of the unfit, and, as a consequence, would soon cease to progress. If some scheme of artificial selection were substituted to take the place of natural selection, it is evident that competition would still have to be retained to determine who were the fittest.

A society that would give positions of trust and responsibility to individuals without imposing some competitive test upon them would be like a ship built partially of good and partially of rotten wood,—it would soon go to pieces. This leads us to emphasize the continued necessity of selection in society. No doubt natural selection is often a brutal and wasteful means of eliminating the weak in human societies, and no doubt human reason might devise superior means of bringing about the selection of individuals which society must maintain. To some extent it has done this through systems of education and the like, which are, in the main, selective processes for picking out the most competent individuals to perform certain social functions. But the natural competition, or struggle between individuals, has not been done away with, especially in economic matters, and it is evidently impossible to do away with it until some vast scheme of artificial selection can take its place. Such a scheme is so far in the future that it is hardly worth talking about.

The best that society can apparently do at the present time is to regulate the natural competition between individuals, and this it is doing increasingly. What people rightfully object to is, not competition, but unregulated or unfair competition. In the interest of solidarity, that is, in the interest of the life of the group as a whole, all forms of competition in human society should be so regulated that the rules governing the competition may be known and the competition itself public. It is evident that in politics and in business we are very far from this ideal as yet, although society is unquestionably moving toward it. A word in conclusion about the nature of moral codes and standards from the social point of view. It is evident that moral codes from the social point of view are simply formulations of standards of conduct which groups find it convenient or necessary to impose upon their members. Even morality, in an idealistic sense, seems from a sociological standpoint to be those forms of conduct which conduce to social harmony, to social efficiency, and so to the survival of the group. Groups, however, as we have already pointed out, cannot do as they please. They are always hard-pressed in competition by other groups and have to meet the standards of efficiency which nature imposes. Morality, therefore, is not anything arbitrarily designed by the group, but is a standard of conduct which necessities of social survival require.

In other words, the right, from the point of view of natural science, is that which ultimately conduces to survival, not of the individual, but of the group or of the species. This is looking at morality, of course, from the sociological point of view, and in no way denies the religious and metaphysical view of morality, which may be equally valid from a different standpoint. Finally, we need to note that natural selection does not necessitate in any mechanical sense certain conduct on the part of individuals or groups. Rather, natural selection marks the limits of variation which nature permits, and within those limits of variation there is a large amount of freedom of choice, both to individuals and to groups. Human societies, therefore, may be conceivably free to take one of several paths of development at any particular point. But in the long run they must conform to the ultimate conditions of survival; and this probably means that the goal of their evolution is largely fixed for them.

Human groups are free only in the sense that they may go either backward or forward on the path which the conditions of survival mark out for them. They are free to progress or to perish. But social evolution in any case, in the sense of social change either toward higher or toward lower social adaptation, is a necessity that cannot be escaped. Sociology and all social science is, therefore, a study not of what human groups would like to do, but of what they must do in order to survive, that is, how they can control their environment by utilizing the laws which govern universal evolution. From this brief and most elementary consideration of the bearings of evolutionary theory upon social problems it is evident that evolution, in the sense of what we know about the development of life and society in the past, must be the guidepost of the sociologist. Human social evolution, we repeat, rests upon and is conditioned by biological evolution at every point. There is, therefore, scarcely any sanity in sociology without the biological point of view.

3

The Function of the Family in Social Organization

Instead of continuing the study of social evolution in general it will be best now, before we take up some of the problems of modern society, to study the evolution of some important social institution, because in so doing we can see more clearly the working of the biological and psychological forces which have brought about the evolution of human institutions. An institution, as has already been said, is a sanctioned grouping or relation in society. Now, there can be scarcely any doubt that the two most important institutions of human society are the family and property. In Western civilization these take the form of the monogamic family and of private property. It is upon these two institutions that our civilization rests. The state is a third very important institution in society, but it exists largely for the sake of protecting the family and property. Of the two institutions, the family and property, the family is without doubt prior in time and more fundamental,—more important in human association. We shall, therefore, study very briefly the origin and development of the family as a human institution in order to illustrate some of the principles of social evolution in general. But before we can take up the question of the origin of the family it will be well for us to see just what the function of this institution is in the human society of the present, in order to justify the assertion just made that it is the most important and fundamental institution of humanity.

THE FAMILY THE PRIMARY SOCIAL INSTITUTION

Let us note first of all that in society, as it exists at present, the family is the simplest group capable of maintaining itself. It is, therefore, we may say, the primary social structure. Because it contains both sexes and all ages it is capable of reproducing itself, and so of reproducing society. For the same reason it contains practically all social relations in miniature. It has therefore often been called, and rightly, "the social microcosm". The relations of superiority, subordination, and equality, which enter so largely into the structure of all social institutions, are especially clearly illustrated in the family in the relations of parents to children, of children to parents, of parents to each other, and of children to one another. Comte, for this reason, claimed that the family was the unit of social organization, not the individual. However this may be, it is evident that families do enter, as units, very largely into our social and industrial life. While the tendency may be to make the individual the unit of modern society, it is nevertheless true that the family remains the simplest social structure in society, and from it, in some sense, all other social relations whatsoever are evolved. The Family Differs from All Other Social Institutions, however, in two respects: First, its members have their places fixed in the family group by their organic natures, that is, the relations of husband and wife, parent and child, rest upon biological differences and relations, so that one may say that the family is almost as much a biological structure as it is a social structure. This is not, to any extent, true of other institutions. Secondly, the family is not a product, so far as we can see, of other forms of association, but rather it itself produces these other forms of association. The family, in other words, is not a result of social organization in general, but seems rather to antedate both historically and logically the forms of social life. It is not a product of society, but it itself produces society.

The primary function of the family is continuing the life of the species; that is, the primary function of the family is reproduction in the sense of the birth and rearing of children. While other functions of the family have been delegated in a large measure to other social institutions, it is manifest that this function cannot be so delegated. At least we know of no human society in which the birth and rearing of children has not been the essential function of the family. From a sociological point of view the childless family is a failure. While the childless family may be of social utility to the individuals that form it, nevertheless from the point of view of society such a family has failed to perform its most important function and must be considered, therefore, socially a failure.

THE FUNCTION OF THE FAMILY IN CONSERVING THE SOCIAL ORDER

The family is still the chief institution in society for transmitting from one generation to another social possessions of all sorts. Property in the form of land or houses or personal property, society permits the family to pass along from generation to generation. Thus, also, the material equipment for industry, that is capital, is so transmitted. While it is obvious that the material goods of society are thus transmitted by the family from one generation to another, it is perhaps not quite so obvious, but equally true, that the spiritual possessions of the race are also thus transmitted. For example, language is very largely transmitted in the family, and students tell us that each family has its own peculiar dialect. Literature, ideas, beliefs on government, law, religion, moral standards, artistic tastes and appreciation—all of these are still largely transmitted in society from one generation to another through the family. While public institutions, such as libraries, art galleries, universities, scientific museums, and the like, are often adopted to conserve and transmit these spiritual possessions of the race, yet it is safe to say that if it were possible for society to depend upon these institutions to transmit knowledge, artistic standards, and moral ideals, there would be great discontinuity in social life. The family has been in the past, and is still, the great conserving agency in human society, preserving and transmitting from generation to generation both the material and spiritual possessions of the race.

The Function of the Family in Social Progress

While the conservative function of the family is very obvious, its function in furthering social progress is perhaps not so obvious. Nevertheless, this is one of the greatest functions of the family life, because the family is the chief or almost sole generator of altruism in human society, and it is upon altruism that society depends for every upward advance in cooperation. It is in the family that children learn to love and obey, to be of service, and to respect one another's rights. The amount of altruism in a given group has a very close relation to the quality of its family life. If the family fails to teach the spirit of service and self-sacrifice to its members, it is hardly probable that they will get very much of that spirit from society at large. The ideal of a human brotherhood has no meaning unless family affection gives it meaning. If the family is the chief generator of altruism in human society and if society depends upon altruism for each forward step in moral progress, then the family is the chief source of social progress.

What we have said is a brief presentation of the claims of the family in modern society to count not only as the primary but also as the most important human institution. The family, it is evident, is charged by society with the most important task, not only of producing the new individuals in society, but of training each individual as he comes on the stage of life, adjusting him to society in all of its aspects, such as industry, government, and religion. If the family fails to perform these important functions the chances are that unsocialized individuals will take important places in society, and this means ultimately social anarchy.

The Family Life may be regarded as a School for Socializing the Individual. We need not trace in detail how the family does this for the child. It is evident that the rudiments of morality, of government, of religion, and even of industry and knowledge, must be learned by the child in the family group. If the child fails, for example, to learn morality, to get moral standards and ideals from his family life, he stands but poor chance of getting them later in society. Again, if the child fails to learn what law is and to get proper ideals of the relation of the citizen to the state in his family life, there are good prospects of his being numbered among the lawless elements of society later. In the family, we repeat, the child first experiences all the essential relations of society, learns the meaning of authority, obedience, loyalty, and all the human virtues. Moreover, the family life furnishes the moral and religious concepts which human society has set before it as its goal. The ideal of human brotherhood, for example, is manifestly derived from the family life; so also the religious idea of the Divine Fatherhood. If a nation's family life fails to illustrate these concepts, it is safe to say that they will not have great influence in society generally. The nation whose family life decays, therefore, rots at the core, dries up the springs of all social and civic virtues.

The Family and Industry

From what has been said in general terms it is evident that the family has a very important relation to the industrial activities of society, and industry a very important bearing upon the family. Primitively all industry centered in the family. Modern industry, as has been well said, is but an enormous expansion of primitive housekeeping; that is, the preparation of food and clothing and shelter by the primitive family group for its own existence is the germ out of which all modern industry has developed. The very word economics means the science or the art of the household. In primitive communities and in newly settled districts the family often carries on all essential industrial activities. It produces all the raw material, manufactures the finished products, and consumes the same. But with the growth of complex societies there has come a great industrial division of labor, and the family has delegated industrial activity after activity to some other institution until at the present time the modern family performs scarcely any industrial activities, except the preparation of food for immediate consumption.

Even this, however, in modern cities seems about to be delegated to some other institution. All that need be said at present about the delegation of the industrial activities of the family to other industrial institutions is that the movement is not one which need cause any anxiety so long as it does not interfere with the essential function of the family, namely, the birth and rearing of children. Even though children can no longer learn the rudiments of industry in their home life, still it is possible through manual and industrial training in our public schools to teach all children this. And the removal of industries from the home, even such essential industries as the preparation of food, is to be regarded as a boon if it gives more time to the parents, especially to the mother, for the proper care and bringing up of their children. But the removal of industries from the family group has not always had the beneficent effect of simply giving more time to the parents for the proper care of their children. On the contrary, the removal of these industries has often been followed by the removal of the parents themselves from the home and the practical disintegration of the family. This has been particularly the case where married women have gone into factories. Under such circumstances children have often been neglected, allowed to grow up on the streets, and to grow up as unsocialized individuals in general.

It would seem that the labor of married women outside of the home should be forbidden by the state, except in certain instances, with a view to assuring to the state itself a better citizenship. The labor of children in factories and other industrial institutions has sprung very largely from the same general causes. While child labor may have the merit of giving the child some industrial training, still it has been shown that it dwarfs the child in body and mind, produces a one-sided development, fails to prepare for citizenship in the higher sense, and so must be regarded as altogether an evil. Even the labor of the young unmarried women in factories and shops, when they should be preparing for the duties of wifehood and motherhood, is to some extent an evil in society, though not by any means of the same proportions as the labor of married women. The Subordination of Industry to the Family Life is necessary, therefore, from a social point of view. Industry, as we have seen, was primitively an adjunct of the family life, and all modern industry, if rightfully developed, should be but an adjunct to the family life. Industrial considerations must be, therefore, subordinate to domestic considerations, that is, to considerations of the welfare of parents and their children in the family group. One trouble with modern society is that industry has come to dominate as an independent interest that oftentimes does not recognize its reasonable and socially necessary subordination to the higher interests of society. There can be no sane and stable family life until we are willing to subordinate the requirements of industry, that is, of wealth-getting, to the requirements of the family for the good birth and proper rearing of children.

THE ORIGIN OF THE FAMILY

We must understand the biological roots of the family before we can understand the family as an institution, and especially before we can understand its origin. Let us note, then, briefly the chief biological facts connected with the family life.

The Biological Foundations of the Family

(1) *The Family rests upon the Great Biological Fact of Sex.* While sex does not characterize all animal forms, still it does characterize all except the simplest forms of animal life. These simplest forms multiply or reproduce by fission, but such asexual reproduction is almost entirely confined to the unicellular forms of life. It may be inferred, therefore, that the higher animal types could not have been evolved without sexual reproduction, and something of the meaning or significance of sex in the whole life process will, therefore, be helpful in understanding all of the higher forms of evolution. Biologists tell us that the meaning or purpose of sexual reproduction is to bring about greater organic variation. Now variation, as we have seen, is the raw material upon which natural selection acts to create the higher types. The immense superiority of sexual reproduction over asexual reproduction is due to the fact that it multiplies so greatly the elements of heredity in each new organism, for under sexual reproduction every new organism has two parents, four grandparents, and so on, each of which perhaps contributes something to its heredity. The biological meaning of sex, then, is that it is a device of nature to bring about organic variation. From the point of view of the social life we may note also that sex adds greatly to its variety, enriching it with numerous fruitful variations which undoubtedly further social evolution.

The bareness and monotony of a social life without sex can readily be imagined. While the differences between the sexes have been mainly elaborated through the differences of reproductive function, yet these differences have come to be fundamental to the whole nature of the organism. In the higher animals, therefore, the sexes differ profoundly in many ways from each other. Biologists tell us that the chief difference between the male and female organism is a difference in metabolism, that is, in the rapidity of organic change which goes on within the body. In the male metabolism is much more rapid than in the female; hence the male organism is said to be more katabolic. In the female the rapidity of organic change is less; hence the female is said to be more anabolic. Put in more familiar terms, the male tends to expend energy, is more active, hence also stronger; the female tends more to store up energy, is more passive, conservative, and weaker. These fundamental differences between the sexes express themselves in many ways in the social life. The differences between man and woman, therefore, are not to be thought of as due simply to social customs and usages, the different social environment of the two sexes, but are even more due to a radical and fundamental difference in their whole nature.

The belief that the two sexes would become like each other in character if given the same environment is, therefore, erroneous. That these differences are original, or inborn, and not acquired, may be readily seen by observing children of different sex. Even from their earliest years boys are more active, restless, energetic, destructive, untidy, and disobedient, while little girls are quieter, less restless, less destructive, neater, more orderly, and more obedient. These different innate qualities fit the sexes naturally for different functions in human society, and there is, therefore, a natural division of labor between them from the first. Indeed, the division of labor between the two sexes may be said to be the fundamental division of labor in human society. The causes which produce sex in the individual are not known to any extent and are probably beyond the control of man. In each species the relative number of the two sexes is fixed by nature, probably through some obscure working of natural selection, and in practically all of the higher species of animals, man included, the number of the two sexes is relatively equal. In human society much depends upon this relative numerical equality of the two sexes. Hence it can be readily seen that it is fortunate that man does not know how to control the sex of offspring, for if he did the numerical equality of the two sexes might be disturbed and serious social results would follow.

(2) *The Influence of Parental Care.* Sex alone could never have produced the family in the sense of a relatively permanent group of parents and offspring. We do not begin to find the family until we get to those higher types where we find some parental care. In the lowest types the relation between the sexes is momentary and the survival of offspring is secured simply through the production of enormous numbers. Thus the sturgeon, a low type of fish, produces between one and two million of eggs at a single spawning, from which it is estimated that not more than a dozen individuals survive till maturity is reached. Thus sexual reproduction of itself necessitates no parental care and in itself could give rise

in no way to the family; but quite low in the scale of life we begin to find some parental care as a device to protect immature offspring and secure their survival without the expenditure of such an enormous amount of energy in mere physiological reproduction.

Even among the fishes we find some that watch over the eggs after they are spawned and care for their young by leading them to suitable feeding grounds. In such cases a much smaller number of young need to be produced in order that a few may survive until maturity is reached. In the mammals the mother, obviously, must care for the young for some time, since mammals are animals that suckle their young.

But this care of the young by a single parent only foreshadows the family as we understand it. Among the mammals it is not until we reach the higher types that we find care of offspring by both parents,—a practice, however, which is common among the birds.

It is evident that as soon as both parents are concerned in the care of the offspring they have a much better chance of survival. Hence, natural selection favors the growth of this type of group life and develops powerful instincts to keep male and female together till after the birth and rearing of offspring. Such we find to be the condition among many of the higher mammals, such as some of the carnivora, and especially among the monkeys and apes and man. If it is allowable at this point to generalize from the facts given, it must be said that the family life is essentially a device of nature for the preservation of offspring through a more or less prolonged infancy.

The family group and the instincts upon which it rests were undoubtedly, therefore, instituted by natural selection. Summing up, we may say, then, the animal family group owes its existence, first, to the production of child or immature forms that need more or less prolonged care; secondly, to the prolongation of this period of immaturity in the higher animals, and especially in man; thirdly, to the development, parallel with these two causes, of parental instincts which keep male and female together for the care of the offspring. It is evident, then, that the family life rests, not upon sex attraction, but upon the fact of the child and the corresponding psychological fact of parental instinct. The family, then, has been created by the very conditions of life itself and is not a man-made institution.

The Origin of the Family in the Human Species

Two great theories of the origin of the family in the human species have in the past been more or less accepted, and these we must now examine and criticize. First, the traditional theory that the human family life was from the beginning a pure monogamy. Secondly, the so-called evolutionary theory that the human family life arose from confused if not promiscuous sex relations. The first of these theories, favored both by the Bible and Aristotle, held undisputed sway down to the middle of the nineteenth century. Then, after the publication of Darwin's Origin of Species in 1859, certain social theorists began to put forward the second theory in the name of evolution. In order that we may see precisely what the origin of the human family life was, and its primitive form, we must now proceed to criticize these two theories, especially the last, which is known as the hypothesis of a primitive state of promiscuity.

The Habits of the Higher Animals

We have already spoken of the origin of the family group in the animal world generally, but it must be admitted that there are some difficulties in arguing directly from the lower animals to man. Man is so separated from the lower animals through having passed through many higher stages of an independent evolution that in many respects his life is peculiar to itself. This is true especially of his family life. If we survey the whole range of animal life and then the whole range of human life, we find that there are but two or three striking similarities between the family life of man and that of the brutes, but a great many striking dissimilarities. The similarities may be summed up by saying that man exhibits in common with all the animals the phenomena of courtship, that is, of the male seeking to win the female, also the phenomenon of male jealousy, and we may perhaps add an instinctive aversion to crossing with the other species. These characteristics of his family life man shares with the brutes below him. There are, however, many things peculiar to the human family life that are found in no animal species below man. The most striking of these differences may be mentioned.

(1) Man has no pairing season, as practically all other animals have.

(2) The number of young born in the human species is on the whole much smaller than in any other animal species.

(3) The dependence of offspring upon parents is far longer in the human species than in any other species.

(4) Man has an antipathy to incest or close inbreeding which seems to be instinctive. This is not found clearly in any animal species below man.

(5) There is a tendency among human beings to artificial adornment during the period of courtship, but not to natural ornament to any extent, as among many animal species.

(6) The indorsement of society is almost invariably sought, both among uncivilized and civilized peoples, before the establishment of a new family—usually through the forms of a religious marriage ceremony.

(7) Chastity in women, especially married women, is universally insisted upon, both among uncivilized and civilized peoples, as the basis of human family life.

(8) There is a feeling of modesty or of shame as regards matters of sex among the human beings.

(9) In humanity we find, besides animal lust, spiritual affection, or love, as a bond of union between the two sexes.

None of these peculiarities of human family life are found in the family life of any animal species below man. It might seem, therefore, that man's family life must be regarded as a special creation unconnected with the family life of the brutes below him. But this view is hardly probable, rather is impossible from the standpoint of evolution.

We must say that these peculiarities of human family life are to be explained through the fact that man has passed through many more stages of evolution, particularly of intellectual evolution, than any of the animals below him. If we examine these peculiarities of man's family life carefully, we will see that they all can be explained through natural selection and man's higher intellectual development.

That man has no pairing season, has fewer offspring born, and a longer period of dependence of the offspring upon parents, and the like, is directly to be explained through natural selection; while seeking the indorsement of society before forming a new family, sexual modesty, tendencies to artificial adornment, and the like, are to be explained through man's self-consciousness and higher intellectual development, also through the fuller development of his social instincts.

The gap between the human family life and brute family life is, therefore, not an unbridgeable one. That this is so, we see most clearly when we consider the family life of the anthropoid or manlike apes—man's nearest cousins in the animal world. All of these apes, of which the chief representatives are the gorilla, orangutan, and the chimpanzee, live in relatively permanent family groups, usually monogamous.

These family groups are quite human in many of their characteristics, such as the care which the male parent gives to the mother and her offspring, and the seeming affection which exists between all members of the group. Such a group of parents and offspring among the higher apes is, moreover, a relatively permanent affair, children of different ages being frequently found along with their parents in such groups.

So far as the evidence of animals next to man, therefore, goes, there is no reason for supposing that the human family life sprang from confused or promiscuous sex relations in which no permanent union between male and female parent existed. On the contrary, there is every reason to believe, as Westermarck says, that human family life is an inheritance from man's apelike progenitor.

THE EVIDENCE FROM THE LOWER HUMAN RACES

The evidence afforded by the lowest peoples in point of culture even more clearly, if anything, refutes the hypothesis of a primitive state of promiscuity. The habits or customs of the lowest peoples were not well known previous to the nineteenth century. Therefore it was possible for such a theory as the patriarchal theory of the primitive family to remain generally accepted, as we have already said, down to the middle of the nineteenth century. This was the theory that the oldest or most primitive type of human family life is that depicted in the opening pages of the Book of Genesis, namely, a family life in which the father or eldest male of the family group is the absolute ruler of the group and practically owner of all persons and property. The belief that this was the primitive type of the human family life was first attacked by a German-Swiss philologist by the name of Bachofen in a work entitled Das Mutterrecht (The Matriarchate), published in 1861, in which he argued that antecedent to the patriarchal period was a matriarchal period, in which women were dominant socially and politically, and in which relationships were traced through mothers only.

Bachofen got his evidence for this theory from certain ancient legends, such as that of the Amazons, and other remains in Greek and Roman literature, which seemed to point to a period antecedent to the patriarchal.

In 1876 Mr. J.F. McLennan, a Scotch lawyer, put forth, independently, practically the same theory, basing it upon certain legal survivals which he found among many peoples. With Bachofen, he argued that this matriarchal period must have been characterized by promiscuous relations of the sexes.

In 1877 Mr. Lewis H. Morgan, an American ethnologist and sociologist, put forth again, independently, practically the same theory, basing it upon an extensive study of the North American Indian tribes. Morgan had lived among the Iroquois Indians for years and had mastered their system of relationship, which previously had puzzled the whites.

He found that they traced relationship through mothers only, and not at all along the male line. This method of reckoning relationship, moreover, he found also characterized practically all of the North American Indian tribes, and he argued that the only explanation of it was that originally sexual relations were of such an unstable or promiscuous character that they would not permit of tracing descent through fathers. From these theories sociological writers put forth the conclusion that the primitive state was one of promiscuity, or, as Sir John Lubbock called it in his Origin of Civilization, one of "communism in women."

Post, a German student of comparative jurisprudence, for example, summed up the theory by saying that "monogamous marriage originally emerged everywhere from pure communism in women, through the intermediate stages of limited communism in women, polyandry, and polygyny." Even Herbert Spencer in his Principles of Sociology, while he avoided accepting such an extreme theory, asserted that in the beginning sex relations were confused and unregulated, and that all forms of marriage—polyandry, polygyny, monogamy, and promiscuity-existed alongside of one another and that monogamy survived through its being the superior form.

Before giving a criticism in detail of this theory let us note whether the evidence from the lowest peoples confirms it. The lowest peoples in point of culture are not the North American Indians nor the African Negroes, but certain isolated groups that live almost in a state of nature, without any attempt to cultivate the soil or to control nature in other respects. Such are the Bushmen of South Africa, the Australian Aborigines, the Negritos of the Philippine Islands and of the Andaman Islands, the Veddahs of Ceylon, and the Fuegians of South America.

Now all of these peoples, with a possible exception, practice monogamy and live in relatively stable family groups.

Their monogamy, however, is not of the type which we find in patriarchal times or among civilized peoples, but is a simple pairing monogamy, husband and wife remaining together indefinitely if children are born, but if no children are born, separation may easily take place. Westermarck in his History of Human Marriage has reviewed at length all of the evidence from these lower peoples and shows undoubtedly that nothing approaching promiscuity existed among them.

Promiscuity is apt to be found at a higher stage of social development, and is especially apt to be found among the nature peoples after the white man has visited them and demoralized their family life. But in all these cases the existence of promiscuity is manifestly something exceptional and abnormal. Perhaps civilized peoples such as the Romans of the decadence have more nearly approximated the condition of promiscuity than any savage people of which we have knowledge. At any rate, one must conclude that the lowest existing savages found in the nineteenth century had definite forms of family life, and that the type usually found was the simple pairing monogamy which we have just mentioned.

OBJECTIONS TO THE HYPOTHESIS OF A PRIMITIVE STATE OF PROMISCUITY

We may now briefly sum up the main criticisms of this theory of a primitive state of promiscuity, not only as we may derive them from inductive study of the higher animals and the lower peoples, but also as we may deduce them from known psychological and biological facts or principles.

(1) In the first place, then, the animals next to man, namely, the anthropoid apes, do not show a condition of promiscuity.

(2) The evidence from the lower peoples does not show that such a condition exists or has ever existed among them.

(3) A third argument against this hypothesis may be gained from what we know of primitive economic conditions. Under the most primitive conditions, in which man had no mastery over nature, food supply was relatively scarce, and as a rule only very small groups of people could live together. The smallness of primitive groups, on account of the scarcity of food supply, would prevent anything like promiscuity on a large scale.

(4) A fourth argument of a deductive nature is that the jealousy of the male, which characterizes all higher animals and especially man, would prevent anything like the existence of sexual

promiscuity. The tendency of man would have been to appropriate one or more women for himself and drive away all rivals. Long ago Darwin argued that this would prevent anything like the existence of a general state of promiscuity.

(5) A fifth argument against this theory may be got from the general biological fact that sexual promiscuity tends to pathological conditions unfavorable to fecundity, that is, fertility, or the birth of offspring. Physicians have long ago ascertained this fact, and the modern prostitute gives illustration of it by the fact that she has few or no children. Among the lower animal species, in which some degree of promiscuity obtains, moreover, powerful instincts keep the sexes apart except at the pairing season. Now, no such instincts exist in man. Promiscuity in man would, therefore, greatly lessen the birth rate, and any group that practiced it to any extent would soon be eliminated in competition with other groups that did not practice it.

(6) We have finally the general social fact that promiscuity would lead to the neglect of children. Promiscuity means that the male parent does not remain with the female parent to care for the offspring and, therefore, in the human species it would mean that the care of children would be thrown wholly upon the mother.

This means that the children would have less chance of surviving. Not only would promiscuity lead to lessening the birth rate, but it would lead to a much higher mortality in children born. This is found to be a striking fact wherever we find any degree of promiscuity among any people. Hence, promiscuity would soon exterminate any people that practiced it extensively in competition with other peoples that did not practice it.

From all of these lines of argument, without going over the evidence in greater detail, it seems reasonable to conclude with Westermarck "that the hypothesis of a primitive state of promiscuity has no foundation in fact and is essentially unscientific."

The facts put forth in support of the theory do not justify the conclusion, Westermarck says, that promiscuity has ever been a general practice among a single people and much less that it was the primitive state. Promiscuity is found, however, more or less in the form of sexual irregularities or immorality among all peoples; more often, however, among the civilized than among the uncivilized, but among no people has it ever existed unqualified by more enduring forms of sex relation.

Moreover, because promiscuity breaks up the social bonds, throws the burden of the care of children wholly upon the mother, and lessens the birth rate, we are justified in concluding that promiscuity is essentially an antisocial practice. This agrees with the facts generally shown by criminology and sociology, that the elements practicing promiscuity to any great extent in modern societies are those most closely related with the degenerate and criminal elements. Those elements, in other words, in modern society that practice promiscuity are on the road to extinction, and if a people generally were to practice it there is no reason to believe that such a people would meet with any different fate. The Earliest Form of the Family Life in the Human Species, therefore, is probably that of the simple pairing monogamous family found among many of the higher animals, especially the anthropoid apes, and also found among the lower peoples. This primitive monogamy, however, as we have already seen, was not accompanied by the social, legal, and religious elements that the historic monogamic family has largely rested upon.

On the contrary, this primitive monogamy rested solely upon an instinctive basis, and, as we have seen, unless children were born it was apt to be relatively unstable. Permanency in family relations among primitive peoples depended largely upon the birth of children. Thus we find confirmed our conclusion drawn some time ago that family life rests primarily upon the parental instinct. That it still so rests is shown by the fact, as we shall see later, that divorce is many times more common among couples that have no children than among those that have children.

Some general conclusions, both of theoretical and practical bearing, may here be pointed out. We have seen that the biological processes of life have created the family, and that the family, as an institution, rests upon these biological conditions. Hence it is not too much to say, first, that the family is not a man-made institution; and, secondly, that it rests upon certain fundamental instincts of human nature.

Now, both of these statements are also true to a certain extent as to human society in general. There is a sense in which social organization is not wholly man-made, and it is true that all human institutions rest to some extent upon human instincts.

This is not saying, of course, that man has not modified and may not modify social organization and human institutions through his reason, but it is saying that the essential elements in human institutions and in the social order must correspond to the conditions of life generally and to the instincts which natural selection has implanted in the species. To attempt to reorganize human society or to reconstruct institutions regardless of the biological conditions of life, or regardless of human instincts, is to meet with certain failure.

A practical conclusion which may be drawn also is that those people who advocate sexual promiscuity in present society, or free love, as they please to style it, are advocating a condition which would result in the elimination of any group that practiced it. Promiscuity, or even great instability in the family life, as we have already seen, would lead to the undermining of everything upon which a higher civilization rests.

The people in modern society who advocate such theories as free love, therefore, are more dangerous than the worst anarchist or the most revolutionary socialist. In other words, the modern attack upon the family is more of a menace to all that is worth while in human life than all attacks upon government and property, although it is not usually resented as such; and it is one of the most serious signs of the times that many intellectual people have indorsed such views. We must reemphasize, therefore, the fact that the family is the central institution of human society, that industry and the state must subordinate themselves to its interest.

Neither the state nor industry has had much to do with the origin of the family, and neither the state nor industry may safely determine its forms independent of the biological requirements for human survival. Moreover, it is evident that human society from the beginning has in more or less instinctive, and also in more or less conscious, ways attempted to regulate the relations between the sexes with a view to controlling the reproductive process. While material civilization is mainly a control over the food process, moral civilization involves a control over the reproductive process, that is, over the birth and rearing of children; and such control over the reproductive process, which has certainly been one of the aims of all social organization in the past, whether of savage peoples or of civilized peoples, evidently precludes anything like the toleration of promiscuity or even of free love.

4

The Forms of the Family

The family as an institution has varied greatly in its forms from age to age and from people to people. This is what we should expect, seeing that all organic structures are variable. Such variations in human institutions are due partially to the influences of the environment, partially to the state of knowledge, and partially to many other causes as yet not well understood. The family illustrates in greater or less degree the working of these causes of variation and of change in human institutions.

THE MATERNAL AND PATERNAL FAMILIES

As regards the general form of the family we have to note first of all the two great forms which we may characterize respectively as "the maternal family" and "the paternal family." As we have already seen, Bachofen, Morgan, and others discovered a condition of human society in which relationship was traced through mothers only, and in which property or authority descended along the female line rather than along the male line. Further investigation and research have shown that up to recent times, say up to fifty years ago, one half of all the peoples of the world, if we reckon them by nations and tribes rather than by numbers, practiced this system of reckoning kinship through mothers only, and passed property and authority down along the female line. Ethnologists and sociologists have practically concluded, from the amount of evidence now collected, that this maternal or metronymic system was the primitive system of tracing relationships, and that it was succeeded among the European peoples by the paternal system so long ago that the transition from the one to the other has been forgotten, except as some trace of it has been preserved in customs, legends, and the like. Among many tribes of the North American Indians this metronymic or maternal system was peculiarly well-developed.

Children took their mother's name, not their father's name; belonged to their mother's clan, not their father's clan; and the chief transmitted his authority, if hereditary, not to his own son, but to his eldest sister's son. The relatives on the father's side, indeed, were quite ignored. Frequently the maternal uncle had more legal authority over the children than their own father, seeing that the children belonged to his clan, that is, to their mother's clan. Now, Bachofen claimed not only that in this stage was kinship reckoned through mothers only, but that women were dominant socially and politically; that there existed a true matriarchy, or rule of the mothers. Do the facts support Bachofen's theory? Let us see. The Iroquois Indians, among whom Morgan lived, were a typical maternal or metronymic people. Among them, without any doubt, the women had a position of influence socially and even politically which often is not found among peoples of higher culture. For example, among the Iroquois the government of the clan was in the hands of four women councilors (Matrons), who were elected by all the adults in the clan. These four women councilors, however, elected a Peace Sachem, who carried out the will of the clan in all matters pertaining to peace generally. Moreover, the councilors of the several clans, four fifths of whom were women, met together to form the Tribal Council; but in this Tribal Council the women sat separate, not participating in the deliberations, but exercising only a veto power on the decisions of the men. In matters of war, however, government was intrusted to two war chiefs elected from the tribe generally, the women here only having the right to veto the decision of the tribe to enter upon the warpath. Thus we see that while the women of the Iroquois Indians had a great deal of social and political influence, the actual work of government was largely turned over by them to the men, and especially was this true of directing the affairs of the tribe in time of war. There is no doubt, however, that in the maternal stage of social evolution women had an influence in domestic, religious, and social matters much greater than they had at many later stages of social development. Among the Zuni of New Mexico, for example, another well-developed maternal people, marriage is always arranged by the bride's parents.

The husband goes to live with his wife, and is practically a guest in his wife's house all his life long, she alone having the right of divorce. Indeed, among all maternal peoples the rule is that the husband goes to live with the wife, and not the wife with the husband, the children, as we have already seen, keeping the mother's name and belonging to her kindred or clan. Nevertheless we cannot agree with Bachofen that a true matriarchy, or government by women, ever existed. On the contrary, among all of these maternal peoples, while the women may have much influence socially and politically, the men, on account of their superior strength, are intrusted with the work not only of protecting and providing for the families and driving away enemies, but also largely with the work of maintaining the internal government and order of the people.

Strictly speaking, therefore, there has never been a matriarchal stage of social evolution, but rather a maternal or metronymic stage. We have already said that this stage was probably the primitive one. How are we to explain, then, that primitive man reckoned kinship through mothers only? Was this due, as Morgan thought, to a primitive practice of promiscuity which prevented tracing relationships through fathers? The reply is, that among the many maternal peoples now well known, among whom relationships are traced through mothers only, we find no evidence of the practice of general promiscuity now or even in remote times. The North American Indians, for example, had quite definite forms of the family life and were very far removed from the practice of promiscuity, though they traced relationship through mothers only. It is evident that the causes of the maternal family and the maternal system of relationship are not so simple as Morgan supposed. What, then, were the causes of the maternal system? It is probable that man in the earliest times did not know the physiological connection between father and child. The physiological connection between mother and child, on the other hand, was an obvious fact which required no knowledge of physiology to establish; therefore, nothing was more natural than for primitive man to recognize that the child was of the mother's blood, but not of the father's blood.

Therefore, the child belonged to the mother's people and not to the father's people. If it be asked whether it is possible that there could be any human beings so ignorant that they do not know the physiological connection between father and child, the reply is, that this is apparently the case among a number of very primitive peoples, even down to recent times. It is not infrequent among these peoples to find conception and childbirth attributed to the influence of the spirits, rather than to relations between male and female. While, therefore, a social connection between the father and the children was recognized, leading the father to provide in all ways for his children, as fathers do whether among civilized or uncivilized peoples, yet the blood relationship between the father and the child could not have been clear in the most primitive times. Perhaps an even more efficient cause, however, of the maternal system was the fact that the mother in primitive times was the stable element in the family life, the constant center of the family. The husband was frequently away from home, hunting or fighting, and oftentimes failed to return. Nothing was more natural, therefore, than that the child should be reckoned as belonging to the mother, take her name and belong to her kindred or clan. Moreover, after the custom of naming children from mothers and reckoning them as belonging to the mother's clan was established, it could not be displaced by the mere discovery of the physiological connection between the father and the child. On the contrary social habits, like habits in the individual, tend to persist until they work badly. We find, therefore, the maternal system persisting among peoples who for many generations had come fully to recognize the physiological connection of father and child. Indeed, the maternal system could never have been done away with if social evolution had not brought about new and complex conditions which caused the system to break down and to be replaced by the paternal system.

THE PATERNAL OR PATRIARCHAL FAMILY

At a certain stage we find, then, that a vast revolution took place in human society, especially in the family life, and the family and society generally came to be organized more definitely in regard to the male element. At a certain period, indeed, we find that the authority of the husband and father in the family has become supreme, and that he is practically owner of all persons and property of the family group, the wife and children being reduced, if not to the position of property, at least to the position of subject persons. This is the patriarchal family, classical pictures of which we find set forth in the pages of the Old Testament. How, then, did the transition take place from the maternal system, in which the mother was so important in the family, to the paternal system, in which the father was so all-important? What were the causes which brought about the breakdown of the maternal system and the gradual development of the patriarchal family? Some of these causes we can clearly make out from the study of social history.

(1) War was unquestionably a cause of the breakdown of the maternal system through the fact that women were captured in war, held as slaves, and made wives or concubines by their captors. These captured wives were regarded as the property of the captor. Any children born to them were, therefore, also regarded as the property of the captor. Furthermore, these captured wives were separated from their kindred, and their children could not possibly belong to any clan except their husband's. Manifestly this cause could not have worked in the earliest times, when slave captives were not valuable; but as soon as slavery became instituted in any form, then women slaves were particularly valued, not only for their labor, but because they might be either concubines or wives. It is evident, then, that war and slavery would thus indirectly tend to undermine the maternal system.

(2) Wife purchase would operate in the same way. Among peoples that had developed a commercial life as well as slavery it early became the practice to purchase wives. It is evident that these purchased wives would be regarded as a sort of property, and the husband would naturally claim the children as belonging to him. Among certain North American Indians we find exactly this state of affairs. If a man married a wife without paying the purchase price for her, then her children took her name and belonged to her clan; but if he had purchased her, say with a number of blankets, then the children took his name and belonged to his clan.

(3) The decisive cause, however, of the breakdown of the maternal system was the development of the pastoral stage of industry. Now, the grazing of flocks and herds requires considerable territory and necessitates small and compact groups widely separated from one another. Hence, in the pastoral stage the wife must go with the husband and be far removed from the influence and authority of her own kindred. This gave the husband greater power over his wife. Moreover, the care of flocks and herds accentuated the value of the male laborer, while primitively woman had been the chief laborer. In the pastoral stage the man had the main burden of caring for the flocks and herds. Under such circumstances nothing was more natural than that the authority of the owner of the family property should gradually become supreme in all matters, and we find, therefore, among all pastoral peoples that the family is itself a little political unit, the children taking the father's name, property and authority passing down along the male line, while the eldest living male is usually the ruler of the whole group.

(4) After all these causes came another factor—ancestor worship. While ancestor worship exists to some extent among maternal peoples, it is usually not well-developed for some reason or other until the paternal stage is reached. Ancestor worship, being the worship of the departed ancestors as heroes, seems to develop more readily where the line of ancestors are males. It may be suggested that the male ancestor is apt to be a more heroic figure than the female ancestor. At any rate, when ancestor worship became fully developed it powerfully tended to reenforce the authority of the patriarch, because he was, as the eldest living ancestor, the representative of the gods upon earth, therefore his power became almost divine. Religion thus finally came in to place the patriarchal family upon a very firm basis. Thus we see how each of these two great forms, the maternal family and the paternal family, arose out of natural conditions, and therefore they may be said to represent two great stages in the social evolution of man. It is hardly necessary to point out that civilized societies are now apparently entering upon a third stage, in which there will be relative equality given to the male and the female elements that go to make up the family.

Polyandry

We must notice now the various forms of marriage by which the family has been constituted among different peoples and in different ages. Marriage, like the family itself, is variable, and an indefinite number of forms may be found among various peoples. We shall notice, however, only the three leading forms,—polyandry, polygyny, and monogamy,—and attempt to show the natural conditions which favor each. It is evident that if we assume that the primitive form of the family was that of a simple pairing monogamy, the burden is laid upon us to show how such different types as polyandry and polygyny arose. Polyandry, or the union of one woman with several men, is a relatively rare form of marriage and the family, found only in certain isolated regions of the world. It is particularly found in Tibet, a barren and inhospitable plateau north of India and forming a part of the Chinese Empire. It is also found in certain other isolated mountainous regions in India, and down to recent times also in Arabia. In none of these places does it exist exclusively, but rather alongside of monogamy and perhaps other forms of the family. Thus in Tibet the upper classes practice polygyny and monogamy, while among the lower classes we find polyandry and monogamy. In all these regions where polyandry occurs, moreover, it is to be noted that the conditions of life are harsh and severe. Tibet is an exceptionally inhospitable region, with a climate of arctic rigor, the people living mainly by grazing. Under such circumstances it is conceivably difficult for one man to support and protect a family. At any rate, the form of polyandry which we find in Tibet suggests that such economic conditions may have been the main cause of its existence.

Ordinarily in Tibet a polyandrous family is formed by an older brother taking a wife, and then admitting his younger brothers into partnership with him. The older brother is frequently absent from home, looking after the flocks, and in his absence one of the younger brothers assumes the headship of the family. Under such circumstances we can see how the natural human instincts which would oppose polyandry under ordinary circumstances, namely, the jealousy of the male, might become greatly modified, or cease to act altogether. Certain other conditions besides economic ones might also favor the existence of polyandry, such as the scarcity of women. Summing up, we can say, then, that this rare form of the family seems to have as its causes:

(1) In barren and inhospitable countries the labor of one man is sometimes found not sufficient to support a family.

(2) Also there probably exists in such regions an excess of males. This might be due to one of two causes: First, the practice of exposing female infants might lead to a scarcity of women; secondly, in such regions it is found that from causes not well understood a larger number of males are born. It may be noted as a general fact that when the conditions of life are hard in human society, owing to famine, war, or barrenness of the soil, a larger number of male births take place. We may therefore infer that this would disturb the numerical proportion of the sexes in such regions.

(3) A third cause may be suggested as having something to do with the matter, namely, that habits of close inbreeding, or intermarriage, might perhaps tend to overcome the natural repugnance to such a relation. Moreover, close inbreeding also, as the experiments of stock-breeders show, would tend to produce a surplus of male births, and so would act finally in the same way as the second cause.

POLYGYNY

The word "polygamy" is too broad in its meaning to use as a scientific term for this form of the family. "Polygamy" comes from two Greek words meaning "much married;" hence it includes "polyandry" (having several husbands) and "polygyny" (having several wives). or the union of one man with several women, is a much more common form of marriage. It is, in fact, to be found sporadically among all peoples and in all ages. It has perhaps existed at least sporadically from the most primitive times, because we find that at least one of the anthropoid apes, namely, the gorilla, practices it to some extent. It is manifest, however, that it could not have existed to any extent among primitive men, except where food supply was exceptionally abundant. In the main, polygyny is a later development, then, which comes in when some degree of wealth has been accumulated, that is, sufficient food supply to make it possible for one man to support several families. Polygyny came in especially after women came to be captured in war and kept as slaves or wives. The practice of wife capture, indeed, and the honor attached to the custom, had much to do in making the practice of polygyny common among certain peoples. Wherever slavery has existed, we may also note, polygyny, either in its legal form or in its illegal form of concubinage, has flourished. Polygyny, indeed, is closely related with the institution of slavery and is practically coextensive with it. In the ancient world it existed among the Hebrews and among practically all of the peoples of the Orient, and also sporadically among our own Teutonic ancestors. In modern times polygyny still exists among all the Mohammedan peoples and to a greater or less degree among all semicivilized peoples. It exists in China in the form of concubinage. It even exists in the United States, for all the evidence seems to show that the Utah Mormons still practice polygyny to some extent, although it may be doubted whether polygynous unions are being formed among them at the present time.

Two facts always need to be borne in mind regarding polygyny: First, that wherever it is practiced it is relatively confined to the upper and wealthy classes, for the reason that the support of more than one family is something which only the wealthy classes in a given society could assume. Secondly, it follows that under ordinary circumstances only a small minority of a given population practice polygyny, even in countries in which it is sanctioned. In Mohammedan countries like Turkey and Egypt, for example, it is estimated that not more than five per cent of the families are polygynous, while in other regions the percentage seems to be still smaller.

The reason for this is not only the economic one just mentioned, but that everywhere the sexes are relatively equal in numbers, and therefore it is impossible for polygyny to become a widespread general custom. If some men have more than one wife it is evident that other men will probably have to forego marriage entirely. This is not saying that under certain circumstances, namely, the importation of large numbers of women, a higher per cent of polygynous families may not exist. It is said that among the negroes on the west coast of Africa the number of polygynous families reaches as high as fifty per cent, owing to the fact that female slaves are largely imported into that district, and that they serve not only as wives, but do the bulk of the agricultural labor, the male negro preferring female slaves, who can do his work and be wives at the same time, to male slaves. But such cases as these are altogether exceptional and manifestly could not become general. Summing up, we may say that the causes of polygyny are, then:

(1) First of all, the brutal lust of man. No doubt man's animal propensities have had much to do with the existence of this form of the family. Nevertheless, while male sensuality is at the basis of polygyny, it would be a mistake to think that sensuality is an adequate explanation in all cases. On the contrary, we find many other causes, chiefly, perhaps, economic, operating also to favor the development of polygyny.

(2) One of these is wife capture, as we have already seen. The captured women in war were held as trophies and slaves, and later became wives or concubines. Among all peoples at a certain stage the honor of wife capture has alone been a prolific cause of polygyny.

(3) Another cause, after slavery became developed, was the high value set on women as laborers. Among many barbarous peoples the women do the main part of the work. They are more tractable as slaves, and consequently a high value is set upon their labor. As we have already seen, these female slaves usually serve at the same time as concubines, if not legal wives of their masters.

(4) Another cause which we can perhaps hardly appreciate at the present time is the high valuation set on children. We see this cause operating particularly in the case of the patriarchs of the Old Testament. Under the patriarchal family great value was set upon children as necessary to continue the family line. Where the device of adoption was not resorted to, therefore, in case of barrenness or the birth exclusively of female children, nothing was more natural than that polygyny should be resorted to in order to insure the family succession. In the patriarchal family also a high valuation was necessarily set upon children, because the larger the family grew the stronger it was.

(5) Finally, religion came to sanction polygyny. The religious sanction of polygyny cannot be looked upon as one of its original causes, but when once established it reacted powerfully to reenforce and maintain the institution. How the religious sanction came about we can readily see when we remember that very commonly religions confuse the practice of the nobility with what is noble or commendable morally. The polygynous practices of the nobility, therefore, under certain conditions came to receive the sanction of religion.

When this took place polygyny became firmly established as a social institution, very difficult to uproot, as all the experience of Christian missionaries among peoples practicing polygyny goes to show. We may note also the general truth, that while religion does not originate human institutions or the forms of human association, it is preeminently that which gives fixity and stability to institutions through the supernatural sanction that it accords them. Some judgment of the social value of polygyny may not be out of place in connection with this subject. Admitting, as all students of social history must, that in certain times and places the polygynous form of family has been advantageous, has served the interests of social survival and even of civilization, yet viewed from the standpoint of present society it seems that our judgment of polygyny must be wholly unfavorable. In the first place, as we have already seen, polygyny is essentially an institution of barbarism. It arose largely through the practice of wife capture and the keeping of female slaves. While often adjusted to the requirements of barbarous societies, it seems in no way adjusted to a high civilization. Polygyny, indeed, must necessarily rest upon the subjection and degradation of women. Necessarily the practice of polygyny must disregard the feelings of women, for women are jealous creatures as well as men. No high regard for the feelings of women, therefore, would be consistent with the practice of polygyny. Finally, all the evidence that we have goes to show that under polygyny children are neglected, and, at least from the standpoint of a high civilization, inadequately socialized.

This must necessarily be so, because in the polygynous family the care of the children rests almost entirely with the mother. While we have no statistics of infant mortality from polygynous countries, it seems probable that infant mortality is high, and we know from experience with polygynous families in our own state of Utah, according to the testimony of those who have worked among them, that delinquent children are especially found in such households. Fatherhood, in the full sense of the word, can hardly be said to exist under polygyny. Those philosophers, like Schopenhauer, who advocate the legalizing of polygyny in civilized countries, are hardly worth replying to. It is safe to say that any widespread practice of polygyny in civilized communities would lead to a reversion to the moral standards of barbarism in many if not in all matters. That polygyny is still a burning question in the United States of the twentieth century is merely good evidence that we are not very far removed yet from barbarism.

MONOGAMY

As we have already seen, has been the prevalent form of marriage in all ages and in all countries. Wherever other forms have existed monogamy has existed alongside of them as the dominant, even though perhaps not the socially honored, form. All other forms of the family must be regarded as sporadic variations, on the whole unsuited to long survival, because essentially inconsistent with the nature of human society. In civilized Europe monogamy has been the only form of the family sanctioned for ages by law, custom, and religion. The leading peoples of the world, therefore, practice monogamy, and it is safe to say that the connection between monogamy and progressive forms of civilization is not an accident. What, then, are the social advantages of monogamy which favor the development of a higher type of culture? These advantages are numerous, but perhaps the most important of them can be grouped under six heads.

(1) The number of the two sexes, as we have already seen, is everywhere approximately equal. This means that monogamy is in harmony with the biological conditions that exist in the human species. The equal number of the two sexes has probably been brought about through natural selection. Why nature should favor this proportion of the sexes can perhaps be in part understood when we reflect that with such proportion there can be the largest number of family groups, and hence the best possible conditions for the rearing of offspring.

(2) Monogamy secures the superior care of children in at least two respects. First, it very greatly decreases mortality in children, because under monogamy both husband and wife unite in their care. Again, monogamy secures the superior upbringing and, therefore, the superior socialization of the child. In the monogamous family much greater attention can be given to the training of children by both parents. In other forms of the family not only is the death rate higher among children, but from the point of view of modern civilization, at least, they are inferiorly socialized.

(3) The monogamic family alone produces affections and emotions of the higher type. It is only in the monogamic family that the highest type of altruistic affection can be cultivated. It is difficult to understand, for example, how anything like unselfish affection between husband and wife can exist under polygyny. Under monogamy, husband and wife are called upon to sacrifice selfish desires in the mutual care of children. Monogamy is, therefore, fitted as a form of the family to foster altruism in the highest degree, and, as

we have seen, the higher the type of altruism produced by the family life, the higher the type of the social life generally, other things being equal. It is especially to the credit of monogamy that it has created fatherhood in the fullest sense of the term, and therefore taught the male element in human society the value of service and self-sacrifice. Under polygynous conditions the father cannot devote himself to any extent to his children or to any one wife, since he is really the head of several households, and therefore, as we have already noted, fatherhood in the fullest sense scarcely exists under polygyny.

(4) Under monogamy, moreover, all family relationships are more definite and strong, and thus family bonds, and ultimately social bonds, are stronger. In the polygynous household the children of the different wives are half brothers and half sisters, hence family affection has little chance to develop among them, and as a matter of fact between children of different wives there is constant pulling and hauling. Moreover, because the children in a polygynous family are only half brothers this immensely complicates relationships, and even the line of ancestors. Legal relations and all blood relationships are, therefore, more entangled. It is no inconsiderable social merit of monogamy that it makes blood relationships simple and usually perfectly definite. All of this has an effect upon society at large, because the cohesive power of blood relationship, even in modern societies, is something still worth taking into account. But of course the main influence of all this is to be found in the family group itself, because it is only under such simple and definite relations as we find in the monogamous family that there is ample stimulus to develop the higher family affections.

(5) From all this it follows that monogamy favors the development of high types of religion and morals, family affection being an indispensable root of any high type of ethical religion. That form of the family which favors the development of the highest type of this affection will, therefore, favor the development of the highest type of religion. We see this even more plainly, perhaps, in ancient times than in the present time, because it was monogamy that favored the development of ancestor worship through making the line of ancestors clear and definite, and thus monogamy helped to develop this type of religion, which became the basis of still higher types.

(6) Monogamy not only favors the preservation of the lives of the children, but also favors the preservation of the lives of the parents, because it is only under monogamy that we find aged parents cared for by their children to any extent. Under polygyny the wife who has grown old is discarded for a young wife, and usually ends her days in bitterness. The father, too, under polygyny is rarely cared for by the children, because the polygynous household has never given the opportunity for close affections between parents and children.

That monogamy, therefore, helps to lengthen life through favoring care of parents by children in old age is an element in its favor, for it adds not a little to the happiness of life, and so to the strength of social bonds, that people do not have to look forward to a cheerless and friendless old age. In brief, the monogamic family presents such superior unity and harmony from every point of view that it is much more fitted to produce a higher type of culture. From whatever point of view we may look at it, therefore, there are many reasons why civilized societies cannot afford to sanction any other form of the family than that of monogamy. The Relation of the Form of the Family to the Form of Industry.—As we have already seen, the form of the family is undoubtedly greatly influenced by the form of industry. This is so markedly the case that some sociologists and economists have claimed that the form of the family life is but a reflection of the form of the industrial life; that the family in its changes and variations slavishly follows the changes in economic conditions. That such an extreme view as this is a mistake can readily be seen from a brief review of the causes which have produced certain types of family life in certain periods. Thus, the maternal type of the family cannot be said by any means to have been determined by economic conditions. On the contrary, primarily the maternal family, as we have seen, was determined by certain intellectual conceptions, namely, the absence of knowledge of the physiological connection between father and child, though the economic conditions of primitive life tended powerfully to continue the maternal family long after intellectual conditions had changed. Again, it has been said that the patriarchal family owed its existence entirely to a form of industry, namely, pastoral industry, but, as we have seen, other factors also operated to produce the patriarchal type of the family, such as war, religion, and perhaps man's inherent desire to dominate. Moreover, religion continued the patriarchal family in many cases long after pastoral industry had ceased to be the chief economic form.

So too with the forms of marriage. While polygyny has been claimed to be due entirely to economic causes, we have seen that these so-called economic causes have only been the opportunities for the polygynous instincts of man to assert themselves. These polygynous instincts of man have asserted themselves more or less under all conditions of society, but under certain conditions, when there was an accumulation of wealth, and especially with the institution of slavery, they had greater opportunity to assert themselves than elsewhere. Thus the basic cause of polygyny is not economic, but psychological; and given certain moral and economic conditions of society, these polygynous tendencies assert themselves. Monogamy, on the other hand, has in no sense been determined by economic conditions but is fundamentally determined by the biological fact of the numerical equality of the sexes. This is doubtless the main reason why monogamy has been the prevalent form of the family everywhere. Certain moral and psychological factors which go along with the development of higher types of culture have, however, powerfully reenforced monogamy. It is doubtful if economic conditions can to any extent be shown to have equally reenforced the monogamic life. Our conclusion must be, then, that while the form of the family and the form of industry are closely related, so closely that the form of industry continually affects more or less the family life, yet there is no reason for concluding that the form of the family is wholly or even chiefly determined by the form of industry.

5

The Historical Development of the Family

While we cannot enter into the historical evolution of the family as an institution among the different civilized peoples, still it will be profitable for us to consider the history of the family among some single representative people in order that we may see the forces which have made and unmade the family life, and incidentally also to a great degree, the general social life of that people. We shall select the ancient Romans as the people among whom we can thus best study in outline the development of the family. While the family life of the ancient Hebrews is of particular interest to us because of the close connection of our religion and ethics with that of the Hebrews, yet in the family life of the ancient Romans constructive and destructive factors are more clearly marked and, therefore, the study of ancient Roman family life is best fitted to bring out those factors. The ancient Romans were among the earliest civilized of the Aryan peoples, and their institutions are, therefore, of peculiar interest to us as representing approximately the early Aryan type. What we shall say concerning Roman family life, moreover, will apply, with some modifications and qualifications, to the family life of other Aryan peoples, especially the Greeks. The Greeks and the Romans, indeed, were so closely related in their early culture that for the purpose of institutional history they may be considered practically one people. Without any attempt, then, to sketch the history of the family as an institution in general, let us note some of the salient features of the family life of the ancient Romans.

The Early Roman Family

(1) Ancestor Worship as the Basis of the Early Roman Family. What we have said thus far indicates a close connection between the family life and religion among all peoples. This was especially true of the early Romans. It may be said, indeed, that ancestor worship was the constitutive principle of their family life. Among them the family seemed to have

lost in part its character as a purely social institution and to have become specialized into a religious institution. At any rate, the early Roman family existed very largely for the sake of perpetuating the worship of ancestors. Of course, ancestor worship could have had nothing to do with the origin of the family life among the Romans. The type of their family life was patriarchal, and we have already noticed the causes which brought about the existence of the patriarchal family. But while ancestor worship had nothing to do with the origin of the family, once it was thoroughly established it became the basis of the family life and transformed the family as an institution. The early Romans shared certain superstitions with many primitive peoples, which, if not the basis of ancestor worship, powerfully reinforced it. They believed, for example, that the soul continued in existence after death, and that persons would be unhappy unless buried in tombs with suitable offerings, and that if left unburied, or without suitable offerings, the souls of these persons would return to torment the living, Inasmuch as in the patriarchal family only sons could perform religious rites, that is, could make offerings to the departed spirits, these superstitions acted as a powerful stimulus to preserve the family in order that offerings might continue to be made at the graves of ancestors. Thus, as we have already said, among the early Romans the family was practically a religious institution with ancestor worship as its constitutive principle. It is supposed by de Coulanges that in the earliest times the dead ancestors were buried beneath the hearth. At any rate, the hearth was the place where offerings were made to the departed ancestors, and the flame on the hearth was believed to represent the spirit of the departed. The house under such circumstances became a temple and the whole atmosphere of the family life was necessarily a religious one.

(2) The Authority in the Early Roman Family was vested, as in all patriarchal families, in the father or eldest living male of the family group. Under ancestor worship he became the living representative of the departed ancestors, the link between the living and the dead. Here we may note that the family was not considered as constituted simply of its living members, but that it included also all of its dead members. Inasmuch as the dead were more numerous and were thought to be more powerful than the living, they were by far the more important element in the life of the family. The position of the house father, as representative of the departed ancestors, and as the link between the living and the dead, naturally made his authority almost divine. Hence, the house father was himself, then, almost a deity, having absolute power over all persons within the group, even to the extent of life and death. This absolute power, which was known in the early Roman family as the "patria potestas," could not, however, be exercised arbitrarily. The house father, as representative of the departed ancestors, was necessarily controlled by religious scruples and traditions. It was impossible for him to act other than for what he believed to be the will of the ancestors. Disobedience to him was, therefore, disobedience to the divine ancestors, and hence was sacrilegious.

(3) Relationship in the Early Roman Family was determined by community of worship, inasmuch as only descendants upon the male side could perform religious rites, and inasmuch as married women worshiped the household gods of their husbands' ancestors; therefore, only descendants on the male side could worship the same ancestors and were relatives in the full religious and legal sense. These were known as "agnates." Later, some relationship on the mother's side came to be recognized, but relatives on the mother's side were known as a "cognates," and for a long time property could not pass to them. Indeed, in the earliest times the property of the family, as we have already implied, was kept as a unit, held in trust by the eldest living member of the family group for the good of all the family. In other words, the house father in earliest times did not possess the right to make a will but the property of the family passed intact from him to his eldest male heir.

(4) The Marriage Ceremony among the Early Romans was necessarily of a religious character. It was constituted essentially of the induction of the bride into the worship of her husband's ancestors. But before this could be done the bride's father had first to free her from the worship of her household gods, in later times a certificate of manumission being given not unlike the manumission of the slave. After the bride had been released from the worship of her father's ancestors, the bridegroom and his friends brought her to his father's house, where a ceremony of adoption was practically gone through with, adopting the bride into the family of her husband. The essence of this ceremony, as we have already said, was the induction of the bride into the worship of her husband's ancestors through their both making an offering on the family hearth and eating a sacrificial meal together. After that the wife worshiped at her husband's altar and had no claim upon the household gods of her father. Under such circumstances it is not surprising that marriage was practically indissoluble. A wife who was driven out of her husband's household or deserted was without family gods of any sort, having no claim upon those of her husband, and became, therefore, a social outcast. Under such circumstances it is not surprising that divorce was practically unknown. It is said, indeed, that for five hundred and twenty years after Rome was founded there was not a single divorce in Rome. While this may be an exaggeration, it is historically certain that divorce was so rare in early Rome as to be practically unknown. In case of a failure of sons to be born there was no taking of a second wife, as among the Hebrews. Polygyny was unknown in early Rome. The Roman device to prevent the failure of the family succession in such cases was adoption. Younger sons of other families were adopted if no sons were born, and these adopted sons, taking the family name, became the same legally as sons by birth. Inasmuch as the position of younger sons in the patriarchal household was not an enviable one there was never lack of candidates for the position of eldest son in some family group in which no sons had

been born. Not only was the early Roman family life the most stable that the world has ever known, but it must also be considered to have been of a relatively pure type. Chastity was rigidly enforced among the women, but of course, as in all primitive peoples, was not enforced among the men. Still it was expected that the married men at least should remain relatively faithful to their wives. On the whole, therefore, the early Roman family life must be judged to have been of a singularly high and stable type. While the position of women and children in the early Roman family was one of subjection, the family itself was nevertheless of a high type. But it was inevitable that it should decay, and this decay began comparatively early. Inasmuch as the early Roman family was based upon ancestor worship, a religion which was fitted for relatively small isolated groups, it was inevitable that the family life should decay with this ancestor worship. How early the decay of ancestor worship began it is impossible to say. Perhaps the nature gods, Jupiter, Venus, and the rest, existed alongside of ancestor worship from the earliest times. At any rate, we find their worship growing rapidly within the period of authentic history and undermining the domestic worship, while at a still later period skeptical philosophy undermined both religions. Along with the decay of ancestor worship went many economic and political changes which marked the dissolution of the patriarchal family. Let us see what some of the steps in this decadence were.

(5) The Decadence, (a) One of the earliest steps toward the breaking down of the patriarchal family which we find is the limiting of the power of the house father. This took place very early—as soon as the Council of Elders, or Senate, was formed to look after matters of collective interest. Gradually the paternal power diminished, until it was confined to matters concerning the family group proper. (b) A second step was when the right to make a will was conceded. This right, as we have seen, did not exist in the earliest Roman times, but with the development of property and of a more complex economic life the house father was given the right to divide his property among his children, at first only on the male side, but later among any of his children, and still later to bequeath it to whom he pleased. (c) Thus women came to be given the right to hold property, a thing which was unknown in the earliest times; and becoming property holders, their other rights in many respects began to increase. Originally the wife had no right to divorce her husband, but in the second century B.C. women also gained the right of divorcing their husbands. (d) The rights of children were increased along with the rights of women, particularly of younger children. (e) The right of plebeians to intermarry with the noble families became recognized. All of these changes we should perhaps regard as good in themselves, but they nevertheless marked the disintegration of the patriarchal family. The decay of the family life did not stop with these changes, however, but went on to the decay of the family bonds themselves.

Later Roman Family Life

By the beginning of the Christian era the relations between the sexes had become very loose. Men not only frequently divorced their wives, but women frequently divorced their husbands. Indeed, a complete revolution passed over the Roman family. Marriage became a private contract, whereas, as we have seen, in the beginning it was a religious bond. Many loose forms of marriage were developed, which amounted practically to temporary marriages. In all cases it was easy for a husband or wife to divorce each other for very trivial causes. Among certain classes of Roman society the instability of the family became so great that we find Seneca saying that there were women who reckoned their years by their husbands, and Juvenal recording one woman as having eight husbands in five years. Women and children achieved their practical emancipation, as we would say. Women, especially, were free to do as they saw fit. Marriages were formed and dissolved at pleasure among certain classes, and among all classes the instability of the family life had become very great. Along with all this, of course, went a growth of vice. It is not too much to say that the Romans of the first and second centuries A.D. approached as closely to a condition of promiscuity as any civilized people of which we have knowledge.

Causes of the Decadence

When we examine the causes of this great revolution in Roman family life from the austere morals and stable family of the early Romans to the laxity and promiscuity of the later Romans, we find that these causes can perhaps be grouped under four or five principal heads,

(1) First among all the causes we must put the destruction of the domestic religion, namely, ancestor worship, through the growth of nature worship and skeptical philosophy. The destruction of the domestic religion necessarily shattered the foundations of the Roman family, since, as we have already seen, there was the closest connection between the family life of the early Romans and ancestor worship. But it is not probable that ancestor worship was destroyed merely through the growth of nature worship and of skeptical philosophy. As we have already seen, it was a religion which was mainly adapted to isolated groups. Changes in economic and political conditions, therefore, were to some extent prior to the decay of the domestic religion.

(2) Changes in economic conditions, that is, in the form of industry, were, then, among the more important causes of the decay of the early Roman family. The patriarchal family, as we have already seen, belonged essentially to the pastoral stage of industry, and as soon as settled agricultural life, commerce, and manufacturing industry developed, this destroyed the isolated patriarchal groups, and so also in time affected even the religion which was their basis. Again, the increase of population going along with the changes in the methods in obtaining a living destroyed the old conditions under which the family had been the political unit.

(3) We have therefore as a third cause the breaking up of old political conditions. Family groups were welded into small cities and the authority of the patriarch was destroyed. Legislation designed to meet the new social conditions often profoundly affected the whole family group, and weakened family bonds.

(4) The growth of divorce and of vice may be put down as a fourth cause of the decay of the Roman family. Some may say that this was an effect of the decay of the Roman family rather than a cause, but it was also a cause as well as an effect, for it is a peculiarity of social life that what is at one stage an effect reacts to become a cause at a later stage; and this was certainly the case with the growth of divorce and vice in Rome, in its effect upon the Roman family. Moreover, much of this came from Greece through imitation. The family life had decayed in Greece much earlier than it had in Rome, and when Rome conquered Greece it annexed its vices also.

While the most radical social changes do not usually come about merely through imitation, yet the imitation of a foreign people is frequently, in the history of a particular nation, one of the most potent causes in bringing about social changes. It was certainly so in the case of the growth of divorce and vice in Rome. To sum up and to generalize: we may say that the causes of the decay of the Roman family life were very complex, and that this is true of nearly all important social changes. It is impossible to reduce the causes of these changes to any single principle or set of causes. While we have seen that changes in economic conditions were undoubtedly very influential in bringing about the profound changes in the Roman family, still we have no ground for regarding the economic changes as determinative of all the rest. We know as yet little of the development of industry in antiquity.

What little we do know, however, furnishes good ground for claiming that changes in the methods of getting a living are among the most influential causes of social change in general; but there is nothing which warrants the sweeping generalization of Karl Marx and his followers, "that the method of the production of the material life determines the social, political, and spiritual life process in general." On the contrary, the evolution of the Roman family clearly shows moral and psychological factors at work quite independent of economic causes. The decay of ancestor worship, for example, cannot be wholly attributed to the change in the method of getting a living.

The very growth of population and accompanying changes in political conditions probably had quite as much to do with the undermining of ancestor worship. Moreover, while religion may not be an original determining cause of social forms, it is, nevertheless, as we have already seen, especially that which gives them stability and permanency, so much so that the life history of a culture is frequently the life history of a religion. The decay of religious ideas and beliefs, therefore, from any cause, frequently proves the important element working for social change in all societies. So, too, changes in political conditions, especially changes in law through new legislation, frequently prove a profound modifying influence in societies. Lastly, there are certain moral causes inherent in the individual, oftentimes involving perverted expressions of instinct, which lead to profound social changes. Such was the vice which Rome copied very largely from Greece, but which proved the final solvent in its family life.

In general we may say, then, that there is no single principle which will explain the evolution of the family from the earliest times down to the present. Any attempt to reduce the evolution of the family to a single principle, or to show that it has been controlled by a single set of causes, must inevitably end in failure. The economic determinism of Marx and his followers, the ideological conceptions of Hegel, the geographical influences of Buckle and his school, and like explanations, are all found wanting when they are applied to the actual history of the family. It is not different with the theories of recent sociologists, who would strive to explain all social changes through a single principle. Professor Giddings' principle of "Consciousness of Kind" and Tarde's principle of "Imitation" will not go further in explaining the changes in the family life than some of the older principles that we have just mentioned. Human life is, indeed, too complex to be explained in terms of any single principle or any single set of causes. The family in particular is an organic structure which responds first to one set of stimuli and then to another. Now it is modified by economic conditions, now by religious ideas, now by legislation, now by imitation, and so on through the whole set of possible stimuli which may impinge upon and modify the activity of a living organism. So it is with all institutions.

The Influence of Christianity upon the Family

While we cannot study further the evolution of the family in any detail, still it is necessary, in order to avoid too great discontinuity, to notice in a few sentences the influence of Christianity upon the family in Western civilization. Early Christianity, as we have already seen, found the family life of the Greco-Roman world demoralized. The reconstruction of the family became, therefore, one of the first tasks of the new religion, and while other circumstances may have aided the church in this work, still on the whole it was mainly the influence of the early church that reconstituted the family life. From the first the church worked to abolish divorce, and fought as evil such vices as concubinage and prostitution, that came to flourish to such an extent in the Pagan world.

Only very slowly did the early leaders of the church win the mass of the people to accepting their views as to the permanency of the marriage bond. In order to aid in making this bond more stable the early church recognized marriage as one of the sacraments, and, as implied, steadily opposed the idea of the later Roman Law that marriage was simply a private contract. The result was, eventually, that marriage came to be regarded again as a religious bond, and the family life took on once more the aspect of great stability. After the church had come fully into power in the Western world, legal divorce ceased to be recognized and legal separation was substituted in its stead. Thus the church succeeded in reconstituting the family life upon a stable basis, but the family after being reconstituted, was of a semipatriarchal type. Nothing was more natural than this, for the church had no model to go by except the paternal family of the Hebrew and Greek and Roman civilization. Nevertheless, the place of women and children in this semipatriarchal religious family established by the church was higher on the whole than in the ancient patriarchal family.

The church put an end to the exposure of children, which had been common in Rome, and protected childhood in many ways. It also exalted the place of woman in the family, though leaving her subject to her husband. The veneration of the Virgin tended particularly to give women an honored place socially and religiously. Only by the advocacy and practice of ascetic doctrines may the early church be said to have detracted from the social valuation of the family. On the whole the reconstituting of the family by the church must be regarded as its most striking social work. But the thing for us to note particularly is that the type of the family life created by the church was what we might call a semipatriarchal type, in which the importance of husband and father was very much out of proportion to all the rest of the members of the family group. It was this semipatriarchal family which persisted down to the nineteenth century.

6

Poverty and Pauperism

While the many social problems arising from the presence in society of abnormal or socially unadjusted classes, namely, the dependent, defective, and delinquent classes, cannot be discussed in this book adequately, yet they must be briefly noticed in order to correlate them with other social problems, and even more in order to call the attention of the student to the vast literature which exists concerning these problems.

DEFINITIONS OF POVERTY AND PAUPERISM

Poverty is a relative term, difficult to define, but as generally employed in sociological writings at the present it means that economic and social state in which persons have not sufficient income to maintain health and physical efficiency. All who do not receive a sufficient income to maintain the minimum standard of living necessary for efficiency are known as the "poor," or are said to live below the poverty line. Pauperism, on the other hand, is the state of legal dependence in which a person who is unable or unwilling to support himself receives relief from public sources. This is, however, legal pauperism. The word as popularly used has come to mean a degraded state of willing dependence. A pauper in this popular sense is a person unwilling to support himself and who becomes a social parasite. Poverty is closely related to dependence or pauperism, because it is frequently the anteroom, so to speak, to pauperism, although only a small proportion of those who live in poverty actually become dependent in any one year.

The Extent of Poverty and Pauperism in the United States

The census reports showed that in the year 1904 there were about 500,000 dependents in institutions in the United States. While the number who received relief outside of institutions from public and private sources is not known, it is certain that it is many times the total of those in institutions. It is generally estimated that about five per cent of our population are recipients of some sort of charitable relief in a single year. In our large cities the number who receive relief from public and private sources, even in average years, is very much higher. In New York apparently the number who receive relief in an average year reaches fourteen per cent, while in Boston the number who receive relief has reached as high as twenty per cent in a single year. It seems probable, therefore, that taking the country as a whole nearly five per cent of our population have to have some sort of help every year. That would make the number who received relief in 1904 about 4,000,000, and probably this is not an excessive estimate. Upon the basis of these and other known facts Mr. Robert Hunter has estimated that the number of people in the United States living below the poverty line is about 10,000,000 in years of average prosperity.

If negroes are included in this estimate of those below the poverty line, it is certainly not excessive. Probably 10,000,000, or fourteen per cent of our population, understates rather than overstates the number of persons in the United States who live upon such a low standard that they fail to maintain physical and mental efficiency. Moreover, investigations in the countries of Europe show that the estimate of fourteen per cent of our population living in poverty is far from excessive. Mr. Charles Booth, in his Life and Labor of the People of London, says that about thirty per cent of the population of London live below the poverty line, and Mr. B.S. Rowntree found in the English City of York about the same proportion. While poverty is more prevalent in the old world than in the United States, it would seem that in view of our large negro population it is evidently not excessive to estimate the proportion of our people living in poverty at about fifteen per cent.

Moreover, when we extend our view in history we find that poverty has been oftentimes in the past even much more prevalent than it is at present. This question of poverty is, in other words, a world-old question and is intimately bound up with the question of material civilization—that is, man's conquest of nature—and with social organization,—the relations of men to one another. At certain times in history certain institutions like slavery have either obviated or concealed poverty, and particularly its extreme expressions, in dependence and legal pauperism. Nevertheless we can regard these questions of poverty and pauperism as practically existing in all civilizations and in all ages. This is not saying, however, that modern poverty and pauperism may not have certain peculiar foundations in modern social and industrial conditions. It is only saying that it is useless to search wholly for the causes of poverty in conditions that are peculiar to the modern world, because poverty and pauperism are not peculiarly modern problems.

The Genesis of the Depressed Classes

So complex a problem, it might be said at once, cannot manifestly have a simple explanation, yet this has been the mistake of many social thinkers of the past. They have sought some single simple explanation of human misery, and particularly in its form of economic distress or poverty. Malthus, as we have already seen, attributed all human misery to the fact that population tends to increase more rapidly than food supply, and that it is the pressure of population upon food which sufficiently explains poverty in human society. Karl Marx offered an equally sweeping explanation when he attributed all poverty to the fact that labor is not paid a sufficient wage; that the capitalist appropriates an unjust share of the product of labor, leaving to the laborer just enough to maintain existence and reproduce. Henry George in the same spirit, in his Progress and Poverty, attributed all poverty to one cause,—the landlord's appropriation of the unearned increment in land values. There is, of course, some truth in all of these sweeping generalizations, but it must be said that there is not sufficient in any of them to stand the test of concrete investigation; rather these men have made the mistake of attempting to explain a very complex social phenomenon in terms of a single set of causes, which, as we have already seen, has been the bane of social science in the past.

Even the theory of evolution itself fails to explain, as ordinarily stated, the genesis of the depressed classes in human society. It may explain it in part, however. As we have already seen, biological variations are always found in individuals, making some naturally superior, some naturally inferior, and in the struggle for existence we know that the inferior are more liable to go down; they are less apt to maintain a place in society, and hence more readily fall into the depressed classes. Many well-endowed persons, however, also fall into the dependent classes through accidents and causes inherent in our social organization but in no way natural. Thus, owing to our industrial system and to our laws of property, inheritance, and the like, it often happens that a superior person through sickness or other accident gets caught in a mesh of causes which bring him down to the dependent classes, and on the other hand inferior individuals, through inheritance or "social pull," oftentimes enjoy a very large economic surplus all their lives. It may be admitted, however, that slight defects in personal character or ability enter into practically all cases of dependence. This is more apt to be the case also in a progressive society like our own, where rising standards of efficiency make the economic struggle more severe all the time.

Formerly, for example, any employee could drink and retain his position, but now the drinker quickly loses his position in many industries and gives place to the sober man. Oftentimes, however, such defects that give rise to dependence are not inherent but are produced by social conditions themselves, like faulty education, bad surroundings, and the like. Through the improvement of social conditions, therefore, there is no doubt that much of the present poverty of the civilized world can be wiped out. This is not saying, however, that poverty and dependence will ever be wholly eliminated. Probably, no matter how ideal social conditions might be, even under the most just social organization, there would be some accidents and variations in individuals which would produce a condition of dependence. Moreover, the elimination of poverty and pauperism is not so simple as some suppose. It is not wholly a question of the improvement of social conditions; it also involves the control of physical heredity, because many of the principal defects that give rise to dependence are inherent in heredity. But man can control to some extent even the birth of the inferior or unfit classes.

This may seem, however, so far in the future that it is idle to discuss it, although, as we shall see, society is undoubtedly taking steps to prevent the propagation of the unfit. In the meantime, however, so long as humanity progresses through natural selection we shall have poverty, to some extent at least, no matter how much industrial and social conditions may be improved. Yet without the control of physical heredity or the substitution of artificial for natural selection, poverty can be undoubtedly greatly lessened, and it is the rational aim of applied social science to discover how this may be done. It would seem that the existence of 10,000,000 persons in the United States living below the poverty line cannot be justified upon either moral or economic grounds; that it represents a great waste of human life and human resources, and that much of the social maladjustment which this poverty is an expression of might easily yield to wisely instituted remedial measures. If the social maladjustment which is undoubtedly the cause of the bulk of modern poverty were done away with, it is safe to say that it would be reduced to less than one third of its present dimensions.

The Concrete Causes of Poverty

It is necessary to inquire somewhat more minutely into the concrete conditions, social and individual, which give rise to poverty and dependence. Manifestly the poor do not constitute any single class in society. All classes, in a sense, are represented among the poor, and the causes of poverty which are manifest will depend very greatly upon the class of the poor that is studied. If, for example, we should study the causes of dependence among defective classes, naturally personal defects of various sorts would be emphasized. Again, if we should study almshouse paupers, we should expect to find the causes of their dependence different from the causes of the temporary dependence of those who are dealt with outside of institutions and largely by private societies, especially the charity organization societies of large cities. It is especially, however, this latter class of temporary dependents that we are most interested in, because they show most clearly the forces operating to produce the various classes of permanent dependents. There are two great classes of causes of poverty: objective causes, or causes outside of the individual, that is, in the environment; and subjective causes, or causes within the individual. We shall take up first the objective causes.

The Objective Causes of Poverty

The objective causes of poverty may be again divided into causes in the physical environment and causes in the social environment. The causes in the physical environment should not be overlooked, even though to a great extent they may not be amenable to social control. Much poverty in certain regions is caused simply by the unpropitious physical environment, such as unproductive soil, bad climate, and the like. Added to these unpropitious factors in the environment we have also great natural calamities, such as tornadoes, floods, earthquakes, and volcanic eruptions. Every one is familiar with the great amount of misery which is caused, temporarily at least, by such calamities. Again, certain things in the organic environment, particularly in the way of disease-producing bacteria, are also productive of much poverty. Certain bacteria exist, we now know, plentifully in nature, such as the malaria germ, to which rightfully has been ascribed the physical degeneracy of people living in certain sections of the earth. But the most important objective causes of poverty are undoubtedly those found in the social environment,—those which spring from certain social conditions or faults in social organization. Among these we may mention:

(1) Economic Causes. Defective industrial organization and economic evils of various sorts are thought by many persons to be the main productive causes of poverty and dependence in modern society, and there can be no doubt that a very large per cent of poverty may be traced directly to economic evils. This is shown by the fact that in the schedules of all charity organization societies "lack of employment" figures as the first or second most conspicuous cause of distress in the cases with which such societies deal. It is usually estimated that from twenty to forty per cent of all such cases of dependence may be attributed to lack of employment, not due to the employee. It is well known that in periods of industrial depression the number of applicants for aid in our large cities increases enormously, and local strikes and lockouts frequently have the same effect. Again, changes in methods of production through the introduction of new machinery frequently displace large numbers of workingmen, who, on account of age or other reasons, fail to get employment along new lines. Changes in trade brought about through changes in fashions have to some extent at least a similar effect. Again, fluctuations in the value of money may undoubtedly depress a debtor class to the point of dependence. Unwise methods of taxation, such as levying heavy taxes on the necessaries of life, produce a great deal of poverty and economic distress. Systems of land tenure such as prevail in England and even to some extent in the United States, may also be another economic cause of poverty. The free land which has up to the present time existed in this country has been a great aid against poverty. The employment of women and children in factories is another cause of poverty which needs to be mentioned under this head. As we have already seen, this breaks up the home, and in the case of the employment of children stops the development of the child. Still another economic cause of poverty is unhealthful and dangerous occupations. The disease-begetting occupations in modern industry are very numerous, such as hat making, glass blowing, the grinding of tools, and the like—any work in which there is a great deal of dust. Among dangerous occupations must also be included those in which there are numerous accidents, such as mining and railway occupations. The accidents in mines and on railways in the United States each year cause as many deaths and serious injuries as have often resulted in many a petty war. Thus, on the railways of the United States in 1904 there was a total of 10,046 persons killed and 84,155 injured, about three fourths of those injured being employees,—one employee being killed in every three hundred and fifty-seven and one injured in every seventeen. While it is improbable that our great industries can be carried on without some sacrifice of health and life, it seems reasonable to believe that the number of those who are sacrificed at present is

far greater than is necessary, and that reasonable precautions in industry might greatly increase the healthfulness of the occupations and diminish the number of accidents to employees. On the whole, it is probable that these economic causes of poverty figure in from 50 to 80 per cent of all cases, not operating alone, to be sure, but often in connection with faults of character or physical or mental defects in the individual; for it is always to be remembered in discussing the causes of poverty that one never finds a case which can be fairly attributed to a single cause. The complexity of causes operating in the case of a single dependent family frequently makes it impossible for any one to say with certainty what is the chief and what are the contributing causes. Oftentimes what appears to be the chief cause, such as lack of employment, has back of it defects in individual character which are not apparent to the investigator. Researches along this line have shown that the number of cases of distress which may be attributed to lack of employment, for example, may be very greatly reduced when all individual defects are taken into consideration. This, however, is not an argument for regarding the economic causes of poverty as any less important than has been indicated.

(2) Unsanitary conditions of living are frequent causes of poverty. Among these unsanitary conditions may be mentioned especially the housing of the poor. The housing of the poor in badly ventilated, poorly lighted, and unsanitary dwellings greatly increases sickness and death and undoubtedly contributes greatly to their economic depression. Thus in New York city in the first ward, where there is only one house on each lot, the death rate is 29 per 1000 of the population, but where rear tenements have been erected it is 62 per 1000 of the population. The importance of public sanitation, and especially of the prevention of overcrowding and the securing of properly lighted and ventilated dwellings for the people, is so great that we need not enlarge upon it.

(3) Defects in our educational system are certainly productive of poverty. Ignorant and illiterate persons are much more liable to become dependent. In particular the lack of industrial training in our public schools is a prolific cause of dependence in our complex industrial civilization.

(4) Defects in government, permitting corruption on the one hand, or failing to check economic or sanitary evils on the other hand, are manifest causes of poverty. Indeed, inasmuch as government exists to regulate the whole social order, wherever it fails to perform this work properly some economic distress must ensue.

(5) Corruption in social institutions and customs is certainly a cause of poverty: such, for example, is the custom of social drinking, and such also the unwise and indiscriminate charity which has so often existed in the past.

(6) Unrestricted immigration, especially in our Eastern states and cities, is, as we have already seen, a prolific cause of dependence.

The Subjective Causes of Poverty are the causes within the individual. Among these must be enumerated:

(1) Physical and mental defects of all sorts, especially those arising from sickness and accidents. Sickness causing temporary or permanent disability figures in from 25 to 40 per cent of all cases applying for relief in our large cities. Probably it is the most common and most important single cause of poverty with which charity workers have to deal. Back of sickness, however, are often remote causes in the environment or in personal character. We have already spoken of accident as a cause of poverty in connection with dangerous occupations. It is only necessary to add that good authorities estimate that there are over 1,000,000 serious accidents in the United States every year, in order to see that disabilities resulting from accident are prolific as causes of poverty, especially in our large industrial centers. The physical and mental defects which manifest themselves in the defective classes proper, such as the feeble-minded, the insane, the epileptics, the deaf-mutes, and the blind, do not need to be dwelt upon as causes of dependence.

(2) Next after sickness in the list of subjective causes of poverty comes intemperance. While the effect of intemperance in producing poverty has often been exaggerated, there can be no doubt that intemperance is one of the most important causes with which we have to deal. Back of intemperance, of course, may often be again causes in the social environment, or other remote causes, but these do not detract from the fact that practically one fourth of all the cases of distress with which charity organization societies have to deal are attributable, more or less, to intemperance. The Committee of Fifty who investigated this subject found that, in thirty-three cities, out of thirty thousand cases dependence was due to personal intemperance in 18.46 per cent, and due to the intemperance of others in 9.36 per cent, making a total of 27.82 per cent of cases in which intemperance can be traced as a cause of poverty. Other investigations conducted in American cities give substantially the same results, although certain other investigations in English cities give higher percentages. It is noteworthy also that in an investigation conducted by the Massachusetts Bureau of Labor 39 per cent of the cases of poverty were attributed directly or indirectly to drink. Again the Committee of Fifty found that in the case of alms-house paupers a considerably higher per cent owed their condition to the influence of drink either directly or indirectly, the percentage being 41.55.

(3) Sexual vice is undoubtedly a prolific cause of poverty, although it is very hard to trace concretely in the study of specific cases. Dr. Dugdale, however, in his study of the Jukes family places sexual vice even ahead of intemperance as a cause of their degradation, and other similar studies of similar families have reached substantially the same results.

(4) Shiftlessness and laziness are frequently found in the lists of causes of dependence used by charity organization societies, from 10 to 15 per cent of the cases of distress being attributed more or less to these causes. It is now generally agreed, however, that in most

cases these causes may be resolved into more remote causes, laziness being oftentimes attributable to a degenerate or at least undervitalized physical condition.

(5) Old age, which has not been rendered destitute by vice, drink, or other faults of character, is frequently in itself a cause of dependence. Old age seems to figure more largely as a cause of dependence in the European statistics than in American; nevertheless, even in America we frequently find old persons who have worked hard all their lives and yet come to poverty in their old age through no fault of their own. It is for this reason that many are urging old-age pensions as a means of preventing dependence among the aged.

(6) Neglect and desertion by relatives, or the disregard of family ties, in America at least, may be put down as one of the important causes of dependence. From five to ten per cent of all the cases of distress, for example, which charity organization societies in our large cities deal with are those of deserted wives. Again, it is particularly common in America for children to fail to support aged parents and even the desertion of children by parents is of frequent occurrence.

(7) Death of main support must also be mentioned as an important cause of dependence. Widows and their children always figure largely among those helped by charitable societies and institutions. Probably from 10 to 20 per cent of all cases dealt with by societies for relieving temporary distress are cases in which the death of the breadwinner has temporarily rendered the family dependent.

(8) Crime, dishonesty, ignorance, and the like are manifest frequent causes of dependence, and as such need no discussion. We have enumerated in detail some of the more important objective and subjective causes of poverty and dependence in order that the student may see that such causes are very complex, and, as we have already said, there rarely exists a dependent family in which three or more of these causes are not found to be active. Certain questions arise from such a brief presentation as this which we may mention but cannot hope adequately to deal with. Such, for example, is the question whether the subjective causes of poverty can all be reduced to objective causes. In our opinion this cannot be done, because the subjective causes have their roots in biological and psychological conditions, which cannot be attributed directly to causes in the environment.

No doubt, however, many of the subjective causes of poverty are characteristics which have been acquired by individuals from the influence of their environment. When we attribute a certain per cent of poverty to intemperance, for example, it is probable that that particular personal defect may be ascribed almost wholly to the environment. On the other hand, there are other personal defects, such as sickness, vice, and mental deficiency, that cannot always with certainty be traced to environmental factors. It is safest to conclude that while personality is built up largely out of social influences, society is, on the other hand, also rooted in human nature, so that both objective and subjective causes combine to produce practically all social phenomena, and especially the phenomena of poverty and dependence. It is unscientific, therefore, to disregard either the subjective or the objective causes of poverty. Another question which is frequently raised in connection with poverty or dependence is, whether it is due to misconduct or misfortune. This question really has not much meaning in it when it is analyzed. As we have already seen in practically every case of poverty, personal defects and bad environment combine. Only a few of these personal defects, however, can by any proper use of language be regarded as misconduct. The great mass of poverty, therefore, seems attributable to misfortune rather than to misconduct,—using these words in their popular sense.

But such a conclusion as this necessarily rests upon a somewhat superficial examination of the causes of distress which does not enter into the remote springs of personal character and development. On the whole, it seems unwise to attempt to divide the poor into the "worthy" and "unworthy" poor, as has often been done, for no one can say who is the worthy and who is the unworthy in a moral sense. The only sense in which these words may be used scientifically in charitable work is to mean "needy" and "not needy."

Pauperism and Degeneracy

In order to see more clearly the biological roots of dependence we must notice briefly the relation of habitual pauperism to degeneracy. Studies like that made by Dr. Dugdale of the Jukes family show that unquestionably there is in many instances a close relation between habitual pauperism of various types and degeneracy. Out of 709 in the Jukes family studied by Dugdale 500 had been aided. Pauperism was 7 1 2 times as common among the Jukes as in the ordinary population. Along with the pauperism of the Jukes went prostitution, illegitimacy, crime, and physical disease and defects. Many other studies have shown the same intimate relation between physical degeneracy and habitual dependence or pauperism. There can be no doubt, therefore, that general physical degeneracy, or biological unfitness, is, as we have already asserted in the beginning, a conspicuous factor in the worst cases of chronic pauperism.

The Influence of Heredity upon Pauperism

Similar studies to those already mentioned have shown that dependence is often times hereditary in families from generation to generation. This is doubtless based upon the inheritance of physical and mental defects. Indirectly, therefore, there is such a thing as hereditary pauperism. Now we know from the labors of Weismann that acquired characteristics are not inherited, but only congenital, or inborn characteristics. It is not the characteristics, in other words, which are acquired from the influence of environment that are transmitted to offspring, but the characteristics that arise through variations in the germ, caused by forces which are not yet well understood. Defects that are acquired by the individual in his lifetime, in other words, will not be transmitted; but the defects that arise through accident or other means in the germ are transmitted. This being so, it follows that acquired pauperism or dependence is not transmitted but only the pauperism which rests upon congenital defects. This is illustrated by the case of the deaf. Deaf-mutes are of two sorts: persons who are born deaf, or the congenital deaf-mutes, and persons who become deaf-mutes through diseases affecting the ear in early childhood. These latter are styled adventitious deaf-mutes. Now when congenital deaf-mutes marry, they show a strong tendency to transmit their defect to offspring, but the children of adventitious deaf-mutes are always normal. Dr. Fay, in his investigations into the marriages of the deaf in the United States shows that only 0.3 per cent of the children born from the marriages of persons adventitiously deaf and having no deaf relatives are born deaf; while on the other hand, 30.3 per cent of the children born from the marriages of persons congenitally deaf, both parents having deaf relatives, are born deaf. In other words, the number of deaf-mutes born where both parents are congenitally deaf and have deaf relatives is one hundred times greater than where both parents are adventitiously deaf and have no deaf relatives. This is pretty conclusive proof that it is only the congenital defects which are transmissible, but these are so highly transmissible that they may express themselves in pauperism from generation to generation.

The marriage of all persons in whom there is an hereditary taint of feeble-mindedness, insanity, epilepsy, and the like ought, therefore, to be forbidden by law. But unless these defective classes were segregated in institutions, the only result of this might be to increase illegitimacy; therefore, any step in eradicating degeneracy and pauperism must look to the isolation and custodial care through life of the hopelessly defective classes. All this gives point to our conclusion that poverty and pauperism have roots which are quite independent of defects in economic conditions, and that, until heredity itself can be controlled, we cannot expect to eliminate poverty entirely. Proposed Remedies for Poverty and Pauperism.—The scientific remedies for poverty and pauperism, that is, the scientific methods of dealing with the various dependent classes and of preventing their existence, now form the subject-matter of a great independent science, the science of philanthropy, which, as we have already seen, may be considered a branch of applied sociology.

We have not room in this book to discuss adequately these remedies, but we may call the attention of the student again to the vast literature existing upon the subject, and may point out the trend of modern scientific philanthropy in developing scientific methods for removing the causes of dependence and of preventing the existence of the various dependent classes. As we have already seen, poverty is an economic expression of biological or psychological defects of the individual on the one hand, and of a faulty social and industrial organization on the other hand. This implies that the remedies must be along the lines of the biological and psychological adjustment of the individual and of the correction of the faults in social organization. Where biological defects of the individual are the cause of dependence, we have just implied that, unless these defects are relatively superficial, the scientific policy for treating these classes of defective individuals would be that of segregation in institutions. The feeble-minded, the chronic insane, the chronic epileptic, and other hopelessly defective persons, in other words, should be permanently kept in institutions where tender and humane care should be provided, but in such a way that they will not reproduce their kind and burden future generations. The policy of segregating the hopelessly defective is one of the most scientifically approved policies of modern philanthropy. In this way, to a certain extent, the reproduction of unfit elements in society might be lessened, and the spread of degeneracy checked. In the case of slightly defective adults, such as the congenitally deaf and the congenitally blind, it is difficult to say exactly what the policy should be. It would seem that many of these persons may be relatively adjusted to free social life, although if they marry and have offspring we know, if their defect is congenital, that a certain proportion of the offspring, according to Mendel's law, will inherit the defect. In the case of those individuals whose dependence is due to psychological defects, or defective character, it is evident that we have a different problem. Here, in general, the wise policy would seem to be, not to segregate, but to overcome the defective character. Psychological defects, we know, are much more frequently acquired than biological defects and much more easily remedied. The work of scientific philanthropy in dealing with this class of individuals must be, therefore, a work of remedying defects in individual character. This is, perhaps, best done through personal relations between the dependent person and those who may help him. Defective character is, on the whole, therefore, best remedied by such means as education, religious influences, friendly visiting, and the like.

The class of dependents whose condition is due to defective character may be on the whole, therefore, best treated outside of institutions, and probably better through voluntary private charity than through public relief systems. There remains another class of dependents whose condition is not due either to biological nor to psychological defects in themselves, but to faulty social and industrial conditions. For these, the best method of treatment consists in remedying the faulty conditions or in removing them, if possible, from them. This means that, in many cases, society must provide pensions, insurance against accident and sickness, legislation to check social abuses, and, above all, proper facilities for education. Here comes in the need of child-labor legislation, of better housing, of industrial insurance, of industrial education, and the like. In the light of these principles, let us review very briefly the different methods of dealing with dependent classes at the present time.

Public and Private Outdoor Relief

By outdoor relief we mean relief given to the poor outside of an institution. Usually, outdoor relief refers simply to the public relief of dependents outside of institutions, but we shall use the phrase to cover both public and private relief. It is evident from what has already been said that the class of persons to whom this form of relief is appropriate are those in temporary distress, whose condition of dependence is not a permanent one and, therefore, usually those whose condition is due either to defective personal character or to faulty social organization. If the temporary dependence is due to defective personal character, it is evident that the aid may be so given, if given wisely, as to stimulate the overcoming of the moral defect. Hence the need of carefully planned measures of relief in all such cases. Hence, also, the need of the friendly visitor, who by personal contact with such a family will help them to become socially adjusted. If, on the other hand, the temporarily dependent person is simply a victim of circumstances, there is, then, also, the need of wise charity in order to overcome those adverse circumstances without impairing the character of the individual who is helped by destroying his self-respect and the like. It is evident that the task of relieving temporarily dependent persons outside of institutions is a delicate and difficult one, and requires carefully trained workers to do it successfully.

For this reason, many have argued that outdoor relief should not be undertaken by the state in any of its branches, such as the city or county. In general, it must be admitted that the private society is, in many cases, naturally better fitted to accomplish this delicate and difficult task of restoring the temporarily dependent person. But, on the other hand, it must be said that the whole matter is simply a question of administration. Private societies may be quite as lax and unscientific in their charity as the state, and it is conceivable that the state can develop a system of outdoor relief which will be administered by experts quite as carefully as any private organization could administer it. Indeed, this is what has been practically done in Germany under the Elberfeldt System, which is a state system for dispensing outdoor relief to the temporarily indigent. In the United States, however, this work of relieving the temporarily dependent in their own homes has been, in our large cities, undertaken with great success by the charity organization societies, which, in general, do the work with such thoroughness as to obviate the necessity for public outdoor relief in our large cities.

State Charitable Institutions

Indoor relief, or relief within institutions, for the permanently dependent classes is probably best undertaken by the state. Originally, the only institution of this sort was the almshouse or the poor house; but with the development of our complex civilization many of the permanently dependent have been provided for in other institutions than the almshouse, and it would seem that ultimately all the permanently dependent would be cared for in specialized state institutions. Thus, the permanently dependent, through various sorts of defects, such as the feeble-minded, chronic epileptic, chronic insane, and the like, are properly cared for in institutions especially provided for the purpose by the state and manned by experts. Into the details of public care of the unfit and defective of various types it is not necessary to go further than to say that such public care should be of the most scientific character, and with the double aim of reclaiming all those that can be reclaimed, and of providing permanently tender and humane care for those who cannot be fitted for free social life. State institutions then, should be manned by experts, and their activities should be coordinated by some central board. In accordance with this principle, it would seem that the best state policy would be to provide expert commissions for the care of different classes, such as the insane, and the like, and a supervisory board to watch over the work of these commissions and the institutions.

Dependent Children

The care of dependent children is manifestly one of the most important forms of remedial philanthropic work, for it is manifest that the dependent child will make a dependent adult unless proper measures are taken to secure his adjustment to the social life. The dependent child is rarely biologically defective. The problem is, usually, in his case, the development of character under proper social conditions. For this reason, both the state and private societies have claimed the field of care of dependent children. While private societies have accomplished in this respect some of the most notable work, it would seem, however, that the work is one which properly belongs to the state in its capacity of legal guardian of all dependent children. The state, through a properly organized system of child helping, could conceivably guarantee that every neglected and dependent child should have normal opportunities to become adjusted to the social life. The system in the state of Michigan, with its Public School for Dependent Children at Coldwater, and its plan of placing these children, after a few months, in good homes, is a system which cannot receive too high commendation. In general, it is practically agreed by experts that the dependent child cannot be well adjusted to the social life by being reared in an institution, but that the better plan is to find suitable homes in which these children can be placed and reared under state supervision. In this way, practically every dependent child can be guaranteed a good chance in life. In the United States, private societies called "Childrens' Home Societies" are also doing this work with great success.

Public and Private Charity

As has ordinary line to be observed between is that to private charity should be difficult tasks, such as readjusting already been indicated, the private charity and public relief given the more delicate and the temporarily dependent persons, the care of, in some cases, dependent children and the like, while to public charity should be given the cases which need permanent relief in institutions. This is only a conventional line, however, between private charity and public relief. As has already been pointed out, the state can conceivably, also, undertake the more delicate and difficult tasks of charitable aid, and probably it should do so as rapidly as it demonstrates its fitness to undertake this work, as the state, when once it has achieved certain standards, is a more certain and reliable agency than private institutions or societies. But there is in philanthropic work, a large place for the private society or institution. There will probably always be debatable cases which may better be looked after by private agencies than by public.

There is, therefore, in every well-developed community, room for both public and private agencies, although there should be close cooperation where both exist one with the other. The church, through all its history, has undertaken philanthropic work with notable success, and it would be regrettable if the philanthropic activities of the church were to cease at this time, when they are needed as never before, in spite of the large development of public philanthropy. Church charity should, however, be made as scientific as any other form of charity, and should be carefully coordinated with the work of the state and other secular agencies. Among the secular agencies we have already mentioned the charity organization society as typifying in many ways the highest type of philanthropic activity of the present. It would seem that this society, organizing as it does all the philanthropic forces and agencies of the community, could scarcely be displaced by state activity; and that there would remain to this society, as well as many other private philanthropic societies, a very large field of activity in the future. State activity in the field of charity is, therefore, to be encouraged, but it must not be supposed that such activity can take the place of private charity.

Preventive Agencies

A very large task for both private societies and the state is to be found in the field of prevention. This field is so broad, however, that we cannot attempt to even mention the many different movements alone which characterize our present social development. Such are the movements for better housing, for better sanitation, for purer food, for juster economic conditions, for the prevention of disease, and the like. The main thing to be said with respect to these movements is that they need to be guided by the larger social view, they need synthesis in order that they may work toward a common goal, and in harmony, also, with the activities of the state. In the field of prevention the state has much to do, especially in forwarding education along lines of social need and in creating juster economic conditions. We may, perhaps, sum up this chapter by saying that it is evident that the cure of poverty is not to be sought merely in certain economic rearrangements, but in scientific control of the whole life process of human society. This means that, in order to get rid of poverty, the defects in education, in government, in religion and morality, in philanthropy, and even in physical heredity, must be got rid of. Of course, this can only be done when there is a scientific understanding of the conditions necessary for normal human social life. What some of these requirements for a normal life are will be seen in a subsequent chapter, and it is only necessary to say in conclusion that the wisest measures for removing pauperism will be directed toward the prevention of its causes rather than toward the reclaiming of those who have already been caught in its meshes.

7

Socialism in the Light of Sociology

There have been many "short-cuts" proposed to the solution of social problems. Among these the various schemes for reorganizing human society and industry, brought together under the general name of "socialism," have attracted most attention and deserve most serious consideration. In criticizing the most conspicuous of these schemes of social reconstruction, the so-called "scientific socialism," it should be understood at the outset that there is no intention of questioning the general aims of the socialists. Those aims, as voiced by their best representatives, are in entire accord with sound science, religion, and ethics. That humanity should gain collective control over the conditions of its existence is the ultimate and highest aim of all science, all education, and all government. No student of sociology doubts that human society has steadily moved, though with interruptions, toward a larger control over its own processes; and no sane man doubts that such collective control over the conditions of existence is desirable. These general aims, which the socialists share with all workers for humanity, are not in question. What is in question are the specific means or methods by which the socialists propose to reconstruct human society—to gain collective control over the means of existence. In order to criticize socialism we must see a little more narrowly what socialism is and what it proposes to do.

SOCIALISM DEFINED

As a recent socialist writer has declared, socialism, like Christianity, is a term which has come to have no definite meaning. It is used by all sorts of people to cover all sorts of vague and indefinite schemes to improve or revolutionize society. It has been said that the word "socialism," as currently used, has four distinct meanings:

(1) Utopian socialism, i.e., schemes like More's Utopia;

(2) the socialist party and its program, i.e., "the socialization of the instruments of production;"

(3) The Marxist doctrine of social evolution, i.e., "the materialistic conception of history;"

(4) a vague body of beliefs of the working classes, more or less derived from (2) and (3).

It is of course only socialism in the second and third senses which is discussed in this chapter. Such a vague conception would, of course, be impossible of scientific criticism. But fortunately the word historically has come to have a fairly clear and definite meaning. It has come to stand for the social and political program of a party, the Social-Democratic party of Germany and other European states. Karl Marx and his associates were the founders of this party, hence historical socialism is synonymous with Marxian socialism, and we shall so use the word. The cardinal tenet or principle of the socialist party is the public ownership of all capital, that is, of the means of production. Certain other things are, however, involved in this, and we may define the full program of Marxian socialism by saying that it proposes:

(1) The common ownership of the means of production (abolition of private property in capital);

(2) Common management of the means of production (industry) by democratically selected authorities;

(3) Distribution of the product by these common authorities in accordance with some democratically approved principle;

(4) Private property in incomes (consumption goods) to be retained. It is evident from this outline of "orthodox" or Marxian socialism that it is primarily and dominantly an economic program. It is true that it emphasizes democratic forms of government, but this is only incidental to its main purpose of securing a just distribution of economic goods. Strictly speaking, in a correct use of scientific terms, Marxian socialism should be called "economic socialism."

THE THEORETICAL BASIS OF MARXIAN SOCIALISM

Marx's socialism is frequently called scientific socialism, because its followers believe that it rests upon a scientific theory of social evolution. This theory is best stated in Marx's own words, as he gives it in his Critique of Political Economy, namely, that "the method of the production of material life determines the social, political, and spiritual life process in general." We find it stated in other words, though in substance the same, by Engels, Marx's friend and coworker. Engels says, "In every historical epoch, the prevailing mode of economic production and exchange, and the social organization necessarily following from it, form the basis upon which is built up, and from which alone can be explained, the political and intellectual history of that epoch." In other words, according to Marx and his followers, the economic element in human society determines all other elements; if the other elements cannot be fully derived from the economic, their form and expression is at least determined by the economic. This is the so-called "materialistic conception of history" upon which Marxian socialists believe their program to have a firm scientific foundation.

The followers of Marx, indeed, declare that with this principle Marx explains social evolution quite as fully as Darwin explained organic evolution through natural selection; and they do not hesitate to compare Marx's work in the social sciences with Darwin's work in the biological sciences. It may certainly be agreed that this social philosophy which we have already said is best characterized as "economic determinism," is the logically necessary foundation of economic socialism.

If the change of the economic or industrial order of human society is going to work such wonders as the socialists claim, then it must follow that the economic element is the fundamental and determining element in the social life. If what is wrong with human society is chiefly wrong economic conditions, then the changing of those conditions should, of course, change the whole social superstructure. It would seem, therefore, that the dominantly economic program of Marxian socialists must stand or fall with the economic interpretation of social organization and evolution which Marx proposed. If it can be shown that Marx's philosophy of human society is essentially unsound, then the proposition to regenerate human society simply by economic reorganization is also unsound. Let us see whether the positions of the economic socialists are tenable in the light of the sociological principles which have been emphasized in the previous chapters of this book.

Criticism of Marxian Socialism

The student has already been told that human society is a complex of living organisms, responding now this way, now that, to external stimuli in the environment. These stimuli in the environment we have roughly, but inaccurately, spoken of as causes, though they are not causes in a mechanical sense. The responses which are given to these stimuli by individuals and groups vary greatly according to heredity, instincts, and habits,—the inner nature, in other words, of the organisms composing society. Now, the stimuli in the environment which give rise to the activities of individuals and societies, though not in any mechanical way, may be classified into several great groups, such as the economic, the reproductive, the political, the religious, and so on.

The economic stimuli would be those that have to do with the processes of production, distribution, and consumption of wealth; that is, the economic stimuli are those which are concerned with economic values.

Now, while the student has not been even introduced to the psychological theory of human society, he perhaps knows enough of individual human nature to see that there is no reason in the nature of things why one's responses to economic stimuli, those connected with economic values, should determine his response to all other stimuli; and this is what scientific sociology and scientific psychology exactly find; namely, that there is no reason for believing that economic stimuli determine in any exact way or to any such extent, as Marx thought, responses to other stimuli. It is true that our habits of response to a certain class of stimuli affect to a certain extent our habits of response to all other classes. Thus it follows that the economic phase of human society affects to a very great degree all other phases of human society. But this is simply the doctrine of the unity of personality and the interdependence of all phases of the social life, and it is very different from Marx's theory that the economic determines all the other phases; for under the doctrine of social interdependence we can see it is quite as reasonable to state that the religious and political phases of the social life determine the economic as it is to state that the economic determines the political and religious. Let us bring the discussion down to more concrete terms.

The student has seen that in every social problem there are a multitude of factors or stimuli (causes) at work, and that in no problem is the economic factor so all important that it may be said that the other factors are simply subsidiary. On the contrary, in such a problem as crime the methods of production and distribution of material goods, while important factors in the problem of crime, in no way determine that problem; and ideal conditions of the production and distribution of wealth would in no way solve the problem of crime. So, too, the negro problem is hardly touched by the question of the forms of industry or the economic organization of society. We might go on with a whole list of social problems and show that in every case the economic factor is no more important than many other factors, and that the economic reorganization of society would in some cases scarcely affect these problems at all.

The social problem, therefore,—the problem of the relations of men to one another,—is not simply nor fundamentally an economic problem; rather it is fundamentally a biological and psychological problem, —if you please, a moral problem. This brings us to a second criticism of socialism, namely, that it proposes to reorganize human society upon an economic basis, not upon a biological basis. The program of the socialist looks forward to the satisfaction of economic needs, but it has failed to take into account the biological requirements for existence. It would be far more scientific to reorganize society upon the basis of the needs of the family than to reorganize it simply upon the basis of industry.

The reproductive process which the economic socialists ignore, or leave unregulated almost entirely, is far more important for the continued existence of human society than all its economic processes,—if by the reproductive process we mean the rearing as well as the birth of offspring; and if by the economic process we mean merely the forms and methods of the production and distribution of material goods.

In other words, the socialistic program leaves the future out of account, and aims simply to satisfy the present generation with a just distribution of material goods. If it could be shown that a just distribution of material goods would insure the future of the race and of civilization, then, of course, the socialist plea would be made good. But this is just what is doubtful. On the whole, it must be said that the socialist program is based upon the wishes and desires of the adult, not upon the needs of the child or of the race. The extreme emphasis which Marxian socialism throws upon economic and industrial conditions in human society is, therefore, not justified by the scientific facts which we know about collective human life. Rather it must be said that this is the vital weakness of Marxian socialism,—that it over-emphasizes the economic element. Of course, we are not saying that control over economic conditions is not necessary to collective control over the general conditions of existence, which society is undoubtedly aiming at, but it is saying that conceivably collective control over the social life process might be upon some other basis than the economic. It might emphasize, for example, the health and continuity of the race, or individual moral character, far more than the distribution of economic values. Modern economic socialism proposes simply to carry a step further our already predominatingly economic social organization by frankly recognizing the economic as the basis of all things in the social life.

Modern economic socialism is, therefore, rightfully judged as materialistic. It is really an expression of the industrial and commercial spirit of the present age. When the perspective of life becomes shifted again to the more important biological and spiritual elements in life, socialism will lose its prevailingly economic character, or it will cease to exist. It must be emphasized here that all the material and economic progress of the modern world has not added greatly to the happiness or betterment of man. It is true that material progress is important, yes, necessary for spiritual progress. But material progress alone does not lead to spiritual progress, and therefore mere material progress can never add anything to the real happiness and social betterment of the race. On the contrary, it is possible to conceive of a society in which every one has an economic surplus,—a society rolling in wealth, approximately equally divided, and yet one in which human misery in its worst forms of vice and crime, pessimism and self-destruction, prevail. It is an old truth that making men "better-off" does not necessarily make them "better," and one which cannot be too often emphasized, but one which the modern socialist gets angry at when it is mentioned to him. It is therefore a matter of comparative indifference, from the standpoint of the happiness and ultimate survival of the race, whether economic goods are distributed relatively evenly in human society or not.

We say comparative indifference, because, of course, no one can be indifferent to the material needs of life, inasmuch as they are the basis of its higher development. But after a certain minimum is assured it is extremely doubtful whether a surplus will be of benefit or not, and this minimum necessary for the higher spiritual development of the social life can be secured through the reform of present society without trying the doubtful social revolution which the socialists advocate. This brings us to a third criticism of Marxian socialism. Traditionally Marxian socialism has been revolutionary socialism. The vast mass of the socialist party to-day look forward to some revolution which will, as they say, "socialize the instruments of production," that is, transfer capital from private ownership and management to public ownership and management. Probably rightly, many socialists hold that such a wholesale transfer from private to public ownership would be the only way in which a socialistic regime could be successfully inaugurated.

But if this revolution were accomplished it is evident that it is highly uncertain whether its results would be permanent. For all that we have learned concerning human society leads us to say that social organization at any particular time is very largely a matter of habit. Now collective habits are less easily changed than individual habits, because any change in collective habits practically necessitates the consent of all the individuals who make up the social group.

We know also that even in individual life old habits are not easily supplanted by new ones and that there is always a tendency to revert to the old. All historical evidence shows that revolutions are always followed by periods of reaction, and that this reaction is usually proportionate to the extent and suddenness of change in social organization. Some modern socialists have argued from de Vries's mutation theory in biology that in social evolution we must expect mutations also, and that, therefore, the great changes in human society are normally accomplished by means of revolution. But this argument rests wholly on analogy, and arguments from analogy in science are practically worthless. It may be asserted, on the other hand, that all the great changes in human society which have been desirable have come about only after prolonged preparation and after a series of gradual steps which led up to the final change.

The Greco-Roman world, for example, was becoming ripe for Christianity before Christianity finally appeared and became triumphant. The centuries from the fourteenth to the sixteenth had prepared for the protestant reformation in the countries of modern Europe before the reformation became an established fact. Thus, radical reconstruction of the social life by means of revolution is scarcely possible.

The instincts and habits of individual human nature upon which the social order rests cannot be easily changed by revolutionary programs in legislation or in institutions. The only probable result of such an attempt would be the collapse of the new social order, because it would have insufficient foundations in individual character upon which to rest. The idea of ushering in the social millennium through some vast social revolution is therefore chimerical. It is not the place in this book to take up the practical objections to economic socialism. These practical objections are for the most part of a political and economic nature, and they accordingly can be better dealt with in treatises on politics and economics than in one on sociology. It is perhaps sufficient to say that the political and economic objections to socialism are not less weighty than the sociological objections.

Government, for example, exists in human society to regulate, and not to carry on directly, all social activities. If the state were in its various forms called upon to own and manage all productive wealth in society, it is extremely probable that such an experiment would break down of its own weight, since the state would be attempting that which, in the nature of things, as the chief regulative institution of society, it is not fitted to do. But it is not our purpose, as has just been said, to go into the political and economic objections to economic or Marxian socialism. To understand these the student must consult the leading works on economic and political science.

Substitutes for Economic Socialism

Certain steps sociology and all social sciences already indicate as necessary for larger collective control over the conditions of social existence. These steps, however, aim not at instituting a new social order, but at removing certain demonstrated causes of social maladjustment which exist in present society; and as in the solution of special social problems we have seen reason to reject "short-cuts" and "cure-alls," so in a scientific reconstruction of human society we have good reason to reject the social revolution which the followers of Marx advocate, and to offer as a substitute in its stead some social reforms which will make more nearly possible a normal social life.

Perhaps the necessary steps for bringing about such a normal social life have never been better summed up than by Professor Devine in his book on Misery and its Causes. Rather than offer a program of our own we shall, therefore, give a brief resume of the conditions which Professor Devine names as essential to normal social life, believing that these offer a program upon which all sane social workers and reformers can unite. Professor Devine names ten conditions essential to a normal social life:

(1) The securing of a sound physical heredity, that is, a good birth for every child, by a rational system of eugenics;

(2) The securing of a protected childhood, which will assure the normal development of the child, and of a protected motherhood, which will assure the proper care of the child;

(3) A system of education which shall be adapted to social needs, inspired by the ideals of rational living and social service;

(4) The securing of freedom from preventable disease;

(5) The elimination of professional vice and crime;

(6) The securing of a prolonged working period for both men and women;

(7) A general system of insurance against the ordinary contingencies of life which now cause poverty or dependence;

(8) A liberal relief system which will meet the material needs of those who become accidentally dependent;

(9) A standard of living sufficiently high to insure full nourishment, reasonable recreation, proper housing, and the other elementary necessities of life;

(10) A social religion which shall make the service of humanity the highest aim of all individuals.

It is sufficient to say, in closing this chapter, that if these ten essentials of a normal social life could be realized—and there is no reason why they cannot be—there would be no need to try the social revolution which Marxian socialism advocates. There can be no question that the ultimate aim of the social sciences is to provide society with the knowledge necessary for collective control over its own life processes. Sociology and the special social sciences are aiming, therefore, in an indirect way to accomplish the same thing which political socialism aims at accomplishing through economic revolution. There would seem to be no danger in trusting science to work out this problem of collective control over the conditions of existence. There are no risks to run by the scientific method, for it proceeds step by step, adequately testing theories by facts as it goes along.

The thing to do, therefore, for those who wish to see "a humanity adjusted to the requirements of its existence" is to encourage scientific social research along all lines. With a fuller knowledge of human nature and human society it will be possible to indicate sane and safe reconstructions in the social order, so that ultimately humanity will control its social environment and its own human nature even more completely than it now controls the forces of physical nature. But the ultimate reliance in all such reconstruction, as we will try to show in the next chapter, must be, not revolution, nor even legislation, but education.

8

Education and Social Progress

As has just been said, the ultimate reliance in all social reform or social reconstruction must be upon the education of the individual. Social organization can never be more complex or of a higher type than the individual character and intelligence of the members of the group warrants. At any given stage of society, therefore, the intelligence and moral character of its individual members limits social organization. Only by raising the intelligence and character of the individual members of society can a higher type of social life permanently result. Another fact to which the student needs his attention called is that all progress in human society, it follows, from what has just been said, depends upon the relation between one generation and its successor. Only as new life comes into society is there opportunity to improve the character of that life. If at any given time intelligence and character limit the possibilities of social organization, then it is equally manifest that only in the new individuals of society can that intelligence and character be greatly improved.

There are, of course, two possible ways of bringing about such improvement:—first, through the selection of the hereditary elements in society, eliminating the unfit and preserving the more fit; but, as we have repeatedly pointed out, such a scheme of artificial selection is far in the future, and in any case its inauguration would have to depend upon the second method of improving individual character, which is through education and training. As we have insisted, not only may the natural instincts and tendencies of individuals be greatly modified by training but through education the habits and hence the character of individuals can be controlled. Therefore the main reliance of society in all forward movements must be upon education, that is, upon artificial means of controlling the formation of character and habit in individuals. The finality of education in social betterment can be, perhaps, further illustrated by reconsidering for a moment some of the social problems which we have just studied. Take for example the problem of crime. There are only three possible means, as we have already seen, of eliminating crime from human society:—first, through changes in individual human nature, brought about by biological selection, that is, through a system of selective breeding, eliminating all who show any criminal tendencies. This method would, perhaps, eliminate certain types of criminals as we have already seen, namely, those in whom the hereditary tendency to crime is dominant. A second means of attacking the problem of crime would be by improving social and economic conditions by means of the interference of the organized authority of society in the form of the state.

Legislation and administration directed to social ends might accomplish much in reducing the temptations and opportunities for crime in any group. The correction of evils in social and industrial organization would, no doubt, again greatly lessen crime but it is entirely conceivable, from all that we know of human nature and human society, that crime might still persist under a just social and industrial organization. Crime could be completely eliminated only through a third means, namely, the careful training of each new individual in society as he came on the stage of life, so that he would be moral and law-abiding, respecting the rights of others and the institutions of society. Moreover, neither selective breeding nor governmental interference in social conditions could accomplish very much in eliminating crime unless these were backed by a wise system of social education. Now what is true of crime is equally true of all social problems. They may be approached from either of three sides:—first, from the biological side, or the side of physical heredity; second, from the side of social organization, or the improvement of the social environment; third, from the side of individual character, or the psychical adjustment of the individual to society.

As Professor Ward and many other sociologists have emphasized, it is this latter side which is the most available point of attack on all social problems; for when we have secured a right attitude of the individual toward society all social problems will be more than half solved. Thus, as we said at the beginning of this book, education has a bearing upon every social problem, and every social problem also has a bearing upon education. Just how important this reciprocal relationship between education and social life is, we can appreciate only when we have considered somewhat more fully the nature of social progress.

THE NATURE OF SOCIAL PROGRESS

Social progress has been defined in many ways by the social thinkers of the past. Without entering into any formal definition of social progress, we believe that it will be evident to the reader of this book that social progress consists, for one thing, in the more complete adaptation of society to the conditions of life. We regard those changes as progressive whether they be moral, intellectual, or material, which bring about a better adaptation of individuals to one another in society, and of social groups to the requirements of their existence. Social progress means, in other words, the adaptation of society to a wider and more universal environment. The ideal of human progress is apparently adaptation to a perfectly universal environment, such an adaptation as shall harmonize all factors whether internal or external, present or remote, in the life of humanity. Social progress means, therefore, greater harmony among the members of a group. It means also greater efficiency of those members in performing their work. Finally, it means greater ability on the part of the group to survive.

Social progress includes, therefore, the ideals of social harmony, social efficiency, and social survival. Things which do not ultimately conduce to these ends can scarcely be called progressive. Now it is evident that adaptation on the part of individuals and groups to the requirements of life may be in part accomplished by biological selection, that is, by eliminating the least adapted. But selection is, after all, a very clumsy and imperfect instrument for securing the highest type of adaptation. Again, it is evident that a certain degree of adaptation can be secured through the constraint of government and law; but only a relatively low type of adaptation can be secured in such an external way. It is finally evident, therefore, that the highest type of adaptation in either individual or social life can be secured only by training the intelligence and moral character of individuals so that they will be sufficient to meet the requirements of existence. Another feature of social progress which we have not yet mentioned in this chapter, though we have noted it repeatedly in earlier chapters, is the increased complexity of social organization. This increased complexity is in part due to the mere increase in numbers. It is also due to the various processes themselves by which wider and more universal adaptation is brought about in society.

Thus, while every useful mechanical invention aids man to conquer nature, it at the same time increases the complexity of social life. Now in a more complex society there is more opportunity for conflicts of habit between individuals, more opportunity for social maladjustment, and therefore more opportunity for the failure of some part or all of the group in achieving a social life characterized by harmony, efficiency, and capacity for survival. Hence, the adaptation of individuals in the large and complex groups of modern civilized societies becomes a greater and greater problem. The regulative institutions of society, such as government, law, religion, and education, have to grapple with this problem of adjusting individuals to the requirements of an increasingly complex social life. No doubt religion, government, and law have a great function to perform in increasing social regulation, but they can only perform it effectively after they enlist education on their side. The Social Function of Education.—We are now prepared to understand the meaning of educational systems in civilized society and to see what the true function of education is.

Education exists to adapt individuals to their social life. It is for the purpose of fitting the individual to take his place in the social group and to add something to the life of the group. Educational systems exist not to train the individual to develop his powers and capacity simply as an individual unit, but rather to fit him effectively to carry on the social life before he actively participates in it. In other words, the social function of education is to guide and control the formation of habit and character on the part of the individual, as well as to develop his capacity and powers, so that he shall become an efficient member of society. This work is not, at least in complex civilizations like our own, one which we carry on simply in order to achieve social perfection, but it is rather something which is necessary for the survival of large and complex groups. Otherwise, as we have pointed out, the conflicts in the acquirement of habit and character on the part of individuals would be so great that there would be no possibility of their working together harmoniously in a common social life. Just so far as the system of education is defective, is insufficient to meet social needs, in so far may we expect the production of individuals who are socially maladjusted, as shown in pauperism, defectiveness, and crime. Education is, then, the great means of controlling habit and character in complex social groups, and as such it is the chief means to which society must look for all substantial social progress. It is the instrument by which human nature may be apparently indefinitely modified, and hence, also, the instrument by which society may be perfected. The task of social regeneration is essentially a task of education.

EDUCATION AS A FACTOR IN PAST SOCIAL EVOLUTION

Does past social history justify these large claims for education as a factor in social development? It must be replied that the history of human society undoubtedly substantiates this position, but even if it did not, we should still have good ground for claiming that education can be such an all-powerful factor in the social future. The sociological study of past civilizations, however, shows quite conclusively that all of them have depended in one way or another upon educational processes, not only for continuity, but largely, also, for their development. As we have already seen, the life history of a culture or a civilization is frequently the life history of a religion. But religious beliefs, together with the moral and social beliefs, which become attached to them, were effectively transmitted only through the instruction of the young. The religious element did scarcely more than afford a powerful sanction for the moral and social beliefs upon which the social organization of the past rested; hence, when we ascribe great importance to the religious factor in social evolution, we also ascribe, at the same time, great importance to education, because it was essentially the educational process, together with religious sanction, which made possible most of the civilizations and social progress of the past. Indeed, we have no record of any people of any very considerable culture that did not employ educational processes to the largest degree to preserve and transmit that culture from generation to generation.

Culture has been passed down in human history, therefore, essentially by educational processes. These educational processes have controlled the formation of habits and character, of ways of thinking and ways of acting, in successive generations of individuals. The educational processes have had much more to do, therefore, with the civilizations and social organization of the past than industrial conditions. Industrial conditions have been rather relatively external factors in the social environment to which society has had to adapt itself more or less. In the same way, political authority has rested on, and been derived from, the social traditions rather than the reverse. It is therefore not too much for the sociologist to say, agreeing with Thomas Davidson, that education is the last and highest method of social evolution. The lowest method of evolution was by selection, and that, as we have already emphasized, cannot be neglected. The next method of social evolution apparently to develop was the method of adaptation by organized authority, and, as we have already seen, organized authority in society, or social regulation by means of authority, must indefinitely persist and perhaps increase, rather than diminish; but the latest and highest method of social evolution is not through biological selection nor through the exercise of despotic authority, but through the education of the individual, so that he shall become adjusted to the social life in habits and character before he participates in it. Human society may be modified, we now see, best through modifying the nature of the individual, and the most direct method to do this is through education.

The Socialized Education of the Future

If what has been said is substantially correct, then education should become conscious of its social mission and purpose. The educator should conserve education as the chief means of social progress, and education should be directed to producing efficient members of society. The education of the future must aim, in other words, not at producing lawyers, physicians, engineers, but at producing citizens. Education for citizenship means that there must be radical reconstruction in the educational processes of the present. The education of the nineteenth century aimed at developing largely power and capacity in the individual as such. Its implicit, and oftentimes its avowed, aim was individual success. The popularity of higher education in the nineteenth century especially rested upon the cult of individual success. It became, therefore, largely commercialized, and emphasized chiefly the professions and occupations which best assured the individual a successful career among a commercial and industrial people. It is needless to say that the individualistic, commercialized education of the latter years of the nineteenth century very often failed to produce the good citizen. On the contrary, with its ideal of individual power and success, it frequently produced the cultured freebooter, which our modern industry has so often afforded examples of.

Education, instead of being a socializing agency and the chief instrument of social regeneration, became an individualizing agency dissolving the social order itself. Very slowly our educators are becoming conscious of the fact that this type of education is a social menace, and that our educational system needs reformation from bottom to top in order to become again equal to the social task imposed upon it by the more complex social conditions of the twentieth century. Hence the demand for a socialized education, which is proceeding, not only from sociologists and social workers, but from the progressive leaders of education itself. What this socialized education of the future shall be is not the province of this book to discuss, but a few of its essential characteristics may be noted. As has already been said, such education will aim, first of all, at producing the citizen before it aims at producing the lawyer, the engineer, the physician, or any other professional or occupational type.

No doubt, this means, for one thing, that all individuals shall be taught to be good fathers and mothers, good neighbors and members of communities, even more than they are taught the accomplishments of life. No doubt, also, the socialized education of the future will emphasize the adjustment of the individual to the industrial order of society, because it is necessary that individuals shall be producers if they are to be efficient citizens. The necessity and value of industrial training in our system of education has already been emphasized in discussing other social problems. Such training has its place and that place, as we have already seen, is a very important and fundamental one; but it must not be forgotten that the relations of men to one another are more important than the relations of men to nature. In industrial training, the element which is apt to be emphasized is the relations of the individual to the physical facts and forces of nature; but this is only a beginning of the training for citizenship, because good citizenship consists essentially in harmonious and efficient functioning in the social group.

Therefore, the study of the relationships of men to one another must be the final and crowning element in a system of social education. Such studies as history, government, economics, ethics, and sociology must occupy a larger and larger place in the education of the future if we are to secure a humanity adjusted to the requirements of its existence. Historical and sociological instruction should lead up, moreover, to direct ethical instruction. If the industrial element in the social life is important, the moral element is even more so, since it is, as we have already said, the ideal aspect of the social. In some way or another, our public schools, from the kindergarten up, must make a place for social and ethical instruction of a direct and explicit character. In the higher education, the social sciences must be especially emphasized, because it is those who receive higher education who become the leaders of society, and it is important, no matter what occupation or profession they may serve society in, that they understand the bearings of their work upon social welfare.

They must know their duties as citizens and understand how society may best be served. In other words, our higher education should put to the front the ideal, not of individual power and success, but of social service; and this means that, in addition to the technical or professional education which the more highly educated are giving, there must be a sufficient knowledge of social conditions and of the laws and principles of social progress given them to enable them to serve society rightly. Intelligent social service cannot exist without social knowledge. All this implies that the older idea that education can be given regardless of content is, from the social point of view, a great mistake. Social knowledge is necessary, as we have just said, for efficient social service, and a socialized education can have no other end than social service. Therefore, sociological knowledge in the broadest sense should be required in the education of every citizen, and particularly those who are to become social leaders.

Professor Ward has ably argued that if sufficient information of the facts, conditions, and laws of human society could be given to all, that alone would bring about in the highest degree social progress. Whether we agree or not that the mere giving of information will of itself lead to progressive or dynamic action in society, it must be admitted that right social information is indispensable for right social action. As Professor Cooley has said, "We live in a system, and to achieve right ends, or any rational ends whatever, we must learn to understand that system." Hence, the commanding place which sociology and the social sciences should occupy in the education of all classes, and especially in the training of the teacher himself. It is not unreasonable to believe that the development of the social sciences will show us the way to remove many, if not all, social evils; and it is also not unreasonable to believe that the knowledge which these sciences will furnish will stimulate in the vast mass of individuals an impetus to remove these evils.

Moreover, training in the social sciences will check many of the most menacing tendencies of our present civilization. For one thing, training in the social sciences will lessen the practical materialism of modern civilization, for it will throw the emphasis on the relations of men to one another rather than on the relations of man to nature. The social sciences, aiming at the control of the social conditions and of social progress, necessarily emphasize the higher life of man, and they therefore set before the student as the goal, not material achievement or individual success, but the service of man. Again, training in the social sciences will check the exaggerated individualism, which, as we have already seen, is one of the most menacing tendencies of our time; for the social sciences show the solidarity of the society and the interdependence of its parts. They show that no individual lives to himself, and that his acts evidently affect the whole of society. Finally, training in the social sciences will insure the development of true moral freedom in our social life, for these sciences involve a searching but impersonal criticism of social institutions and public policies. Now the very breath of life of a free society is intelligent public criticism of its institutions and policies.

Without this, there can be no change, no progress. But intelligent criticism implies scientific criticism, that is, criticism based upon adequate scientific knowledge and without personal bias. This means the scientific study of institutions and social organization. If the American people are to perfect their institutions, they must maintain and develop their moral freedom; and to maintain true moral freedom, they must encourage the scientific study of social conditions and institutions. To secure an unbiased attitude toward social and political problems, to train every citizen for social service, to reconstruct social organization along scientific lines, it is necessary, therefore, to give the social sciences an honored place in the education of all classes and professions.

9

Political Sociological Theories

THEORIES OF THE STATE AND POWER

1) PLURALISM

Based on functionalism with emphasis on equilibrium, stability and gradual change, conservative perspective.

Key features:

- Societal power is decentralized, widely shared, diffuse and fragmented, deriving from many sources, i.e. power pie divided into many pieces
- Society consists of many diverse groups and associations (e.g. business, labour, professional, religious, etc...) and constitutes a conglomeration of dissimilar and often conflicting interests, no none of which plays a singularly dominant role, through a process of democratic competition the nature and direction of society are determined
- Society is made up of a multitude of conflicting interest groups balanced by the state, groups are equally influential in their impact on government policy and major institutions
- Assumption of a natural balance of power among various groups which is preserved through bargaining and compromise, win some and lose some, give and take, and thus equilibrium is reached in group struggle
- Existence of shared acceptance of basic political framework, i.e. consensus of values, democratic traditions, procedures & principles
- Economic and governmental institutions are separate not overlapping power sources
- Tension between necessity for strong, modernizing, central coordinator on one hand and a relatively equal distribution of social powers on other reflects cross-pulls of two allegedly functional pre-requisites – need of autonomy and need of integration

Role of the state

- Society is a struggle of competing groups within an arena refereed by the state
- State represents institutionalized power and authority
- State is supreme guardian of representative democracy in modern society, from tension paves way for political competition and pluralist democracy
- State serves neither its own interests nor those of any single group or class
- State can act as bargaining agent or mediator
- Primary task of state is to balance interests of a multitude of competing groups, represents interests of society as a whole, coordinating the other major institutions OR
- Primary function is to promote harmony within system to secure equilibrium and order OR
- Or to police conflicts of interest
- From these roles, state is able to institutionalize its rule and maintain order in society
- Separation of governmental power: plurality of competing governmental agencies, divisions and branches, existence of political parties, thus individuals/groups can have various points of access to decision-makers

Role/nature of the individual and of groups

- Individuals with common interests exert influence on decision-makers by collective action thus average citizens can have meaningful input into decision-making
- Political power is distributed over as many citizens working through their associations as want to take responsibility for power, through the voluntary association the ordinary citizen can acquire as much as power in the community or nation as their free time, ability and inclinations permit them (Arnold Rose)
- Political process is made up of social groups and policy outcomes are result of group process, each group being autonomous and democratic
- Potential groups: people who have shared attitudes, unorganized could organize
- Cross cutting group membership: overlapping membership of groups, one individual may have many memberships and each group may have conflicting views on one issue, thus never have one all powerful group agreeing on all issues

In US, pluralism is popular; consider slogans of "government of, by and for the people", "equality before the law" and "separation of power"

ELITE PLURALISM

Seymour Martin Lipset, Robert *Dalh's* polyarchy, or democratic Elitism or strategic Elites

- Fuses reality of Elite rule and democratic principles

- Meaning of democracy is changed from one of direct popular rule to that of competition between and within Elites to control the state
- Elites are not single integrated group, multiple centers of political power
- Assumption of balance
- Assumption that minority will have influence on Elite
- Distrusts of mass participation in politics

CRITIQUE

Pertains to voluntary associations, class bias of interest group activity, inequality of power resources, role of the state, consensus of political values, and democracy

- Rationale for status quo, defense of current US political system, parochial focus, not widely applicable – just to US
- Actual versus perceived role of voluntary associations, simply another level of bureaucracy
- US society is not one of joiners, few are members of voluntary associations, usually the better educated, wealthier and higher social status
- Those who are members of voluntary associations, the groups are social, cultural, youth, church or other whose primary interests are not political, and many of these groups lack any democratic control by ran an file and are bureaucratically structured which prevents direct individual participation in decision-making
- Voluntary associations are asymmetrical in the amount of power they wield per member, e.g. union versus business association
- Assumption that there is a balance of power among various groups, from religious groups to business groups, and pervasiveness of economic institutions ignored, balance of power as it is favors some and not others
- State is not neutral mediator, rules change, agenda setting occurs
- Assumption of widespread agreement on rules of the game, whose rules and who agrees, what of those who oppose
- Modern version of democracy or perversion of democracy in complex, modern industrialized societies
- No concern for minimal participation of masses
- Focus is governmental, public and not including private sector politics, what of Elites in educational sector, corporate sector, communication sector, labour sector, thus picture of societal power is limited
- Pluralists are preoccupied with analyzing formal political institutions, confuses how politics is supposed to work and how it actually works under capitalism

2) ELITE THEORY

Societal power is concentrated in elite groups who control resources of key social institutions and are not accountable to the masses, origins of societal power lie in control of social organizations, regardless of how (un)democratic a society maybe, Elites hold the bulk of power; use all and any means to retain power, power becomes end in itself.

Debated issues among Elite theorists

- Initially are all societies stratified?
- Is power used for society's benefit and welfare or for personal gain?
- Necessary for society or not?
- Elites closed and cohesive units or open and diverse?
- One or more ruling Elites?
- What are the characteristics and patterns of Elites?
- Are Elites and powerful persons the same?

CLASSIC ELITE THEORY (ARISTOCRATIC VERSION)

Based on two ideas:

1) Fundamental psychological difference sets Elites apart from masses, natural process, having personal resources such as intelligence, cunning or skill, and masses are apathetic, incompetent and unable to govern themselves OR
2) Unavoidable product of modern social organization such that organizational complexity necessitates a leader, i.e. functionally necessary, power lies in positions of authority in key political and economic institutions

Pareto

- Stressed the psychological and irrational aspects of Elites, i.e. psychological and intellectual superiority
- Elites are the highest achievers essentially in any and all areas of intelligence, character, skill, capacity, etc...
- Have two types of Elites-governing Elites and non-governing Elites who govern by means of coercion or cunning
- Developed fundamental idea of circulation of Elites comprised of two processes – process in which individuals circulate between elite and nonelite, and process in which a whole elite is replaced by a new one

Mosca

- Stressed the sociological, organizational and personal characteristics

- Elites are an organized minority
- The ruling/political class includes the ruling Elite and sub-Elite (technocrats, managers, civil servants)
- Masses are not organized
- Personal characteristics include the intellectual, material and moral superiority which is highly esteemed and very influential in the society in which they live
- Dominant interests of society which are the social and political forces, i.e. prevailing ideas and institutions of the time, become reflected in the ruling class and thus they dominate the structures and values
- Believed that all societies are divided into two groups, the ruling class and the class that is ruled and thus argued for the universal necessity and inevitability of class rule.

Michels: Iron law of oligarchy

- Tendency for most social and political organizations to be run by a few individuals who make most of the decisions
- Oligarchy arises out of complexity and size of organization – the organizational form-where there is a delegation of power in terms of specialized expertise initially for efficiency and stability but transformed into self-serving conservative Elite
- Social organization and division of labour are key variables
- Have combination of apathy, insufficient time, lack of expertise and need for guidance of the masses and the natural greed for power of the Elites
- Elites have resources of information and control its flow, credibility and prestige and cohesive organization
- Three basic principles of Elite formulation that take place within bureaucratic structure of political organization – the need for specialized staff, facilities, and above all leaders; the utilization of such specialized facilities by leaders within these organizations; and, the psychological attributes of the leaders (e.g. charisma)
- Believed all organizations to be elitist, the organizational form is basis for conservatism and this conservatism is inevitable outcome of power attained through political organization

WEBER'S THEORY OF BUREAUCRACY (not per say a theory of power or political sociology but relevancy is clear)

- Having arrived at the conclusion that economic relations, i.e. class relations based on wealth and income, lie at the source of power and politics, Weber focused on manifestation of class power exercized through the state
- Assigns a quasi-autonomous role to the state in which state bureaucrats appear to be serving their own interests and the bureaucracy appears to be a power unto itself

- Bureaucracies are skilled bodies of specialists and experts, a rational form of organization organized on the basis of specific functions, not on basis of authority of personalities and traditions, a social machine with individuals as depersonalized objects
- With modernization of society and greater legal-rational authority, there is increasing professionalization of leadership, power becomes concentrated in bureaucracies which maintain control over vast human, material and intellectual resources – they have monopoly of expertise and have capacity to carry out or not policies of political leaders (policy administration)
- Bureaucracies are stable but intransigent with a remote and unanswerable bureaucratic elite, thus with citizens removed from control of and input into political decision-making
- Question is determining who controls and directs the complex bureaucratic machine
- Does not believe bureaucracy to be an autonomous power unto itself (as Michels does) but rather it is a tool or instrument of power, argues bureaucracy and power are the manifestations of the real material forces that dominate social-economic structure of modern society, to give primacy to analytic strength of these concepts is to study surface phenomena

CONTEMPORARY ELITE THEORY

Power Elite theory aka Radical Power Elite theory-C.W. Mills

- Societal power rests in control of key societal institutions-corporation, executive branch of government and Pentagon in US, i.e. the economy, the state and the military
- Elites not inevitable or natural, nor that masses are incompetent, apathetic or untrustworthy, masses are manipulated and exploited and kept in a state of ignorance and thus powerless by Elites who rule in own interest, this accounts for non-participation
- Elites are from upper class and perpetuate themselves through selective recruitment and socialization to Elite values

Governing Class model-W. Domhoff

- Class hegemony framework combining Power Elite theory and Class theory, reconceptualizes the power Elite in class terms
- Argues in US there is a corporate upper class that owns major business assets and controls the bulk of wealth, including major banks, corporations; major newspapers, radio, television and other mass media; elite universities; foundations; important advisory groups and organizations e.g. Council of Foreign Relations and Committee for Economic Development; executive branch of government, cabinet, judiciary, military and the regulatory agencies
- This class by virtue of its economic power, also controls and influences important departments and agencies of the state and in this way becomes a governing class – the American business aristocracy

CRITIQUE Concerns Elite inevitability, cohesiveness and Elite-mass relations

- Does there maybe exist an iron law of democracy instead due to persistence off democratic ideals & tendencies
- Consider how do organizations inhibit authority not just democracy
- Idea of coalitions, power changing moment to moment, issue to issue
- Increased specialization and complexity so different Elite groups, and several classes not just two
- Accountability functions of electoral politics and public opinion ignored
- Altruistic motives do exist
- Other groups benefit from Elites' actions
- As social class rises apathy decreases

3) MARXISM-CLASSIC MARXIST THEORY

Society is ruled by those who control the means of production – the economic system

Key features:

Marx

- Class basis of politics is the major determinant of political phenomena, must ask which class controls and dominates the state
- Reality is world of human effort – WORK, people realize themselves through work and around this productive process history unfolds
- Dynamics of society originate in its economic activity which is essentially the production of material life – food, clothing, shelter-and culture arises out of this process of economic activity
- Foundation or basis of society is the economy from which the legal, political, religious, cultural and educational institutions derive; i.e. societies in different stages of developments create different productive systems which are the economic institutions which in turn shape general nature of beliefs and practices in all areas of social life including political organization
- A form of economic determinism
- Obedience of all classes is found not on coercion but on virtual dependence of working class on capitalist class for subsistence and false consciousness
- *Power* flows from economic relations, who rules, those who control the economic resources, societal power is a product of economic forces, *Political power* is not centered in the state but in the nature of the class relations, who owns and controls the means of production

- Economic dominance is translated into power in all other societal realms, especially the state, thus dominant economic class is ruling political class
- Since classes are political groups, political conflict is class conflict

Gramsci

- Focused on the ideological apparatuses of the capitalist state
- Introduced concept of cultural ideological hegemony – the ruling class controls and shapes the ideas and hence consciousness of the masses, the dominant class uses its political, moral and intellectual leadership to establish its view of the world as all inclusive and universal, and to shape the interests and needs of subordinate groups
- The ideological hegemony of the ruling class operates through the state itself

Role/Functions of the state

- Perpetuation and legitimation of the social class system:
  - Maintaining and reproducing the capitalist system and its class relations
  - Protecting system of property relations
  - Propagating dominant values in schools, media and other social institutions, fostering dominant ideology
- Accumulation function
  - Guaranteeing the conditions for capital production and accumulation
  - Intervening directly in this process through tax collection & spending
  - Financing economic growth

MARXISM-CONTEMPORARY MARXIST THEORIES

Althusser

- Structural Marxist – combines Marxism which relies on social & historical analysis with structuralism which relies on ahistorical and asocial analysis
- Does this by distinguishing between ideologies (historical/social) and ideology (structural): IDEOLOGIES are specific, historical and differing, there are various ideologies i.e. Christian, democratic, feminist, Marxist ideologies; IDEOLOGY is structural and eternal and has no history since ideology is part of the superstructure, (links structure of ideology to the idea of the unconscious from Freud and Lacan); because ideology is a structure its contents will vary but its form remains the same; ideology is a representation of the imaginary relationship of individuals to their real conditions of existence, ideology doesn't represent the real world per se but human beings' relation to that real world or to their perceptions of the real conditions of existence

- Expands analysis of the base-superstructure relationship to include such other superstructural institutions as the cultural, religious, educational, legal and family
- As hegemony of ruling class in these spheres becomes critical for its control over the dominated classes, and society in general, the class struggle takes on a tri-level character consisting of economic, political and ideological levels
- State is a kind of governmental formation that arises with capitalism, i.e. a state is determined by the capitalist mode of production and formed to protect its interests
- Identifies two major mechanisms for insuring that people within a state behave according to the rules: (1) repressive states apparatuses (RSA), e.g. police, armed forces, prisons (criminal justice and prison systems); (2) ideological state apparatuses (ISA), e.g. schools, religions, family, legal systems, politics, cultural activities such as arts and sports, system of mass communication, which are institutions which generate ideologies (systems of ideas and values) which we as individuals and groups then internalize

Poulantzas-STRUCTURALISM

- Emphasis is on the structural imperatives of the capitalist system as they affect the state and its relative autonomy, emphasized ideological factors
- Focus on structural constraints of the capitalist system that set limits to the state's autonomy and force it to work within the framework of an order that yields results invariably favourable to the dominant capitalist class
- Argues that it is by virtue of the system of production itself in capitalist society that the state becomes a capitalist state even in the absence of direct control of the state apparatus by capitalists
- The direct participation of members of the ruling class in the state apparatus is the effect, not the cause
- Structure of political and economic institutions in capitalist society constrain the political Elite so that it serves those interests regardless of direct/indirect role of business in state affairs, i.e. mechanisms are built into the modern capitalist political economy
- Viability of state dependent on healthy economy, state leaders must promote interests of big business
- Belief that capitalist class is internally divided and thus state protects capitalist interests in general, i.e. on behalf of all capitalists and thus state is autonomous

Miliband-INSTRUMENTALISM

- Simplistically and initially government serves interests of capitalist class
- The idea is that the state is an instrument of the capitalist class as a whole and this class contains fractions thus it has relative autonomy from one fraction

- Emphasis is on the direct and indirect control of the state by the dominant capitalist class
- Focuses on the special relationship between the state and the capitalist class, and the mechanisms of control of the state by this class that, de facto, transform the state into a capitalist state
- Capitalists do not govern, i.e. do not occupy political offices, but they rule by controlling political officials and institutions, directly through manipulation of state policies or indirectly through exercise of pressure on state
- Social and strategic ties among corporate and government leaders is key, between individuals occupying positions of power in different institutional spheres

NOTE: There is a convergence of 2 positions where the state is both controlled by and at the same time relatively autonomous from various fractions of the capitalist class in order to perform its functions in advancing the interests of the capitalist class as a whole, and maintain its legitimacy over society

Offe (comes from Hegelian-Maxist tradition of the Frankfurt School, once a student of Jurgen Habermas, similar to Poulantzas)

- Explains state through economic role
- Emphasis on state's necessity for capital accumulation involving extraction of surplus and the reproduction of capitalist relations
- Focuses on internal mechanisms of the state in terms of its dependence on capital accumulation which is vital for its survival
- Introduced concept of selective mechanisms: negative selection-selective mechanisms that systematically exclude anti-capitalist interests from state activity; positive selection-from the range of remaining alternatives, the policy which is in the interests of capital as a whole is selected over policies serving the parochial interests of specific capitalist groups; disguising selection – the institutions of the state must somehow maintain the appearance of class neutrality while at the same time effectively excluding anti-capitalist alternatives
- Mechanism are contradictory in nature and present problems for state in carrying out its dual role of maintaining accumulation and legitimation, results in crisis of legitimation

4) REALISM-*Machiavelli* & *Hobbes*: "end justifies the means", "might makes right"

- Politics is the way it is
- It is autonomous-separate from moral or other nonpolitical struggles
- National interests of nation-states are what is key and from which there are struggles with other nation-states vying for power
- Belief in absolute power of the state, single minded pursuit of power, national security and interest

Six principles

1. Politics and society are governed by objective laws that have their roots in human nature (determinism & darwinism)
2. Political realism is defined in terms of interest with interest being defined in terms of power, not concerned with motives and ideological preferences (not psychology or emotions)
3. Realm of moral principles and ethics is separate from realm of politics
4. Moral aspirations of nation are not identical to moral laws which govern universe, e.g. foreign policy based on national interest not moral interest
5. Objectivity

Neorealists focus more on international relations and foreign policy

CRITIQUE

- Reductionist
- Separating ethics from politics not possible
- Not objective

5) CORPORATISM (post-Pluralism – reformulation of the pluralist problematic; more sophisticated form of Elite Pluralism; within capitalism, aka as Keynesian corporatism, see it in Europe more than US)

- Strong central state, state is the supreme organ responsible for organizing and leading society under its own directives
- Representing the common good, state is guardian of order and moral authority then can bring about class harmony and national unity
- State takes on responsibility of leading the nation by taking an active role in major institutions of society including the economy, i.e. direct intervention
- A partnership/alliance between state/government, business/corporations and union/ organized labor creating political stability, reciprocal relationships, i.e. agreement between the state, capitalists (management) and trade unionists (workers) to guarantee high levels of employment, capital investment and accumulation, and citizen consumption
- Corporatist state included aims of economic redistribution and extension of citizenship rights, reducing levels of unemployment and inflation in order to bring workers into the mainstream of the capitalist system
- Organized interests are legitimate
- State interventions are acceptable as long as they fall within capitalist principles

Two types:

- State (top down) corporatism which is closer to elitism
- Societal (bottom up) corporatism which is closer to pluralism

CRITIQUES

- Designed to protect interests of monopoly capital
- Results in consolidation of capitalist class power since state is controlled by capitalist class
- Can give rise to authoritarian states in crisis ridden states, and ultimately providing material base for emergence of fascism in response to economic and political crises of advanced capitalism, e.g Germany & Italy

10

Elite Theory in Political Sociology

Elite theory's origins lie most clearly in the writings of Gaetano Mosca (1858-1941), Vilfredo Pareto (1848-1923), and Robert Michels (1876-1936). Mosca emphasized the ways in which tiny minorities out-organize and outwit large majorities, adding that "political classes" – Mosca s term for political elites – usually have "a certain material, intellectual, or even moral superiority" over those they govern (1923/1939, 51). Pareto postulated that in a society with truly unrestricted social mobility, elites would consist of the most talented and deserving individuals; but in actual societies elites are those most adept at using the two modes of political rule, force and persuasion; and who usually enjoy important advantages such as inherited wealth and family connections (1915/ 1935, paras. 2031-34, 2051). Pareto sketched alternating types of governing elites, which he likened, following Machiavelli, to lions and foxes. Michels rooted elites ("oligarchies") in the need of large organizations for leaders and experts in order to operate efficiently; as these individuals gain control of funds, information flows, promotions, and other aspects of organizational functioning power becomes concentrated in their hands (1915/1962; see Linz,, 2006). Emphasizing the inescapability and also the relative autonomy of elites, all three men characterized aspirations to fully democratic and egalitarian societies as futile.

Many democrats and social radicals have rejected this "futility thesis" (Femia, 2001). They have sought to demonstrate that particular elites are not those with superior endowments or organizational capacities, but merely persons who are socially advantaged in power competitions. Adherents of this view have argued that the existence of elites can be terminated either by removing the social advantages that some people enjoy or by abolishing the power concentrations that spur competitions among them – remedies that often go hand-in-hand. There are no historical instances, however, where these remedies have been successfully applied in a large population for any significant length of time. The writings of Mosca, Pareto, and Michels constitute a paradigm from which a general theory of elites and politics might be derived (Field and Higley,

1980). But efforts to produce such a theory have not been conspicuously successful. Linking elites causally to major regularities in politics remains elusive; there is no accepted typology of elites and no accepted specification of the circumstances and ways in which one elite type replaces another; political interactions between elites and non-elite populations are captured only piecemeal. Nevertheless, political scientists and sociologists pay much attention to elites and their key roles in democratic transitions and breakdowns, revolutions, political regimes of all kinds, mass movements, democratic politics, globalization, and many other political phenomena. By outlining a general treatment of elites and politics, this paper seeks to provide elite theory and the attention paid to elites with more coherence and direction.

ELITES

Elites derive from a fundamental and universal fact of social life, namely, the absence in any large collectivity of a robust common interest. While it is true that most large collectivities rest on a base of social and cultural understandings, these tend to be ambiguous and rough. The satisfactions some of their members seek are only partly compatible with the satisfactions sought by other members. Members constantly claim statuses and other valued goods for themselves, their kin, friends, and allies that other members do not accept as fully legitimate. Acceding to these claims is often more a matter of judging that it is dangerous or inexpedient to resist them than of recognizing that the persons and groups making the claims have some right to do so. In large collectivities common interest is fairly minimal and must always be supplemented by authoritative decisions that dissenters and opponents dare not or find it inexpedient to resist.

Common interest is even more limited as regards the detailed features of any large collectivity s functioning. Its operations involve day-to-day decisions and, thus, allocations and re-allocations of tasks and statuses. Merely for a large collectivity to survive, „intelligent and „objective decisions that transcend individual interests must regularly be taken. But there can seldom be any firm consensus among a collectivity s members about the rightness of these decisions. This is partly because only a few are in positions that afford a relatively comprehensive view of the collective effort and its present location in time and space relative to its goals. Yet such a view is usually necessary for knowing if a particular decision is "right". Moreover, the need for constant decision-making deprives members of the time they would need to reach agreement about how their interests apply to current problems and needs. Even a relatively unimportant decision changes the line-up of influence for the next decision so that the details of a collectivity s structure and needs are always different today from what they were yesterday. This means that any incipient consensus among its members necessarily focuses on yesterday s structure and needs.

These aspects of collectivities give to elites their importance in political and social theory. Collectivities of any size and complexity require decisions by persons who happen to be strategically located in them. Because such collectivities are concentrations of power in the wider society, their top decision-makers have disproportionate societal power and influence, and they nearly always enjoy disproportionate privileges and protections. If we call these persons elites we can say that large and complex collectivities necessarily create elites. In this sense only are elites an inherent feature of societies; all other reasons for the existence of elites are less persuasive and more debatable. Recognizing this is not, however, merely to echo Michels dictum that "Who says organization says oligarchy." For oligarchy, aristocracy, and other euphemisms for elites imply or impute specific structural and behavioral features. Whether elites are cohesive, conspiratorial, self-conscious, and so on is answerable only through empirical investigation. While elites are the inescapable consequence of conflicting interests in all large and complex collectivities, their configurations vary according to political and social circumstance.

Elites may be defined as *persons who, by virtue of their strategic locations in large or otherwise pivotal organizations and movements, are able to affect political outcomes regularly and substantially.* Put differently, elites are persons with the *organized capacity* to make real political trouble without being promptly repressed. They consist not only of prestigious and "established" leaders – top politicians, important businessmen, high-level civil servants, senior military officers – but also, in varying degrees in different societies, relatively transitory and less individually known leaders of mass organizations such as trade unions, important voluntary associations, and politically consequential mass movements. "Counter-elites" are subsumed by this definition because they clearly have the organized capacity, although perhaps mainly through negation, to affect political outcomes regularly and substantially.

It is important to stress that this is a limited and specifically political definition of elites. It is restricted to persons who are at the top of the pyramid or pyramids of political, economic, and social power (Putnam, 1976, 14). It does not consider all those in a society who enjoy high occupational, educational, or cultural statuses to be elites in a political sense. As defined, national political elites are not large in number. Geraint Parry (1969/2005) has observed that the entire British elite could be seated with ease in a soccer stadium. Using strict organizational and positional criteria, as well as data about sizes of elite networks, some researchers have estimated that the national political elite in the United States numbers perhaps ten thousand persons (Dye, 2002), maybe half this number in medium-sized countries like France (Dogan, 2003), Australia (Higley, Deacon & Smart, 1979) or Germany (Hoffmann-Lange, 1992), and about fifteen hundred in small countries like Denmark (Christiansen, Möller & Togeby, 2001) and Norway (Gulbrandsen and Engelstad, 2002). This last estimate of fewer than two thousand persons is probably the most plausible for all countries during the early modern historical period and all but the most populous developing countries today.

ELITES AND POLITICAL STABILITY

The presence or absence of stable political institutions is one of the major differences between political systems that can be explained on the basis of differences between elites. It is unusual for political power to be institutionalized effectively, as it has been for many years in

Great Britain, the United States, the Netherlands, Sweden, Switzerland, and a few other Western countries. Stable political institutions are marked by the *absence* of irregular seizures of government executive power or obvious military influence in policy-making through threats of military intervention. Every four years since 1789 a president has taken office in the United States on the basis of election and has served out a term, unless dying in office, as the more or less effective head of the American political system. In Britain over an even longer time span prime ministers and cabinets have regularly succeeded each other as the chief political authority in accordance with principles and rules that, in spite of being largely informal, are well known.

The personalized manipulation of political institutions through individual and direct control of military and police forces has been, and is, much more common. Typically, there is a distinct elite group that effectively commands organized coercive forces and is prepared to arbitrate political decisions no matter what existing institutions prescribe. It is of little consequence analytically whether this group centers on a traditional monarch, a civilian coalition tied closely to professional military commanders, or it is an overt military junta. What is consequential analytically is that elites, no matter what their partisan inclinations may be, see power as personalized and directly dependent on the support of organized coercive forces. Elites critical of current social organization, for whatever reason, necessarily view political change in terms of removing or altering the group that effectively commands those forces. In their eyes and the eyes of their opponents, power flows from gaining at least temporary control over the principal means of coercion. Attempts to seize government executive power by force are seen by all as plausible, even probable, eventualities.

This is the basic aspect of a *disunited elite.* For long periods, as in Spain, Portugal, and Latin America during the nineteenth and most of the twentieth centuries, governance oscillates between "dictatorial" and "democratic" poles. These oscillations are transitory and circumstantial manifestations of the political system s inherent instability so long as most elite persons believe that the hold on government power is subject to sharp and sudden changes. The historical record shows overwhelmingly that politics in most countries normally approximate an unrestrained struggle among mutually distrustful elites to defend and advance their interests with little regard for cost or propriety. Of supreme interest in political analysis, therefore, are the relatively few countries in which political instability is not the order of the day. For, as noted, a few countries have displayed patterns of institutionalized authority and procedure that have been respected and perpetuated over long periods. In them, irregular seizures of government power by force are unknown and informed observers consider such seizures highly unlikely. Elite theory holds that these deviant cases are explicable *only* in terms of elite behavior. More specifically, the historically normal situation of political instability has been abrogated in countries only when a *united elite* has formed.

There are, however, two markedly different types of united elites and, consequently, two quite different forms of political stability. One type is an *ideologically united elite*, which is marked by the uniform profession of a single and defined ideology by all or nearly all elite persons. These persons consistently avoid taking conflicting positions in public about current policies and political beliefs; they foster the image of a single and homogeneous leadership group. But given the conflicting interests that exist in any society, this image is more apparent than real. To some extent it arises from the determination of uppermost leaders imbued with a specific ideology to afford no opening for the intrusion of "unsound" outsiders into policy-making. But even for elite insiders the ideological uniformity is in part coerced. Behind the public profession of more or less complete agreement about current policies and goals – behind the expression of a single and defined ideology – there exists an apparatus of power sufficient to force all or most current and aspiring elite persons to harmonize their public statements with the views that are currently orthodox. Defining what is orthodox is the task of a few individuals in the highest elite positions, and adhering to this orthodoxy obviously blocks the expression of divergent interests.

The content of the single ideology that marks an ideologically united elite is of little analytical importance. It must probably be sufficiently diffuse and removed from present conditions to permit flexibility in interpreting always changing realities. It must probably be focused on some future, imaginary social condition toward which society is allegedly moving. It must, in short, be substantially utopian. But analytically speaking, whether the ideology describes a future classless society or one in which eternal salvation or pastoral contentment for all will be realized is of little consequence for the enforced unity that prevails among elite persons. Because the only permissible public position for organizing endeavors is defined and monopolized by those in power, political institutions can be centralized to a degree unknown elsewhere. Individuals and groups who want to alter those institutions can be identified easily, and they possess few means with which to appeal for public support. Evidence indicates that, once established, institutions operated by an ideologically united elite are stable for long periods.

The other type of united elite, a *consensually united elite*, does not depend on all elite persons taking essentially the same political position in public. There is no single and defined ideology to which all must adhere. Instead, persons with power and influence take clearly divergent positions on public matters. These positions often accord with opposing ideologies, as in the long conflict between conservatives and liberals within British and Swedish elites during the nineteenth century, and the subsequent conflict between liberals and socialists within the same elites during the first half of the twentieth century. The striking aspect of these conflicts is that they occur under a set of rules that is nowhere comprehensively codified but is tacitly and widely understood to remove serious personal danger from elite contests and competitions. These informal rules emanate from a structuring of power that gives all or most elite persons and groups sufficient access to decision-making so that it is in their collective interest to avoid seriously disruptive actions and keep the political situation manageable. Although elite members disagree and oppose each other in limited struggles for ascendancy, power is distributed so that all or most can have influence on political decisions sufficient to deter them from translating their oppositions into attempts to seize government power by force. Political institutions are, accordingly, stable for long periods.

Origins of Elite Types

Ideologically united elites originate in revolutionary circumstances that enable a movement dogmatically expressing a specific ideology or creed to suppress and supplant previously existing elites. Examples are Russia 1917-1921, Italy 1922-1925, Germany 1933-1934, North Korea 1946-1948, China after 1949, Cuba 1959-1961, and Iran 1979-1981. Ideologically united elites may also originate when an external power possessing such an elite imposes its clone on a conquered or otherwise subordinated country, as in East Germany and Eastern Europe following World War II. By contrast, consensually united elites sometimes originate through dramatic changes in the situations and attitudes of the key groups that have constituted a disunited elite. This involves an *elite settlement* in which warring elite camps manage to bring their major disputes to a close and establish a basis for mutual trust (Burton and Higley, 1987; 1998). The first historical instance of an elite settlement occurred in England's „Glorious Revolution of 1688-1689, and it is worth recalling its basic features.

English elites had been bitterly and deeply disunited, as evidenced by the Civil Wars and Interregnum between 1642-1660. In 1660 the monarchical system was restored, albeit with some shifting of positions and blurring of lines between the previously warring elites. Thereafter one main elite camp, the Tories, sought to exploit their association with the monarchy, while the other main camp, the Whigs, maintained its anti-monarchical stance. The Tories were thoroughly identified with the religious doctrine and institutions connected to the Church of England. But when in 1685 the birth of a son to James II, who professed both Roman Catholicism and an absolutist version of monarchical power, made an indefinite Catholic succession to the throne likely, the Tories were as discomfited as their Whig rivals.

Fearing a resumption of civil war, key leaders of the two elite camps conspired to invite the successful military intervention of the Dutch *stadtholder*, William of Orange, and the elite camps subsequently agreed, in early 1689, to establish William as king under terms that effectively guaranteed them joint political influence. Occurring in a predominantly agrarian society where the elite stratum was necessarily small and exclusive, these events marked the beginning of the limited and restrained political contests with understood informal rules that have characterized the British polity ever since (for a fuller account and the English Settlement s ramifications for American political stability, see Barone. 2007). Essentially similar events constituting elite settlements occurred among Swedish elites in 1809 after a century of infighting (Higley and Burton, 2006, 68); Swiss elites in 1848 following a brief civil war between contending elite camps (Tilly, 2004, 168-205); and, more debatably, among Mexican elites in 1928-1929 when they created an omnibus party, eventually known as the PRI, to operate a stable presidential system after a long experience of bloody turmoil (Knight, 1992).

Consensually united elites have also originated in the attainment of independence by former colonies in which local or "native" elites have been able to practice a restrained home-rule politics while waging long, in some cases violent, struggles for independence. As illustrated by elites in Britain s North American colonies, both American and Canadian, local elites in partially self-governing colonies may develop a high enough level of mutual trust when resisting the colonial power s interventions and seeking independence that they are consensually united from the date of independence or the grant of full home rule. In addition to the U.S. and Canada, this was the experience of elites in Australia and New Zealand during the latter part of the nineteenth century, and of white South African, Indian, and Malayan elites during the twentieth century s first half (Higley and Burton, 2006, 107-38). It is worth noting that Dutch elites became united in this manner before and during their successful struggle for independence from Spain late in the sixteenth century, although full integration of the seven Dutch provinces did not occur until after the Napoleonic Wars.

In cases where consensually united elites formed as an outgrowth of colonialism, colonial governments had active representative institutions that afforded elites a considerable practice of limited and restrained politics. But this was not the situation in the Latin American colonies of Portugal and Spain, where, moreover, there was little clear understanding of territorial boundaries when independence was gained. Consequently, military leaders and local political bosses (*caudillos*) tended to predominate in Latin America at independence and for long periods thereafter. Nor were the political experiences of elites under colonial rule and when struggling for independence propitious for the formation of consensually united elites in more than a few of the scores of ex-colonies that achieved independence during the decades following World War II. Except in India, Malaya (later Malaysia), Senegal, and no more than a handful of other ex-colonies, such as Jamaica and Barbados, independence brought with it disunited elites and long-lasting political instability.

To summarize, there have been two ways in which disunited elite became consensually united historically: (1) through basic and sudden elite settlements in societies at relatively low levels of socioeconomic development; (2) through colonial home rule and struggles for independence where local elites had already received, or received in the course of those struggles, experience in political bargaining and restrained competitions. Neither origin appears relevant to the situation of most disunited elites in today s world. A necessary condition for an elite settlement appears to be a level of socioeconomic development lower than that of most developing countries with disunited elites today. At higher development levels elites are probably too numerous and closely tied to particular non-elite interests to be able to fashion a settlement. Colonial dependency is obviously a condition necessary for creating a consensually united elite through home rule and independence struggles, but it is a condition that is no longer seriously present. These observations raise the question of whether there may be a third way in which consensually united elites form. To address this, let me outline briefly what might be termed an *elite convergence*.

In countries that have transited to democratic elections, the opposing camps and factions making up a disunited elite may begin to converge if some of the opposing elites form a broad political coalition that mobilizes enough voters to win the elections repeatedly. This enables the coalesced elites to dominate government executive power and obtain the greater security that derives from this domination. An elite convergence may continue if factions hostile to the winning coalition conclude that seizing power by irregular means is not a realistic possibility and they must beat the winning coalition in election contests if they are to escape permanent political subordination. This means acknowledging the value of elections and promising to accept their results. An elite convergence may be considered complete when the formerly hostile and losing factions gain government executive power in an election and then govern in a way that is respectful of established institutions and tacit live-and-let-live reciprocities with the previously dominant elite coalition. As happens more clearly and quickly in elite settlements, through convergences elites gradually reach an underlying consensus about the norms of restrained political competition so that political institutions become stable.

Elite convergences occurred in several European countries and in Japan during the twentieth century s second half. All were at a relatively high level of socioeconomic development and general prosperity when the convergences took place. The four clearest cases were France once General de Gaulle s associates formed a winning electoral coalition after his return to power in 1958; Italy once the "organic" Christian Democrat-Socialist winning coalition took clear shape in 1963; West Germany after several victories by the Christian Democrat – Christian Socialist – Free Democrat winning coalition formed in 1953; Japan once the Liberal Democrats and centrist parties constituted a winning coalition starting in 1964. In each of these countries, dissident and hostile elite camps eventually came to see that they had no real political alternative to moderating their stances in order to compete effectively in elections, and in each what had previously been a disunited elite gradually became consensually united – by 1981 in France when the previously dissident Socialists won power and governed with moderation, during 1979 in Italy when the "revolutionary" Communist Party cooperated with the dominant Christian Democrats to repress extra-parliamentary terrorist groups; in West Germany when the dissident Social Democrats entered into a "grand" governing coalition with their previous nemesis, the CDU-CSU coalition (minus the Free Democrats); and in Japan once the Socialist Party jettisoned its Marxist baggage during the mid-1980s (Higley and Burton, 2006, 139-79).

Elite Theory and Democracy

Although an elite theorist s personal preference may be for democratic politics, he or she does not believe that in most countries and circumstances a practical and stable form of democratic politics can be achieved. Meaningfully democratic institutions and practices depend upon the type of elite that a society has. No type of elite is compatible with the full democratic ideal, and only one of the three types is reasonably compatible with the stable democratic politics that are practiced in Western countries and a few others today. However, none of the three elite types is *reliably* conducive to even this limited form of democracy.

The most common political situation, that of disunited elites, has the basic feature of institutional instability. While institutions operated by some part of a disunited elite may at times have a formally democratic façade, the institutions are hardly worth much promotion or defense because they are unlikely to survive a serious political crisis. Commonly, any substantial increase in normal political tensions leads, with or without a military coup, to a more authoritarian and repressive government. Although such a government may eventually mellow or even be replaced by a more democratic one that has the tacit consent of the elite veto group associated with the military, this improvement is likely to be merely an interval in a succession of more or less repressive governments. As noted, historical evidence is overwhelming that disunited elites and the unstable institutions they create persist through most vicissitudes and that each government is in practice one permitted by those who happen to control military and police forces.

The circumstances in which disunited elites become ideologically or consensually united are unlikely to appeal to people with democratic sentiments. An ideologically united elite does not allow competitive politics, and where it exists meaningful actions motivated by democratic sentiments are nearly impossible. The basic settlements in which a few consensually united elites originated historically had as their principal features substantial elite autonomy from mass pressures together with the sacrifice of deeply held political principles for which opposing elites and their supporters had long stood. The colonial origins of consensually united elites involved empires that are odious to convinced democrats and are, in any case, no longer feasible politically and economically. Where opposing camps in a disunited elite have gradually converged, those who have most liked to consider themselves genuine democrats have found themselves consistently in the minority, while more conservative and traditional persons who are part of the majority to which the winning coalition appeals are inclined to merely pretend that they are democrats (cf. Power, 2000; Alexander, 2002). Moreover, although a consensually united elite may emerge via an elite convergence and open the way to a more widely accepted and stable democratic regime, the process depends on socially radical groups becoming disillusioned with their democratic ideals.

It is also the case that the regime created and operated by a consensually united elite may not, in fact, be very democratic. It can be based, as in most historical cases, on a highly restricted suffrage. Even temporary dictatorship or the long dominance of a high-handed chief executive is possible so long as the elite remains internally trusting and is prepared to cooperate in removing the dictator or chief executive if he or she becomes seriously incapacitated or incompetent. Fundamentally, practical democracy depends on the ability of a consensually united elite to keep political tensions moderate. Where such an elite exists the problem for people imbued with democratic ideals is deciding how much public attention they should try to center on issues that they consider morally right but that are also potentially explosive. The champions of such morally charged issues are likely to find that members of a consensually united elite distort, partially suppress, or simply confuse the issues if doing so seems necessary to maintain institutional stability. Morally charged issues will be subject to "benign neglect" if elites conclude that the issues have reached a threshold of articulation and antagonism beyond which political stability is endangered.

Should those who cannot get the hearings that they believe their moral causes deserve acquiesce in such elite actions? If it is correct that consensually united elites are ordinarily quite capable of managing political tensions, the question is without significance. Yet, suppose that the elite cannot quite do this in the face of embittered demands and vehement mass demonstrations. On the assumptions of the approach to elites outlined here, this would break up the elite and in all probability create a disunited elite with the usual consequence of covert or overt military rule and the suppression of political dissent. Would it be right for staunch democrats to help bring this outcome about on behalf of a high moral cause? The answer is obvious.

Elite theory teaches, in other words, that a mature and experienced advocate of democracy must always settle for a political order that is considerably less than ideal. An elite that is consensually united, or one that approaches this condition, is necessary for practical democracy. Only such an elite will effectively manage conflicting interests whose open and dogmatic expression would create disastrous internal conflict. Where an elite does this over the course of many years, representative political institutions guided by reasonably competitive and influential elections are possible, although not inevitable. But where groups within the elite fully and openly reflect and express and conflicting non-elite interests, then at some point political freedom for considerable numbers of elite and non-elite persons alike will be suppressed or the polity will not survive. Elite theory rejects the fashionable but fatuous notion that the most desirable political system is one in which the divergent interests of a population are clearly represented and forcefully articulated at the elite level. Posing "a real choice, not an echo" in practical democratic politics threatens to weaken a consensually united elite and concomitant institutional stability. Recognizing this, proponents of elite theory cannot properly feel compelled to pursue the democratic ideal in all circumstances and at all costs.

Elites and Revolution

There is no agreed definition of revolution that attaches the term to a clearly specified political event or process. It is sometimes used to mean almost any irregular and forcible seizure of power, thereby covering the many coups and sporadic uprisings that occur where elites are disunited. "Revolution" is also often used to label civil wars and wars of liberation that center on dynastic, ethnic, regional, or religious divisions. This definitional vagueness makes it a matter of subjective judgment whether to call a regime, movement, or violent conflict "revolutionary" – a judgment that is, indeed, frequently made after the fact, as happened with the so-called Cuban Revolution that established the Castro regime. When they were fighting the Batista dictatorship, Castro s insurgents portrayed themselves as, and were widely believed to be, liberal and populist, not revolutionary. It was only after a year or two in power that Castro and his associates proclaimed themselves "revolutionaries" and a Cuban Revolution was widely perceived. By not distinguishing between many kinds of violent upheavals, "revolution" has lacked the precision required of a concept that can be utilized seriously in an elite theory of politics.

There is, however, one special kind of upheaval with features that are objectively different from those of coups, civil wars, secessions, and popular outbursts. This is an upheaval that begins when normal government authority, most manifest in disciplined military and police forces, suddenly and dramatically collapses. During the shorter or longer interval that follows, maintaining order against riot or pillage becomes highly problematic until government authority and military and police discipline are either restored or built anew by some victorious group. One cannot say that an elite of any of the three types exists during this interval. Power resides, as radicals like to say, "in the people" or, more precisely, in persons who assemble fairly spontaneously, usually under arms, and respond to immediate propaganda and oratory with mass actions. Such assemblages typically include bodies of rank-and-file troops who have either liquidated their officers or are simply ignoring officers orders.

As Pareto clearly saw (1915/1935, paras. 2056-57), an upheaval of this kind eventually brings a substantially different body of persons to elite status, and it changes political and especially economic institutions in fundamental ways. But before such sweeping alterations become apparent, whoever attempts to restore or construct a semblance of organized power in the area where government authority has collapsed usually comes under attack from areas to which the government collapse did not extend. To survive this attack, the new power organizers must quickly create some degree of bureaucratic centralization accompanied by disciplined military and police units. Sooner than later, the popular assemblages that have held forth are policed and suppressed. When this happens, the observer can again speak of a regime operated by one or another type of elite. In the English and French upheavals of 1642-1645 and 1789-1794, respectively, the new elite was again disunited. But after the upheaval in Russia, 1917-1921, the elite was ideologically united as a consequence of the victorious Bolsheviks tight organization and doctrinal coherence during the upheaval.

If for purposes of conceptual order and terminological consistency "revolution" refers only to an upheaval involving the collapse of government authority and an ensuing interval when coercive power is located in more or less spontaneous popular assemblages, it is a rare and unlikely event (Brinton, 1938). A revolution in this sense can probably occur only in societies at low levels of socioeconomic development, that is, largely agrarian or peasant societies. In more bureaucratized societies at higher development levels the widespread collapse of government authority and disciplined military and police forces seems even more implausible today than it did when proponents of revolution counted, for the most part mistakenly, on large numbers of citizen-soldiers turning on governments after hardships and defeats in large-scale warfare. Moreover, advances in military technology, especially nuclear weaponry, suggest that wars fought by mass armies may now be relics of history. Whether or not they are any longer likely, do revolutions in the present sense of the term bring political improvements? From the standpoint of democratic and liberal criteria, the answer is an emphatic No. Because of the searing enmities and political scars they create, revolutions never eventuate in consensually united elites. Their consequences are either disunited or ideologically united elites, neither of which is congenial to reliable democratic practices. Although much has been heard from persons outraged by what they regard as fundamental moral deficiencies of contemporary political regimes, not least Western democracies, the sweeping "revolutionary" changes that these persons have demanded lie well beyond what elite theory depicts as possible; they are just dreams and wishful thoughts that are from a liberal and democratic standpoint deeply imprudent.

Elites and Non-Elites

How does elite theory treat non-elite populations and link them to elites? The bulk of Pareto s million-word *Treatise* was an attempt to answer this question and it is self-evident that no satisfactory answer to it can be offered here. The question requires conceptualizing a dynamic relationship between elites and non-elites in which, under specifiable conditions, elites override non-elites, but under different and equally specifiable conditions non-elites override elites. Where elites prevail, a theory must be content to specify the *outer limits* of possible elite behavior and, thus, of political outcomes. Where non-elites prevail, political outcomes can be forecast with greater certainty. Specifying the changing predominance of elites and non-elites theoretically is, therefore, the crucial task.

To illustrate how this might be tackled, consider the proposition that at low levels of socioeconomic development a leftist or leveling propensity is potentially widespread among non-elites. In extreme political circumstances, this propensity may eventuate in a revolutionary collapse of government authority and military discipline of the kind just discussed. But such leveling revolutions appear possible *only* in an early phase of development, and even then they are exceedingly rare: the English, French, and Russian revolutions are the classic instances and all three occurred in pre-industrial conditions. Much more normally in pre-industrial societies, bodies of peasants and artisans are not greatly aggravated by the encroachments of elites, and their fundamentally leftist or leveling propensity is not strongly activated. Non-elite propensities become more enflamed, however, when societies reach the industrial stage of development. In this stage, manual industrial workers, who are numerous, hold consistently to egalitarian sentiments and a hostile view of elites, clearly articulated by the powerful trade unions and leftist parties that mobilize them. Bureaucratic and service workers, who are also numerous, tend to accept the presence of elites even if they do not condone all of their actions and features. Diminished and now more or less comparable numbers of artisans and ex-peasants, who in industrial conditions typically own small farm properties, are ambivalent about elites and elite actions: they resent elite interferences in their farming and artisan endeavors but are inclined to support those elites who seek to check leveling forces. In extreme political circumstances, an anti-egalitarian and possibly "fascist" upheaval aimed at crushing leveling forces is possible: northern Italy in the 1920s; Weimar Germany in the late 1920s and early 1930s; Spain in the late 1930s; strong fascist movements in Austria, Belgium, France, and most other European countries during the interwar period (Paxton, 2004). Normally in industrial societies, however, the large numbers and political influence of non-manual bureaucratic and service workers, augmented by ambivalent artisans and ex-peasants, are sufficient to prevent strongly egalitarian mobilizations of manual industrial workers from gaining government power. If elections are held, the latter are simply out-voted. Finally, the pervasiveness of non-manual bureaucratic and service workers in socioeconomic development s postindustrial stage (Bell, 1973, 121-64) rules out the dramatic leveling and anti-leveling political changes that are possible in earlier stages of development.

There is an important caveat. In societies that are late-comers to socioeconomic development and in a handful of mostly small societies with large petroleum reserves it is clear that today s production and communication technologies greatly accelerate the conversion of workforces from an overwhelmingly peasant and artisan composition to one that consists predominantly of bureaucratic and service workers. In these accelerated and technologically more sophisticated circumstances, manual industrial workers are at once fewer in relative numbers and, perhaps because of their smaller numbers and more sophisticated work tasks, their outlooks appear to be less intransigently egalitarian and hostile toward elites. The main political problem in societies coming late to socioeconomic development may, consequently, reside less in the composition of their rapidly changing workforces than in the inability of these work forces to provide employment for large parts of swollen and mostly young non-elite populations.

The illustrative point, in any case, is that non-elite configurations, sketched here as distinct workforce compositions and concomitant mixes of orientations toward elites, rule out certain elite actions and political outcomes at different stages in socioeconomic development, but they do not determine what elites will do and what political outcomes they will produce. Thus, early in socioeconomic development non-elites tend toward a hostile view of power exercises by elites, and their impoverished situations give non-elites little reason to fear a general leveling of existing hierarchies. If elites are exceptionally incompetent or unlucky, a collapse of government authority that triggers a leveling revolution is possible. But elites may circumvent this by couching effective appeals for non-elite support in terms of religious and other traditional beliefs. In socioeconomic development s industrial stage, a shift to fascist rule is possible, although entrenched elites may circumvent it by holding elections in which leveling forces simply lack sufficient numbers to prevail. What is not possible in industrial societies – in other words, what is precluded by the non-elite configuration – is a successful leveling revolution, and, *pace* Marx, none has occurred. Meanwhile, industrial societies appear to prevent sudden and deliberate settlements of basic elite disputes because their relative complexity makes the elite stratum large and not sufficiently autonomous from non-elites. Elite actors are numerous and many give their primary allegiance to the partisan interests of the mass organizations and movements they head. Negotiating behind the political stage to compromise principled interest positions that elite factions have repeatedly taken when mobilizing non-elite support and then getting followers to accept such compromises is unlikely. Forming a winning political coalition that successfully defends existing hierarchies is the more plausible option for elites in industrial societies.

Elites and Non-Elites in Postindustrial Conditions

How do elites and non-elites affect each other in postindustrial conditions? By the 1970s all of the Western countries that were experiencing these conditions – the Anglo-American, Scandinavian, and Benelux countries, plus West Germany and perhaps Austria-had consensually united elites and stable political institutions. Disunited elites in several countries that were just then reaching the postindustrial stage of development were becoming more consensually united – French, Italian, Japanese, Greek, and Portuguese elites via convergences; Spanish elites via a dramatic elite settlement in the wake of the *Franquist* regime (Linz and Stepan 1995; Gunther 1992). Initially, postindustrial conditions seemed to accentuate the political stability that consensually united elites produce. This was because the preponderance of bureaucratic and service workers blurred class lines and weakened customary partisan alignments among non-elites. Consequently, elites needed less recourse to ideologies, such as socialism and liberalism, in order to justify their statuses, policy positions, and governing actions. Elite political discourse shifted to discussing affluence and the welfare state as solvents of historic discontents and problems. Observers avidly discussed the „end of ideology, a thesis that is probably best seen in hindsight as rationalizing blandly optimistic views of the postindustrial landscape, especially as viewed by sub-elite commentators. With high productivity and nearly full employment, the absence of serious economic downturns, a shrunken working class acquiring middle-class life styles, and no other large and obviously discontented collectivities in sight, there was the appearance of considerable harmony among non-elite populations (e.g., Beer, 1965). Elites, accordingly, adopted a more blatantly managerial posture and they voiced a complacent belief that mere „fair treatment of individuals and groups would ensure social progress and tranquility (Thoenes, 1966).

With the passage of time, however, the greater non-elite harmony and elite complacency that appeared to be the principal political effects of postindustrial conditions diminished. Increased crime, narcotics use, and other deteriorating social conditions became apparent in many cities; a seemingly intractable form of poverty spread in urban slums and rural backwaters; and many young people with essentially privileged family backgrounds displayed considerable alienation and discontent. These trends suggested that postindustrial conditions could be more difficult politically than they first seemed.

Postindustrial conditions are in important respects the terminus of socioeconomic development. They complete the conversion of workforces that consisted overwhelmingly of peasants and artisans at development s outset into workforces pervaded by bureaucratic and service personnel. It is quite unlikely that some further stage of development, conceived in terms of new basic kinds of work and new workforce components, lies beyond postindustrial conditions. If this is so, it must be asked whether postindustrial societies can over the longer haul remain viable politically without the sense of progress and spread of hope that development engendered historically. Crudely put, can postindustrial societies "stagnate" indefinitely in their non-elite configuration without suffering major political upheavals?

One concern is the increased empathy between elites and non-elites that occurs in postindustrial conditions. The preponderance of bureaucratic and service work intermingles previously distinct social strata. Persons more frequently and routinely ascend to elite positions from non-elite origins and locations than happens in more rigidly stratified societies at earlier development levels. As a consequence, not a few persons holding elite positions in postindustrial conditions see themselves as one of a kind with non-elites, among whom they frequently have intimate personal associates and for whom they have considerable empathy. These close and empathetic ties to non-elites help ensure that elite persons are better able to determine measures that at least partially assuage non-elite discontents and aspirations. But what may happen if it is not possible to assuage non-elites? Presumably, actions and measures ranging from deception to discouragement to outright repression will be more reviled by non-elites and harder for elites to take.

A still wider difficulty confronts elites in postindustrial conditions. In all earlier stages of socioeconomic development political action was not generally required to keep most persons steadily engaged in the performance of necessary work. For the most part, internalized attitudes and customary social controls supplied by neighbors and work mates sufficed. In postindustrial conditions, however, such close social controls, along with most religious and other traditional belief systems, attenuate greatly. In earlier stages of socioeconomic development, moreover, most persons worked diligently in order to stave off dreadful personal circumstances – dismissal, eviction, hunger, etc. – and a significant proportion worked without surcease because they could plausibly believe that by doing so their strong personal ambitions could be realized. In these earlier societies only a small number of specially favored persons – mainly the offspring or friends of the rich and powerful – were unmotivated to work in disciplined ways and were inclined toward a self-indulgent, if perhaps esthetically satisfying, leisure. It is easy to see that the proportion of people who are unmotivated for steady work increases markedly in materially affluent and empathetically indulgent postindustrial conditions. It is useless to ignore this by holding that modern technology greatly reduces the need for human labor. Responsible work is not readily parceled out in little pieces in any society. Some tasks must still – and presumably must always – be performed with care, diligence, and forethought, and those who perform them will not allow a large body of essentially idle people, however decorative they may be, to receive substantial rewards for their idleness. This disjunction between the diligent and the idle signals a growing clash between segments of non-elite populations in postindustrial societies, although it is uncertain if this clash will have a magnitude that consensually united elites are unable to manage.

Elite Theory's Limits

Elite theory's predictive pretensions are necessarily modest. Elite behavior cannot be inferred, let alone projected, from knowledge of non-elite configurations and propensities. For instance, neither the creation nor persistence of a consensually or an ideologically united elite is discernibly linked with non-elite propensities. The probability of a united elite of either kind forming and creating stable political institutions can only be guessed at from knowledge of recent elite history. Does this history display long and costly, but essentially inconclusive, warfare between disunited elite factions who, in consequence, may be disposed toward a basic settlement of their disputes? Have elites recently suffered a defeat so grave that the way may be open for a well-organized but previously peripheral group to seize and consolidate power in revolutionary circumstances? The difficulty is not merely that elite behavior is poorly understood; it always contains enough elements of arbitrariness, capriciousness, or simple lack of obvious explanation to defy deterministic explanation. Thus, while societies have displayed similar non-elite configurations during socioeconomic development, no such regularities in the behaviors and configurations of their elites can be identified. Any theory that recognizes this disjunction between elites and non-elites must allow considerable leeway for political accident and unpredictable political choice, so that its explicative claims must be quite modest.

It must also be recognized that elite theory is distasteful to many because it rules out the more ideal aims and outcomes that are regularly voiced by intellectuals, mass movement leaders, and even loosely predicted by social scientists. Elite theory has no place for idealized visions of democracy or social revolution, nor does it have a place for the spread of new values that dispose human beings toward a consistent and thorough altruism. Human conflicts inevitably dilute social cohesion and constitute political problems that elites must manage as best they can. However well or poorly they accomplish this task, elites are the central actors in politics, but the theory that centers on them is unlikely to have many enthusiastic adherents.

11

Political Sociology in Present World

The main question for political sociology is, as Harold Laswell has it, who gets what, when and how. This approach is different from political science approach because political sociology looks for the answers to these questions in the social formation, in social institutions that underpin both the social and the political. The contemporary global society is marked by a skewed distribution of resources and capabilities accorded to different groups in the world and therefore a skewed distribution of power and capacity. The contemporary global society is also a society in transition, in the sense that some fundamentals changes to the structure of world economy—namely, globalization—are leading to new developments that have not been the purview of political sociology as conceived at the time of bounded nation-state units, the hallmark of the times when political sociology came of age. It is important to remember that the field of political sociology as conceived in those times was also a product of a certain social and cultural milieu—which shows up in the importance accorded to topics that flow from the heart of European philosophy and history.

Therefore I will argue here that the questions asked and the answers given also exhibit the limitations of these perspectives and the questions of power as conceived in political sociology leave out issues that arise in communal settings with religious centrality. Therefore, whether the ideas flow from pluralist, elite or Marxist approaches in political sociology, they contain within them limitations of their answers. The contemporary global society is marked by a skewed distribution of economic resources. It is true that as compared to any other time in human history many more people are living on earth. It is also true that as compared to any other time in human history many more people are living longer and healthier lives. Yet it is also true that the level of economic inequality among different population groups is also bigger than any other time in human history. The question of skewed distribution of economic and cultural resources in the language of political sociology is a question of who has power and how this power is exercised.

Three different perspectives try to answer this question. The first perspective, the pluralist perspective, finds its origin in classical liberal ideas of Hobbes, J.S. Mills and Jeremy Bentham and in work of French aristocrat DeTocqueville. The liberal thought of Hobbes and Mills were concerned with protecting the rights of individuals in the context of English society of 17th and 18th century. For them it was individual liberty—defined in a narrow economic and individualistic basis—that was of foundational importance. Hobbes conceptualized the world in terms of a jungle where the only reason we do not cheat or hurt each other is because of the presence of the institution of state—the Leviathan. But then the problem becomes how to stop the state from taking over the whole sphere of existence. The economic activities in particular were held by the thinkers like Mills and Bentham—whose ideas Marx ridiculed as the view of the bourgeois of the market street—to be sacrosanct and therefore outside the purview of state. The truth is that liberalism in its own time was a revolutionary idea. The ending of royal privileges and the need for individual social dignity—although this for J.S. Mills did not include non-property owners and colonized people—was the goal. The goal was to dethrone the clerical authority. For Mills and Bentham the reason for the existence of human beings and the state was to maximize pleasure and minimize pain, the idea that is known as utilitarianism.

In the modern world, this notion of liberal idea of power came to be encapsulated in the form of pluralist perspective. With the royal privilege destroyed and the clericals in retreat, the freedom to undertake commerce became dominant and the pluralist perspective echoes the individualist, liberal ideas. For pluralists, the society is not dominated by any one particular interest, but rather different people with similar interest come together and they play a part in the electoral process via which the ideas with most appeal to the populace gets into the government and therefore become applied to the society. For pluralists the process of elections as conceived in the present fashion is sufficient; power for them is not concentrated and is in fact dispersed throughout the society. DeTocqueville's construction of the local level of democracy among Americans in 1830s— as described in *Democracy in America*—who self-organized at local level and took initiative without any direction from government or any other centralizing authority, forms the basis of this model of power. The most famous statement of modern pluralist thought is found in Robert Dahl's work, *Who Governs? Democracy and Power in an American City*, in which he studies the distribution of power in local politics in New Haven and argues that there had occurred in New Haven a historical shift from "a system of cumulative inequalities in political resources to a system of non cumulative or dispersed inequalities in political resources" (1961, 228). Pluralists extend this model to the polity at large and argue that there is no concentration of power.

They also downplay the role of state; for them the state in the shape a minority (*homo politicus* as Dahl had it) does not play an important role. Dahl terms most of the people in the society as *homo civicus*, people who do not have much interest in the political affairs. The people who have an active interest in politics are characterizes as *homo politicus*. The population therefore is divided into two strata: apolitical statrum and political stratum. It is the second stratum—which does not require any special qualification for entrance such as wealth and education, except for an interest in politics—that people in government are selected from. The state then is a democratic state in the sense that it is elected by electoral process in which anyone can contend. People make the decisions and the words of Abraham Lincoln—"government of the people, by the people and for the people"—reflects the true nature of government. Democracy in this perception is defined as polyarchy, a system of limited democratic representation. For Dahl the idea of polyarchy is an improvement over the closed hegemonies of the authoritarian societies. William I. Robinson characterizes this notion as "low intensity democracy" since it is associated with democracy in a formal rather than substantive sense. The notion of civil society in this perspective is the font from where the ideas that find representation in state arise. The state is not partial to any interest; it floats over all interest and its actions and policies are reflective of what the people at large want. Class and social movements do not exist in this language, because if they were real issues they will find a voice in the electoral process. To begin with, this model is an idealized model of American society. This model does not even attempt to give a prescription to the world outside the United States. There are those who argue that American society is an exceptional society and that there is no existence of the notion of class in the American society because it does not requite the language of old world. It is a known fact that United States never had a strong socialist party and nor a strong socialist tradition. This for Seymour Martin Lipset had to with American exceptionalism in the sense that America never had a feudal background so Americans were born conservatives and as well the limitations put on government from the beginning made Americans gravitate towards libertarianism and anarchism ideas than socialism. There are things that are truly different about America, but pluralism as a model does not even do justice to capturing how power is exercised, let along power on the global scale. The pluralist perspective applied to a global society will dictate that polyarchy is the answer for different parts of the world. Anywhere there is electoral process, which is nominally free, we have a polyarchy—which is all fine and well with the American government and as well as with capitalists who want to consolidate the present distribution of power in the world: in favor of those with money and power and against those lacking either capital and power. William I. Robinson in his perceptive work, *Promoting Polyarchy*, argues that polyarchy as a political program has been adopted by American foreign policy on the behalf of promoting interest of global capitalist fraction of the capitalist class.

Pluralist's notion of power, that they say exists in the world, is not complete. This conception of power—defined by Dahl as "the ability of A to make B do what otherwise B will not do"—is a relational one, one that is visible in real world transactions. This model of power, as defined in this way, is focused on observable power—what Steven Lukes refers as one-dimensional notion of power. Lukes also points out that the one-dimensional power is about behavior of making policy decisions about conflict of (subjective) observable interests. This kind of focus on what would be a model of behaviorism—which neglects the black box of consciousness—is a reflection of the electoral process that is central to Dahl's model. As the United States preaches polyarchy to Middle East countries at this instance in global political situation—via its Greater Middle East Project—it is clear that they it does not want to let real substantive democracy come into play. Take, for example, of Egypt where supposedly American political pressure is bringing changes in the political structure.

The supposed change that United States wants is the ability of different groups to be able to take part in elections and be able to get selected into government. So the visible conflict in the society is between Islamists and secularists (read American favored)—but even when America is calling for changes in the political restructuring of Egypt, it is not asking for an open elections that will have the real conflicts of interests between the Mubarak regime and the Muslim brotherhood to come to the fore. While Mubarak has declared that he will allow other candidates to run against himself or the nominee of the ruling Nation Democratic Party nominee in the upcoming presidential elections this year, in fact the desire of the Mubarak regime and the American side is very clear in actions of the ground: Mubarak has accepted that other people will run against him in the elections but he has attached an onerous and insuperable condition. Any candidate who would want to run the elections will have to get the signature of 50 members of the parliament (All but 10-15 of whom happen to be from another party); this then blocks out any chance for a real possibility that someone from Muslim brotherhood will run in the elections.

This is the kind of low intensity democracy that comes out of pluralist perspective. The real democratic choice in Egypt today will see Muslim brotherhood in power, but that is not acceptable to the superpower, because it will not be good for its interests.1 Some of the recent examples of regime changes in places as diverse as Serbia, Georgia, Ukraine and the failed regime change effort in Venezuela are examples if what a pluralist world order will want to achieve: formal elections which bring into power those who protect the regime of capital and the associated laws that insure that profits can be taken out and foreign investments allowed in a rationalized fashion. The state-civil society relations implied by pluralism are also partial in truth. For this perspective the state is but the clear representative of the democratic interests of the populace. And civil society therefore is truly represented in the state, which implies that there should not be antagonistic relation between the government and the civil society. It therefore makes no space for the social movements to in this equation.

The only legitimate way of making one's voice heard is via organized lobby and pressure groups. In their reading, if people are not satisfied they can form a lobby or pressure group and influence the government. But for them there is no difference of a lobby group such as National Association of Manufacturers (NAM) and the Sierra club because each has an equal chance to be heard in the system. This, however, is patently false because the economic resources that a group such as NAM can bring to play are widely substantial from the resources that a group such as Sierra club can bring to play. Lastly, in relation to the differential economic resources, there is no sense of class differentials present in this perspective, which will be necessary to understand the contemporary global political and social situation. This then is a perspective that is very local to American society and it is even flawed when applied to that society.

The second perspective in political sociology that tries to answer the question of political power is the elite perspective. This perspective is based upon the work of Gaetano Mosca and Villfredo Pareto. Both these theorists held that societies are divided between elites and masses. This division comes from the differential abilities present in human beings. Those who end up elite have superior ability and those who remain in masses have lower abilities. These theorists point to the existence of a ruling group all through the human history as a factor supporting their theory. Pareto was so sure of his theory that he drew a curve that showed the distribution of elites and masses that parallel the curve of distribution of income among the population. Human nature, for these theorists, explains the persistence of elites and masses all through the history. Human nature for Pareto is an unchanging entity and therefore we have a universal presence of elites and masses throughout human history. Pareto explained the persistence of this division in terms of irrational behavior of human psyche—in terms of "deep residues". He divided the population into two groups: those with "instinct for combination" and those with "instinct for aggregates". Those in the first group possess ability to make combinations and are cunning in their reason and they end up as elites. Those in second group are borne to resist change and have devotionalism to stability.

The combination of these two factors—the Machiavellian foxes and lions—keep society in stability. While the elite theorists are known for their critique of both liberal democracy and Marxism, one of them at least sees a limited role for liberal democracy. Mosca sees a limited liberal democracy as a mechanism for the circulation of elites since the elections will move those born in masses that have the ability of elite. This 'circulation of elites' will give the system an appearance of stability. The second idea that is at the heart of elite perspective is that complex organization need leadership to insure effective functioning. In this context of work of Robert Michaels in *Political Parties* put forward the "iron law of oligarchy". For Michaels, one "who says organization, says oligarchy" (1992: 364). Michaels studied the German Social Democratic Party to see how he can explain the concentration of power in the hand of a few people. His intention was critical, but he came to the conclusion that any organization turns into an oligarchy because of the requirement of concentration of power in the hands of a small number of people—the elite—for effective running of any organization. This kind of idea is also entertained by Marxism, as can be seen from the Lenin's idea of "dictatorship of proletariat" in *State and Revolution*, in which the working class is to be lead through the transition from capitalism to communism via the dictatorship of proletariat, which will wither away as people become prepared for communism. As from the case of Soviet Union, this did not work as the dictatorship of proletariat become another kind of elite rule. Max Weber also drew attention to the process of bureaucratization that gets in the way of real democratic rule. For Weber, the only break out the "iron cage of bureaucracy" was to be provided by charismatic personality. In *Capitalism, Socialism and Democracy*, Schumpeter also talks about democracy as a system that inevitably leads towards elite rule because it bureaucratizes the process of selection of leaders. The democratic process then become only a way for selecting as to who will rule them. The modern variant of the elite theory are found in the work of C. Wright Mills who in *Power Elite* argues that American society is ruled by elites from three different fields: military, corporate and political. Further work in Domhaff's Who *Rules America? Power and Politics* continues Mills tradition of democratic elite theory but with an increasing focus on class.

The notion of notion of power in the elite perspective is identified with the seconddimension of power in Steven Lukes' work, which assumes that there is a hierarchical relationship between groups in which the group in power is able to further its interest in not only the sense of the one dimension of power—that is by making an actor do something that the actor would not do otherwise—but also in the sense of being able to exercise political power by keeping certain issues off agenda. This perspective is identified with managerialism by Alford and Friedland in *Powers of Theory*, because it the power is concerned with the way structures of organization allow the exercise of power by elite. The power flows from the organization of structure via which decisions are made. In this sense the centralization and the institution of bureaucracy becomes a central point of exercise of power. The state then in this perspective is something that stands above the society to exercise in a non-partial manner that is for the good of the system. The bureaucrats in this model have independence from the economic elites. Echoing Weber, there is not only one basis for the societal power. Class, which is understood in a different fashion than the Marxist notion of class, while an important factor is not the sole source of social power, and in addition to class, status and political party are other basis of power. The state in this system reflects two views: the sectional interest and structure of the interests of the dominant group—the elites—in the society and the functional interests of keeping the system going by making decisions that are important for the working of the system. Therefore the centralization and rationalization of the state are accompanied by the increasing coercive power of the elites against rebellious populations.

The nature of democracy in this perspective is limited to an understanding of democracy in which is understood as a result of elite competition. Further democracy is understood to keep the circulation of elites going and in some more generous version of this perspective—namely, Mosca—democracy is a way by which individuals born among the masses can rise to become part of elites. Democracy here works to co-opt the populace. The political imperative that marks this system is one of reform and reaction. It is no accident that most of the major figures of this perspective found attraction in fascism. Pareto was sympathetic to fascism and Michaels left socialism for the fascist work under Benetino Mussolini. The state and civil society relationship in this perspective are organized around interorganizational authority and conflict. The conflict is managed and resolved in this perspective and politics—which allows for the management of conflict—plays a central role in the worldview of this perspective. Given that the state is an autonomous entity in this perspective, the civil society and social movements do not get any importance, because the state can resolve the questions of importance without partiality to any one side.

This is an interesting perspective that works very well in some aspects on the global political situation today. The understanding of the growing role of state in surveillance and the control of human bodies can be understood via this perspective. This perspective also could be used to explain the persistence of inequality and evil in the world. It exists, because it is in human instincts to be unequal—and therefore those with ability can move up and become part of the elite and others will have to be content with being part of masses who will be looked after yet dictated to by state. There is a fundamental level of justification of inequality built into this system. At the national level, the absence of whole groups of peoples from the elite structures points to the problem with this perspective. For example, the lack of representation of minorities in the political power structure can be construed as if the whole of the population lacks in some of the capabilities that are needed in the elites. The elite perspective though if applied to the selection of ruling elites in the United States is not able to answer the question of whether it is possible for someone to be able to rise to a power of political prominence or even within the prominent political structure without a level of economic affluence? It seems as if anyone who runs in the elections has deep pockets. Another related question is whether the bureaucrats making decisions that are autonomous of the interests of the capitalists in their work? On this point, there are a number of instances where it could be argued that a managerial state makes decisions that seem to go against elite interests in the first instance. If elite perspective was the ruling paradigm in the world, the power hierarchy of the world would be made up of bureaucrats who made decisions about what the best way for maintaining the system—and this would have meant that there was more stability in the system. But as it will become clear from my discussion in the Marxist approach section below, the bureaucrats do have some degree of autonomy but in the end the decisions are made by a fraction of populations that has clear relationship with the class structure.

The third approach to global political situation is the Marxist perspective in political sociology. The Marxist political sociology is based upon the work of Karl Marx who stressed that throughout the human history—except in the prehistoric times—there have always existed two classes of people, the oppressors and the oppressed. The oppressed are the ones who sell their capital to make a living and oppressors are the ones who own the means of production. Men make their own history but not the conditions of their own choosing—this sums up how Marx views the relationship of work to the making of history. The social conditions and relationships, according to this perspective, prevailing in a given society reflects its organization of the mode of production.

Different modes of production represent different relationships: the feudal mode of production has the master-slave relationship and the capitalist mode of production has capitalist-workers relationship. In works such as *Capital* Marx worked out the centrality of labor to the production of profit under capitalism. For Marx, the organization of political life is to be understood in relation to the class relationship between its populations. Whenever the mode of production becomes more productive than the social organization that is present in the society, a revolution takes place and brings into being a new mode of society. For both Marx and Engels, as they argue in *The Communist Manifesto*, the history of all societies hitherto has been a history of class struggle and therefore under capitalism the struggle is between the bourgeoisie and the proletariat. The bourgeoisie's power over the proletariat is because of the formers control over the means of production (capital + factories).

The notion of power in Marxist approach flows from the control of economic resources. For Marx the economic differences within the civil society are manifest in the structure of state and the dominance in the realm of economic field implies dominance in the power in terms of state. Those who control capital in the society therefore also control the institution. In *The Communist Manifesto* Marx identities the state as the "executive committee of the bourgeois"—that is, it serves the interests of capitalists in a very straightforward way. Anything that benefits capitalists gets done by the state and anything that benefits the working class is not done by the state of its own volition but is rather forced by the working class if they are strong enough. But it has also to be said that this is not the only way Marx understands state. There are other times in which he gives more leeway to the way state acts. I will return to this when we follow up the discussion on the nature of state in Marxist theory below. The notion of class in this approach is dependent upon the relationship with means of production and is therefore different from the notion of class in elite theory perspective in which it denotes an organized political entity. The economic bases of class are seen to cut through all different parts of social structure. The social structure is marked by the contradictions inherent in the struggle between capital accumulation and class struggle.

The notion of power—a structural one—implied by the Marxist theory is captured in the three-dimensional model of power as captured by Steven Lukes in *Power: A Radical View*. The third degree of power is concerned not solely with what is on the agenda as is the case with pluralist perspectives or as to what is kept of the agenda as is the case of elite theory, but it deals with the latent issues along with observable issues and also with how some potential issues are kept out of politics by sectional interests. In Gramsci's work on hegemony in *Selections from the Prison Notebooks* he is concerned with how the working class—even though it is suffering from exploitation at the hands of the capitalists—does not revolt in keeping with Marx's prediction of revolution. The answer for this for Gramsci is to be found in the way the civil society becomes the place where sectional interests are able to change the cultural modes of thinking via their deployment of hegemony eliciting mechanisms. According to Gramsci, hegemony—the consent to leadership by the capitalist class—is established not in the narrow repressive way but also in ideological way. So the state was not only involved in the establishment of hegemony in repressive terms but more importantly in the ideological sense. Therefore for the resistance to this the real stagy will involve a war of position in the civil society, whose importance between state and economy was established by Gramsci within Marxists, and this will be a slow and long process, one that would need the involvement of organic intellectuals in creating alternative hegemony via cultural work. Gramsci is refreshing because he is saying that a society cannot be just changed by taking over the institution of state, as was the Lenin's program in Soviet Union. In so doing, Gramsci lays the foundation for an alternative understanding of why the revolution did not happen in the advanced industrial revolution, which was Marx's idea of how the transition from capitalism to communism will unfold. It is also important to realize here that this kind of work was later extended by the Frankfurt school scholars who centered culture in their analysis of capitalist societies. In recent times, the ideas of Robert Cox in *Production, Power and World Order: Social Forces in the Making of History*—who builds upon Gramsci's work—are interesting because he argues for understanding power at the global level by examining the "state-civil society" complexes not only in a given nation, but in an international field of power in which some states have maximum degree of external autonomy, and others are dominated by these states with maximum external autonomy.

The Marxist debates around the institution of state are perhaps the most important debates over the institution of state in any of these three approaches. Classical Marx's position—although he gave different stresses to it—was that state acted as the executive committee of the bourgeois. Therefore what was in the favor of the bourgeois was also in the favor of the state. But the debates between Ralph Miliband and Nicos Poulantzas were the modern markers in increasing the understanding the nature of state. For Miliband who follows the instrumentalist approach in *The State in Capitalist Society*—that is, the state is an instrument of capitalist power pure and simple—and therefore argues that all the actions taken by the state are in favor of the ruling class. But Nicos Poulantzas faults Miliband for thinking of the state as an 'empty space' and not as a social relationship. He argues that state has "relative autonomy" from the capitalist class and even though it the state might in the short term take act against what might be the interest of capitalist class in the last instance it will take the side of capitalist class. Fred Block in his article, "The Ruling Class Does Not Rule" argues that the state is not concerned with working for each single capitalist but that in fact the role of the state is to maximize the accumulation of profit and therefore not each single action in case of individual capitalist should be seen as a signification of state's intent.

The idea of democracy favored by this approach is also different from the other conceptions. The democracy here is not limited to the procedural and formal one or as something that is to be managed by the elites within a liberal democracy. The democracy in this approach is a real measure of economic as well as cultural equality for all the populations. Democracy thus takes on the sphere of economy, state and the civil society. Marxists argue that for a democratic system we need to ensure that there is equal opportunity for the development of capacities of each individual from day one. There should be select few who can afford nice cars and schools from day one and others who cannot even afford to go to school. If only does the state provide free education for the children of the poor on par with the rich, argued Marxists, then only can we have a chance at a the establishment of a real democracy. But as studies such as Bourdieu's in *Distinction: A Social Critique of Value of Judgment* show, the markers of class are embedded within the family background so deep that the first institution of socialization—the family itself—cancels out the impact of equalization of education upon the possible establishment of a democratic education. The social movements that arouse out of the Marxist approach were class based and therefore they demanded actions to improve the economic and social position of workers. But since the defeat of the Soviet experiment, the labor movement the world over has suffered a strong blow.

The truth is the contemporary political situation in the world is marked by the shadows of 1989. The death of Soviet experiment in the graveyard of authoritarianism and the victory of capitalism marked the end of an era and the beginning of another. While Fukuyama wrote paeans to the victory of liberal democracy at the end of history, new rumblings were rising inside the very developments that were responsible for the fall of the Soviet Union. The world of today marked at it is by globalization is not the same which was analyzed by the classical perspectives of political sociology—pluralism, elite theory of class perspective. The rise of international trade and the corresponding need for a political structure that facilitates the process of trade and as well the movement of capital and goods across nation-state boundaries has impacted the world political dynamics. The increasing importance of transnational institutions—such as the International Monetary Fund (IMF), World Bank (WB), World Trade Organization (WTO), Group of Eight (G-8), Organization for Economic Cooperation and Development (OECD) and Asia Pacific Economic Cooperation (APEC)—for political coordination of this system of increasing global trade has led to a focus on issues that cannot just be explained by reference to the notions of power and politics conceived in the political sociology literature. There is a need for a rethink in the basis concepts of political sociology. Since most of the concepts of political sociology come from the time when the world economy was divided into neat and bounded boxes of nation-states, the present conjuncture in the world political situation cannot be completely grasped by the concepts of political sociology. Take, for instance, the concept of globalization and its impact upon the institution of state. There three four basic positions that can identified in the impact of globalization in the state. First, there are those who argue that the role of state is weakening under globalization and the importance of transnational institutions is increasing. This position has been called the hyperglobalist position, because it sees the role of nation-state as weakened and therefore it focuses on the transnational. As part of global capitalism school, William I. Robinson's work, A Theory of Global Capitalism: Production, Classes and State in a Transnational

World, can be seen as a representation of this perspective. HE argues that "the apparent declining ability if national state to intervene in the process of capital accumulation and to determine economic policies reflects the newfound power that capital acquired over the nation-state and popular classes..." and that "real power in the global system is shifting to a transnational space that is not subject a 'national control" (2004, 103). Others of view that the nation-state as being weakened by this perspective include Kenichi Ohmae, who argues that the "global civilization" will be the product of the changes brought about by globalization and that nation-state is history. Second, there are those who argue that the world has seen a higher level of globalization in the previous epoch and therefore the institution of nation-state is not weakening and in fact the process of globalization is being controlled and shaped by nation-state (Hirst and Thompson, 1996).

This group is known as the skeptics. Third, the last group is made of those who are known as transformationalists who argue that the world is undergoing complex changes and although the role of nation-state is changing it is not yet okay to argue that its role has weakened. This position is present in the work of Bob Jessop, Held et al. My own position is somewhere in between the transformative and hyperglobalist position. Looking at the world, there is no doubt that the space for action that nation-state had in the past is now constrained. And yet it is also true that I see many obstacles in the path of construction of a transnational state that Robinson argues is in formation via the establishment of a transnational class. The myriad conflicts and the pull of the local in the conflicts world over give me a pause to think that the local will be strong force for quite a long time. Yet I am also very much open to the idea that there is indeed a global fragment in the capitalist class and that this fragment is increasing its power. The very sense in which capital has force over states world over—appearing as a magical force as if it does not have a source but is present everywhere—means that there is the domination of a globalization capital over states.

In terms of democracy, the political situation in the contemporary times is marked by the absence of any real representation by majority of populations in their own political systems. In most of the western democracies, there is certainly a much higher level of formal democracy today than in the past. The level of political participation in formal elections is also healthy, with the sole exception of the United States where political participation at the national level are very low and political culture is heavily dominated by irrational elements. Outside the western world, formal democracy has spread via the third wave of democracy (Huntington, 1993). The biggest mark of this was the fall of Soviet Union and the conversion of the Eastern Europe to formal democracies in 1989. This then is the victory of capitalism that has made it possible for the capitalists to dominate the world political, economic and cultural scene like never before. The discourse of formal democracy has serviced the designs of the powerful countries and by extension the forces that stand behind these nations—the capitalist class. The United States' discourse of support for democracy is about extension of the market and its logic into all parts of the globe and into all facets of human life, without regard for popular democratic ideals. William I. Robinson's path breaking *Promoting Polyarchy: Globalization, US Interventionism and Hegemony* is the best work to capture the deployment of low intensity democracy for controlling the popular forces around the world. The low intensity is being used to make consumers of the people the world over, thereby superceding other more organic identities that people have. The invasion of Iraq and the gunboat democracy that we are seeing today shows the desperate nature of capitalist rule and its interest in consolidating formal democracy, which is integral to the capitalist system in our epoch. If one juxtaposes Venezuela next to the case of Iraq, one can really see the sordid nature of how capitalist power works. Despite coups and repeated attempts of overthrown Chavez, the capitalist interests represented by the United States government cannot bring them to accept that Chavez has the popular support of a solid majority of Venezuelans.

The resistance to exploitation that is part and parcel of capitalism, nonetheless, continues. The fall of the Soviet Union in 1989 was blow to the social movements and class movements that opposed capitalism. The nature of protest and rebellion has changed in the world over. But there is no end of history yet, as protest, rebellion and politics has come back on agenda again. In terms of social movements, there has been a differentiation in the number and types of social movements active in the world. The social movements that held sway in the past, such as the class based movements have suffered a loss of strength in the aftermath of the Soviet demise. The rise of the new social movements in Europe in 1980s has centered the issue of culture. Whereas the social movements before 1980s were based mostly around the issues of class, the NSMs stressed the quality of life issues. In this way, a number of questions that were limited to the class dimension were reconfigured to become questions of quality of life questions and a number of other agendas that were not represented in the class movements were brought forth. Ronald Ingelhart has suggested that the rise of movement like the NSMs (New Social Movements) signify the movement of societies to a set of post-material values, in that the ideas beyond material ideas—which guided the class based opposition to large number of people—have become central to populaces' life. This then shows up in their desire to think of politics in terms of quality of life issues rather than in material terms. This has meant proliferation of movements that range from identity-based movements to peace movements and the environmental movement. But the NSMs are movements that are more present in the advanced industrial countries than in the global south. There is still space in the global south for the kinds of actions that are still concerned with the issues of material well being and economic justice. The rise of an energized global civil society has also made its mark on the global scene. The work of Keck and Sikkink in *Activists beyond Borders* and Jackie Smith in *Transnational Social Movements and Global Politics: Solidarity Beyond State* shows the increasing engagement of global civil society with social justice issues beyond nation-state boundaries. The presence of diasporas—which lead to greater circulation of ideas and peoples across nation state boundaries—and the increasing migration levels point to the possibility of a stratum of population which can be concrete foundations of political action from below. At the same time the work of Michel Foucault gives us a moment for pause because it implies the pervasiveness of power in all sectors of human life. Power, in Foucault's use, is capillary type and it exists everywhere. So the focus on locating power in structures such as politics makes us neglect the presence of power at personal level. The failure of the Soviet Union can be read in these ideas as a problem that neglected the personal level of power in the process of revolutionary change. To conclude, I began this essay arguing that the field of political sociology has its own lineage—a western one—and that therefore leads to its own strength and weakness in interpreting social world. I followed this by examining the three perspectives of political sociology—pluralism, elite theory and the class perspective—in terms of their understanding of the nature of power, state, class, democracy and civil society. I then critically examined these perspectives in relation to the contemporary global society. In the last section I gave an overview of the contemporary world situation in terms of power, state, class, democracy and civil society. I pointed out that the most important process that is influencing political sociology's understanding of world—and simultaneously raising questions about the adequacy of political sociology concepts—is globalization. I want to conclude by looking forward at some of the challenging research directions that need to be undertaken in political sociology. First, if one were to begin from a macro perspective, then there is a need for a rethink of the fundamental understanding of power in political sociology. What other bases of power—such as religion—can be incorporated into political sociology more effectively to understand the world? Second, what needs to be done about political sociology concepts that are not really able to do justice to a global understanding of the world? To answer the first question, political sociology will have to look at the sources of power that are beyond what is examined in the field now—and to answer the second question, political sociologists need to look at new concepts that bridge the nationstate centered foundations with more global concepts.

12

Political Sociology of Poverty

INTRODUCTION

Political sociology of poverty requires an analysis of the relationship between the political, economic and socio-cultural actors, institutions and processes in the context of poverty. It assumes that poverty is a complex and cumulative consequence of power relations over a period of time between groups within a region and between regions in the modern world system. This paper on political sociology of poverty in India is based upon the assumption that (a) the caste system and economic inequality complement each other in the case of the poorer sections of Indian society, (b) Indian society has experienced complexities in identification of class system due to the manifold gradations of social rank, which have evolved in the form of caste and tribe along with quasireligious settings of deprivation, (c) the colonial and post-colonial polity have been organized around the recognition of nebulous coexistence of 'caste' and 'class' principles in the approach of state and political community towards the weaker sections of the society.

The Indian Constitution and political community have given recognition to the grave condition of resourcelessness of the weakest sections of Indian society through the system of 'Scheduled' castes and 'Scheduled' tribes. In other words, while recognizing the heuristic value of 'caste', 'gender', 'tribe' and 'class' as separate analytical and sociological categories, this paper suggests that caste, tribe and class merge into each other in the domain of absolute as well as chronic poverty in India. This clarification is important as there are a large number of instances of 'caste into class' and 'class into caste' as well as tribe-caste convergence in terms of economic conditions. But they do not negate the fact that for the last several decades there is marginal difference in the caste status of the absolutely poor classes and there is very limited evidence of economic prosperity ('creamy layer') among the depressed castes and tribes particularly in the rural domain of the Indian economy.

HISTORICAL CONTEXT

Any attempt to comprehend the Indian experience of poverty eradication through construction of welfare state and political mobilization in the last five decades needs to recognize that India is a post-colonial society where a) the colonial heritage in the statecraft, and b) the legacy of anti-imperialist national movement in the political community and political culture, play critical roles. This relationship between the 'colonial past' and the 'democratic present' is very significant for understanding the changing nature and orientation of the state and society in the context of poverty in India since independence in 1947.

It is also necessary to remember the differences between the rise of democratic polity in Europe and the emergence of welfare state in India. To quote Jawaharlal Nehru, a pioneer of democratic socialism during the anti-colonial movement between 1920s and 1940s and the first Prime Minister of free India from 1947 to 1964, "In Western countries, full blooded democracy with adult suffrage came to the people very late, in the Twentieth Century". They had in the meantime profited from the Industrial Revolution. They got the resources before they gained democracy so that when the demands came for better living conditions they had the resources to fulfil them. In India, we have full-blooded democracy but not the resources.

The results of the Indian endeavour of poverty eradication are not satisfactory in international terms. But the specific and comparative aspects of India help us in contextualising the Indian project of nation building through planning for a poverty free welfare state and a socialistic society between 1950 and the end of the millennium. They also provide insights about the international standing of India in the community of nation-states, where the largest democracy of the world is found to be lagging behind Sri Lanka, China and Indonesia (see Table 1). The Indian political process is being shaped by continuous interaction between the imperatives of interest group dynamics, democratization, decolonization and nation-building. These four factors provide the basis for legitimacy of the post-colonial state. They also give content to the concepts of 'public welfare' and 'national interest'. As a consequence, there were several changes in the state and society relationship in India during this period, which have caused i) decline of politics and rise of economics, ii) rise of dominant caste coalitions and decline of upper caste hegemony, iii) erosion of national constitutional consensus and rise of centrifugal movements, iv) stress on decentralization along with weakening of the process of centerformation including planning, v) rise of movements of erstwhile marginalized categories of people e.g. women, depressed classes like Dalits and Scheduled Tribes, ethnic groups, etc., vi) rise of 'region' instead of 'nation' as the operational category of the party system, vii) weakening of the middle class political culture as well as rise of crime-politics nexus with patronage from the neo-rich classes, and viii) rolling back of the welfare state under the pressure of global forces of liberalization.

The relationship between poverty, politics and state has continued to play a significant role in the political sociology of independent India as it did during the colonial era. The issue of poverty came onto the State's Agenda through different processes after the end of colonial period. First there was a constitutional process which was a consequence of the nationalist discourse where "Community Development" and decolonization were presented as two sides of the same coin. It created an appropriate focus in the making of the constitution of independent India.

Secondly, there came a developmentalist phase which gained importance during the drive for promoting capacity building among the rural cultivators through "Land Reform" in the 1950s. The idea of 'poor peasant' became unacceptable in the discourse of development under the Congress Raj. Of course, it failed to include the landless labourers in its conceptualization of recasting the rural power structure through 'land reforms'.

Then came the phase of nation wide rural agitations in the 1960s. The newly created propertied peasants started asking for increase in state's patronage and, the pauperised peasants urged for radical transformations to ensure jobs, wages, dignity and justice. The states' responses were crystallized as the "Green Revolution".

Finally, India became market oriented in the 1980s as state-centric initiatives became counter productive at worst and ineffective at best. There was a new faith in market mediated system management among the propertied sections of Indian peasantry as well as the urban propertied classes. It was termed "the era of liberalization". Rolling back of the state did show some results in the first few years. But the bifurcation of the propertied and the pauperised was reinforced by the end of the 1990's. Thus there are new indications of pressures about continuity of chronic poverty and creation of 'new poor' in the context of liberalization. In fact, it may be appropriate to suggest that after the 'first generation reforms' or 'structural adjustments' and the consequential rolling back of the state, there is resurfacing of poverty in rural and urban sectors resulting in unrest and conflicts. This rediscovery of poverty is accompanied by refocusing of the political agenda of the India political sectors including political parties, trade unions, peasant bodies and other major components of the power pyramid in India.

In short, the link between active political mobilization (of varying intensity) and rural transformation has played a vital role in shaping the destiny of the poor. The state and its legislative and bureaucratic apparatus have been a secondary factor. Hence the change in the national economic scenario with reference to peasants in general, and poor rural masses in particular has been primarily a political phenomenon (see Mohanty et.al., 1998).

The Constitutional Content

The conceptualization of poverty free welfare state in India has been accomplished in two phases-i) the period of national movement for freedom from foreign rule, and ii) the making of Indian Constitution through a constituent assembly. The Indian national movement was able to focus the attention of the masses on growing poverty and the recurrence of famine which was due to defective policies of the colonial government. It was the view of leading public men like Dadabhai Naoroji (1825-1917), M. G. Ranade (1842-1901) and R. C. Dutt (1848-1909) that the solution to the social and economic backwardness of India could not be found through the British Government's policy of laissez-faire, but that only a national government which actively promoted development by direct government action could bring about improvement in living standards. The resolutions of the Indian National Congress from 1929 onwards emphasized the need "to make revolutionary changes in the present economic structure of the society and to remove grave inequalities in order to remove poverty and ameliorate the condition of the masses". The resolution of 1931 underlined that "political freedom must include real economic freedom of the starving millions" and elaborated the fundamental rights which should be included in the Constitution of free India to provide a basis for it.

It was followed by the formation of a National Planning Committee with Jawaharlal Nehru as Chairman in 1937 on the initiative of Subhash Chandra Bose as the President of Indian National Congress. A complementary process of conceptualization was contributed by the constant debate about the nature and priorities of the state in post-colonial India among the Gandhians, socialists, communists, radical humanists and other ideological groups in the national movement. The charter of demands and agitations by various class organizations of peasants and industrial workers provided the guidelines for the approach of the national movement to poverty and its eradication from villages and towns of India. In fact the decisive push to the colonial rule came with large scale peasant mobilization in the last decades of the freedom movement.

The concept of welfare state became the lodestar of the Constituent Assembly of India. It made its impact on the thinking of the leading lights of the Assembly who wanted to secure 'justice – social, economic and political' for all citizens of the Republic. They were clear that without social and economic democracy, political democracy had no meaning in a poor country like India. The Preamble, Fundamental Rights (Articles 12 to 35), Directive Principles of State Policy (Articles 36 to 51), and the special provisions for Scheduled Castes and Tribes and Backward Classes (Articles 330 to 342) are significant dimensions of the Indian constitution from this perspective. They have created the imperatives for progress from political democracy to social and economic democracy which means "working for a certain measure of well-being for all".

The Preamble of the Constitution commits the state to the development of a free society based on the dignity of the individual in which there would be equality of status, opportunity and justice. The state has to endeavour towards harmonization of interests between individuals, groups, and between individuals and groups on one hand and interests of the community on the other. The Preamble places justice above the other principles of liberty, equality and fraternity. The values embedded in the Preamble are elaborated in the Fundamental Rights and the Directive Principles. The Fundamental Rights have covered all the traditional civil and political rights included in the Universal Declaration of Human Rights. There are six broad categories of the fundamental rights:

i. The right to equality (Articles 1, 15,16,17, and 18)

ii. The right to freedom (Articles 19 and 21)

iii. The right against exploitation (Articles 23 and 24);

iv. The right to freedom of conscience and free profession, practice and propagation of religion (Articles 25 to 28);

v. The right to minorities to conserve their culture, (Articles 29 and 30); and

vi. The right to constitutional remedies for the enforcement of all these Fundamental Rights (Article 32).

The Directive Principles of State Policy are basically inspired by the concept of a welfare state. Article 37 declares that the Directive Principles are "fundamental in the governance of the country" and that "it shall be the duty of the State to apply these principles in making laws". However these are non-justiciable. Article 38 defined the aim as follows; "The State shall strive to promote the welfare of the people by securing and protecting as effectively as it may a social order in which justice – social, economic and political, shall inform all the institutions of the national life".

In Article 39, stress was laid on the right to adequate means of livelihood, equally for men and women; equal pay for equal work for both men and women; conditions of work ensuring health and strength, protection of children and youth against exploitation and against moral and material abandonment. It is also laid down that the state should ensure that 'the ownership and control of the material resources of the community are so distributed as best to subserve the common good'; and that the 'operation of the economic system does not result in the concentration of wealth and means of production to the common detriment'.

Furthermore, the duty is enjoined on the State that 'it should, within the limits of its economic capacity and development, make effective provision for securing the right to work, to education and to public assistance in cases of unemployment, old age, sickness and disablement, and in other cases of undeserved want' (Article 41). The state should also provide for 'securing just and human conditions of work and for maternity relief '; and 'security to all workers-agricultural, industrial and otherwise-a living wage, conditions of work ensuring a decent standard of life and full enjoyment of leisure and social and cultural opportunities' (Articles 42 and 43).

Particular stress is laid on special assistance to the weaker sections of the people, including the Scheduled Castes and the Scheduled Tribes and the other weaker sections with a view to promoting their educational and economic interests and to protecting them from social injustice and exploitation. With regard to rural economy, Articles 40 and 48 enjoin the application of modern scientific methods to agriculture and animal husbandry and the implementation of programmes and improvements through self-governing Panchayats. Promotion of cottage industries on an individual and cooperative basis is mentioned in Article 43.

Article 45 fixed a definite time limit during which the State would endeavour to provide free and compulsory education for all children until the age of fourteen years from the commencement of this Constitution.

The above principles were given a more precise direction when Parliament accepted the socialist pattern of society as the objective of social and economic policy in December 1954. In 1976, the 42nd Amendment Act added certain new directives to the Constitution of India:

(a) That children are given opportunities and facilities to develop in a healthy manner and in conditions of freedom and dignity;

(b) That the operation of the legal system promoted justice on a basis of equal opportunity, and in particular the State provided free legal aid in cases of economic and other disabilities;

(c) That the participation of workers in management of industries is secured; and

(d) That the environment is protected and improved and the forests and wild life are safeguarded.

ANTI–POVERTY MOBILIZATIONS AND THEIR RESULTS

The direction of post-colonial polity in India was evolved during the three Five Year Plans between 1951 and 1965 in the context of peasant mobilization and other protest movements. Self-reliance was the basic goal of the Nehruvian agenda under the hegemony of the Congress Party. It is important to recognize that the response to the peasant movements in the Fifties by the nascent post-colonial state and the hegemonic ruling party, Congress, was:

a) to eliminate intermediaries for creating a broad based proprietary class in the village who took interest in promoting agricultural production;

b) to facilitate infrastructure facilities through a variety of inputs and concessions;

c) to ensure minimum price support through purchase of agricultural products by public sector corporations.

The impact of these reforms created two opposite results –

i) it promoted the expansion of owner-cultivator class which came from upper and upper-middle strata of the caste system; and

ii) it created insecurity among tenants, agrarian workers, and semibonded tillers due to increased pressure of market forces upon the agricultural sector.

Agriculture was changing into a 'market oriented, cash based, and profit claiming occupation, causing deterioration of the situation of the poorer strata in rural India. In short, there was emergence of commercialization, monetization and market/profit oriented production due to the state's plans and programmes between 1950 and 1965. The number of agricultural proletariat-(who belonged to the 'lowest' castes and the Scheduled Tribes) grew at an exponential rate. But the strategy of "incremental democratic modernization" encountered a series of problems from 1963 onwards, which made the Nehruvian approach obsolete in many spheres of State policies. A new set of national issues regarding food scarcity, increase in prices, national defence, foreign dependence, economic stagnation, and regional inequalities generated a cumulative stress between 1963 and 1967. As a consequence a new agenda called Ten Point Programme came into being. The dilemma of dependent accumulation and declining dominance of the Congress Party created a shift in India's direction of development. The slogan of "Jai Jawan-Jai Kisan" (victory to the soldiers-victory to the peasants) symbolized the new thrusts of the State. The 'sixties saw a wave of disenchantment with the entire planning process'. There was visible growth of discontent in the late sixties (Kumar, 1989).

Between anti-Congressism and Naxalism, there was a great range of activism and mobilization all over rural and urban India. This coincided with the 4th Five Year Plan and the 5th Lok Sabha elections. Despite the intelligence and experience, Indian planning had gotten into a rut. The results were disappointing. It was time, therefore, for the planners to ask themselves whether the things they had been trying to do were really correct. Thus the period of the 4th Five Year Plan was marked by political weakness and economic anxieties. The poorer sections of the society and the pro-poor political formations were making impressive moves for collective action. It was the era of second wave of land conflicts after the late nineteen forties and early fifties. The second wave of rural mobilization in the sixties contained two distinct groups of rural masses. There was a movement launched by the newly emerged proprietary classes constituted by rich farmers and middle peasant proprietors. The communists called them 'Kulaks' which was an exaggeration of their economic capacity. They were also named 'Bullock Capitalists'. Their mobilization was aimed at securing increased patronage from the state. They did not come into conflict with the interests of the industrial and commercial urban proprietary classes. It was led by peasant based regional political formations which came into existence in 1960s in several provinces of India. Many of them got amalgamated into a national political party, Bharatiya Lok Dal, led by Charan Singh in 1974.

Another movement was launched by the agrarian poor with increasing prominence of the agricultural workers. The movements of the rural poor in the 1960s and 70s were centred around a combination of economic, social and political issues. Economically, they were in need of security of employment, minimum wages, rights over a certain share of the produce, distribution of surplus lands, and reduction and liquidation of debts. Socially, they were agitated about violation of legally acquired rights, gender discrimination, violence and humiliation by upper caste/class men and public officials. Politically, they were attempting to resist repression and terror of the upper and middle castes who had recently turned into land owning classes in rural India. They found a nexus of the newly emerging proprietors and the nascent post-colonial state. They also felt that the state was paying more attention to the proprietary classes as it considered them as the agents of development. They were led by the left wing parties like Communist Party,

Communist Party (Marxist), Socialist Party and Communist Party (Marxist-Leninist). The rural poor in the 1960s comprised of a) pauperized peasants, b) agrarian workers belonging mostly to the depressed castes and tribes and other marginal groups, and c) a large section of women. Their struggles gave rise to uncomfortable questions regarding the usefulness of the socio-economic framework of developmental planning adopted after independence. They exposed the limits of the development policies as they had failed to improve the condition of the poor even after three Five Year Plans, and a generation long political stability in the form of Congress rule. They brought the nation 'face to face' with the continuity of unimaginable forms of exploitation and oppression of the rural poor. It was an indictment of the post-colonial state and its patronage to newly propertied castes and communities in the name of development and nation building since 1950s. Above all it proved that there is a 'dialectical interconnection' between the various sectors of the society and polity.

Politics of Poverty Eradication

The issue of poverty became a central question during 1964-71. It was triggered by the Lohia-Nehru-Nanda debates in Lok Sabha in 1964 about the nature of poverty and its extent. It became recognized as a political imperative of democratic governance as a large number of people were still trapped in economic settings which forced them to live below the levels of subsistence. It was legitimized by the slogan of Garibi Hatao (eliminate poverty) by the Congress Party under the leadership of Indira Gandhi who routed most of the anti-Congress political parties in the general elections of 1971-72. It appeared that after a long wait, the moment had arrived for fulfilling the dreams of Swaraj by creating an egalitarian social order based upon economic self-reliance and democratic social transformations.

It is another matter that the electoral mandate was not translated into effective socio-economic steps due to a variety of reasons – domestic as well as international. Low savings, limited investment, sluggish industry, a steep rise in the money supply and a sharp decline in agricultural production were the prominent features of economic administration. The problems were further complicated by international 'price revolution' and a phase of 'stagflation' in the world economy. In 1973-74, inflation had turned everything topsy-turvy. It was coupled with the crisis of leadership within the Congress Party at the Central and the provincial levels. The situation gave rise to multiple political pressures, student-youth movements and working class protests which culminated in a national movement against the failures of the government in terms of checking corruption, controlling price rise, creating employment, and providing relief to the poor. It was led by Jayaprakash Narayan, one of the founders of democratic socialism in India (who later devoted himself to the cause of Sarvodaya or Gandhian reconstruction of the Indian society, economy and polity to promote welfare of all) and was supported by socialists and others.

After a phase of indifference and tolerance, the ruling party declared the State of Emergency due to the intensity of internal protests. At the same time, it had to adopt a 20-Point programme of welfare measures to show that even in a situation of crisis, the government is committed to continue the process of relief and welfare.

Inspite of these adversities, the change in the orientation of the political community and the policy makers in the early 1970s, was remarkable. According to C.T. Kurien (1979), "When a small group in the Planning Commission proposed in 1962 that the central concern of our planning has to be the removal of poverty as early as possible, it was a novel and consequently very suspicious idea. But within a decade it had become not only the accepted economic dogma, but also a highly articulated political programme". The new mood was reflected in the Fifth Five Year Plan. For example, Towards An Approach to the Fifth Plan (1974-79) proclaimed "there would seem to be a conspicuous element of historic inevitability in a direct approach to reducing poverty becoming the main thrust of the Fifth Five Year Plan. The Plan is being formulated by a government that has massive mandate from the people, both in the Parliamentary elections of 1971 and the state elections of 1972, on the basis of a programme whose centre piece is Garibi Hatao. The homogeneity of the Governments at the Centre and most of the states during the formulation and early years of the Fifth Plan is guaranteed. This should enable bold and imaginative proposals being put through on the basis of an enlightened national consensus" (Kurien, 1978). Thus, the Fifth Five Year Plan was a landmark due to its special thrust on creating the maximum possible dent on the low end poverty while ensuring that the country moves one more step in the direction of economic independence. It was also remarkable due to its recognition that the Indian economy had reached a stage where larger availability of resources makes it possible to launch a direct attack on – a) unemployment, b) under-employment, and c) poverty. It clearly admitted that the twin causes of poverty are i) underdevelopment, and ii) inequality and it is inadmissible to ignore or underplay either factor. Therefore, it pointed out that the problem of poverty couldn't be overcome within the foreseeable future by efforts in one direction only.

India entered the phase of liberalization in 1980s under Prime Minister Rajiv Gandhi and the process continued inspite of change in leadership at the level of the Prime Minister. The year 1991 was the beginning of an explicit phase of rolling back of the state due to the imperatives of liberalization. Relatively higher growth was recorded during 1980-2000 and particularly during 1990s which was a decade of structural economic reforms. It also showed decline in poverty and improvement in health and literacy levels of the people of India. But India continues to suffer from high levels of illiteracy, high rate of infant mortality, high incidence of disease, disability, and malnutrition even after half a century of freedom and democracy. Allocations for health and education have been only 4.1 percent of the GDP (1996-97) which was lower than several developing post-colonial countries like Malaysia and Sri Lanka.

The sociological consequences of the liberalization-globalisation drive have been summarized by Yogendra Singh (2002) as state versus market dilemma. He argues that the extent to which the power of market increases and expands, the significance of the state as a supreme political institution, undergoes major alterations. Idealistically, some protagonists of the market even anticipate the end of the notion of sovereignty. For societies such as India, where nation-building has still not reached the level of integrative maturity, such fears of the end of sovereignty or a threat to it due to unhindered play of the global market force cause not only acute anxiety but also pose a challenge (Y. Singh, 2002).

Poverty and Conflict Lines: Class, Caste and Tribes

Analysis of poverty-politics relationship needs understanding of power dynamics and conflict patterns because inequality of access to resources generates processes of conflict in the context of interests between the included, the marginal and the excluded sections of any society. The conflicts make reform and strategies and processes of poverty elimination imperative. This requires a multi-dimensional understanding of the interconnectivity of the spheres of state, market and community and the interrelatedness of the local, regional/national, and global domains. All these need special attention in exploring the challenges of chronic poverty.

Poverty and the poor are always associated with (a) resourcelessness, (b) choicelessness, (c) insecurity and (d) deprivation which creates incapacities in the pursuit of dignified life in a given society for a person, household, group or community. Furthermore, those suffering chronic poverty also suffer several simultaneous disadvantages including gender, age, caste, ethnicity, location, etc. According to A.R. Desai (1986) a new class configuration has emerged as a direct consequence of the conjunction of peasant mobilization and government measures over the last few decades. It contains the following categories of rural population: a) *Rich Farmers and Land lords* owning 15 acres and more, possessing 50 per cent of the total land and constituting 7 per cent of the population, b) *Middle Farmers* – with 5 to 15 acres of land, possessing 30 per cent of the total land and constituting 19 per cent of the population, c) *Poor Farmers* owning between 1 and 5 acres, possessing 17 per cent of the total land and constituting 30 per cent of rural population, and d) *Agricultural Labour* without land or owning less than 1 acre of land, possessing about 2 per cent of the total land and constituting 44 per cent of the population. The national picture also suggested presence of five categories on the basis of household income with 10, 19, 12, 192 and 420 million persons in them (Stern, 1993).

The population below poverty line (1993-94) has two major features: i) Overwhelming presence of the Scheduled Castes and Scheduled Tribes population, ii) Assam, Bihar, Madhya Pradesh, Maharashtra, Orissa and Uttar Pradesh were found to be above the national figures of population below poverty line where as West Bengal, Tamil Nadu and Karnataka were within the proximity of national figure (35.9 per cent) (see Table 4). The relation between the resourcelessness of the chronic poor and settings of conflict is rooted in the quest for security and dignity through ending of choicelessness of the chronic poor in a variety of ways. Such households, loaded with a complex set of disadvantages and assetlessness, are usually involved in subsistence type of activities which get them poor returns. Since their earnings are meager, they survive on small amounts of borrowed money or they are forced to suffer from hunger. They are mostly unable to change the power relationships and there are no mechanisms of grievance redressal. The powerful local forces, in conjunction with the corruptible sections of the state apparatus, manipulate and misappropriate the common resources and pubic funds which create further helplessness and frustration. It has been termed as 'web of poverty' with centrality of continuous alienation of the people trapped in it and occasional confrontation in the society. This could lead to social tension, despair or a combination of both (Sharma, 2000).

The increasing visibility of a "fault line of deprivation and conflict" is a consequence of such a setting in India today. It is visible in a number of districts of Uttar Pradesh (13), Bihar (26), Orissa (10), Jharkhand (10), Chattisgarh (4), Madhya Pradesh (16),•Andhra Pradesh (4), Assam (3), Tripura (1) and Arunachal Pradesh (3) (India Today, 2003). In the terminology of bureaucracy and media, these states have a number of districts which are conflict prone due to the effective presence of "Naxalites", "Senas" (private armies), externally aided "extremists", and separatists. Despite the variation of labels, all of them indicate presence of deepening social conflicts around issues of deprivation and poverty. It is another matter that the pattern, form and objectives of mobilization of discontent are defined by: a) social cleavages, and b) the political conditions of the states.

At the same time, the growth of economic, social and cultural disequilibria, rooted in chronic poverty and resourcelessness is a cause of national concern. It affects governability as well as social and economic development. It also promotes increasing togetherness between poverty and political violence, which causes legitimization of crises and invites use of police force to control its proliferation. If the state gets tough, it creates "martyrs" and myths. If the state remains tolerant and mild it faces escalation of violence and disruption of law and order. The feeling of political and economic exclusion invites entrepreneurs of violence. Therefore, the advocates of violence enjoy such settings where a large number of persons are found to be living on the margins of the economy and society. How do we institutionalize the process of conflict resolution, in a volatile setting of chronic poverty and social deprivations ? There is gradual decay of the state apparatus at the micro and meso levels in around 76 districts of India where under-development and poverty provide conducive setting for growth of organised violence. The "fault line" and its growing visibility needs further study.

The issue of chronic poverty and conflict is associated with the persistence of insecurity in the life setting of a person, household, group, or community (UNDP, 1999). Human security suggests that people can exercise their choices in pursuit of secure and dignified existence in society safely and freely. It has two main aspects; a) safety from chronic threats such as hunger, disease and repression, and b) protection from sudden and hurtful disruptions in the patterns of daily life whether in homes, in jobs or in communities. According to the United Nations approach, the many threats to human security, differing for individuals at different times, fall into seven categories:

i. Economic insecurity,
ii. Food insecurity,
iii. Health insecurity,
iv. Personal insecurity,
v. Environmental insecurity,
vi. Community and cultural insecurity,
vii. Political insecurity

These insecurities and threats can affect people everywhere. Famines, ethnic conflicts, social disintegration, terrorism, pollution and drug and human trafficking can no longer be confined within national borders. Some global challenges to human security arise because threats within countries rapidly spill beyond national frontiers, such as greenhouse gases and trade in drugs. Other threats take on a global character because of the disparities between countries-disparities that encourage millions of people to leave their homes in search of a better life, whether the receiving country wants them or not. And frustrations over inequalities in incomes and political power often build up into serious civil conflicts between groups, whether ethnic, religious or social.

Those suffering chronic poverty are caught in the midst of a set of basic conflicts which perpetuate their insecurity through 'capability poverty', resourcelessness and choicelessness. Some of these conflicts are silent and invisible e.g. the crisis due to ecological factors. Several others are visible as demonstrated by the sufferers of class, caste, ethnic gender, religious (communal) and racial discriminations. Together they contribute towards the continuity of chronic poverty in a cumulative manner by sustaining the logic of power relations and marginality of the chronic poor in the discourse of power. They envelop the institutions and processes of state, market and community. The most visible and loud conflicts in the context of chronic poverty are found to exist around a) class, b) caste, and c) tribes (ethno-regional issues).

(a) About Class based Conflicts:

The class based conflicts have industrial and rural spheres. Both kinds of conflicts are sinking into marginality in terms of their impact. In the industrial arena, economic liberalism has led to flexible labour market policies like subcontracting, outsourcing and the engagement of temporary and part-time workers in core activities of the labour process. India's integration into the global economy and far reaching structural adjustment for it in the 1990s has weakened the strategic position of the trade unions. According to the Labour Bureau figures of the Government of India, there has been a decline in the number of man-days lost due to strikes and lockouts in 2000 compared to the figures for 1992. Furthermore, more man-days are lost due to lockouts than strikes (J. John, 2001).

In the rural arena, 298 million persons constitute the labour force engaged in agricultural and allied activities which is 79 per cent of the total workforce. A majority of the workforce engaged in agriculture consists of small and marginal farmers and agricultural labourers. About 80 per cent of total rural labour households (over 30 per cent of total rural households) are agricultural labour households. Of them, the Scheduled Castes and the Scheduled Tribes constitute nearly 50 per cent. In general agricultural labourers suffer from seasonal unemployment, job insecurity, poverty, indebtedness, and lack of access to productive assets. They suffer from lack of social security and inability to form their own organizations. The economic reform measures have worsened their condition due to recent hike in the prices of food grains. There is also decline in their position in comparison to their counterparts in other activities in both rural and urban areas inspite of absolute rise in their wages. The hope of 'land to the tillers' generated before independence has receded beyond the realm of realization.

A significant section of owner-cultivators ('farmers') have become vulnerable to poverty due to the promotion of capital-intensive agriculture. In recent years farmers of Andhra Pradesh, Karnataka, Maharashtra and Punjab have committed suicides in significant numbers due to crop failures and indebtedness. According to newspapers there were 2409 suicides by farmers between 1995 and 1998, but it needs further study (see Table 5). According to one observer our country is a heaven for middlemen who earn their fabulous commissions and a hell for farmers who sweat and toil (Ramarao, 2003). Situations of direct and indirect conflict between the poor in rural and urban spheres of the economy and the propertied sections and the state are spreading in various parts of the country. A cycle of conflicts, control and suppression and re-emergence with added strength appears to occur in significant number of rural areas in most of the poor states. The issues causing conflict in rural areas are security of employment, minimum wages, share in the produce, securing of surplus lands, reduction and liquidations of debts and violence by the land owning classes.

There are also tensions and clashes in the context of sexual and cultural oppression and political denial. In fact the year 2000-01 has been a difficult one for rural economy. Income has declined. Agricultural production has been sluggish; food production has declined by almost 5 per cent. Suicides persist. The rural development programmes have recorded declining growth. A combined view of the situation of the rural labourers, marginal farmers, and the rural sector's contribution to the national economy gives a depressing picture. It is marked by limited growth of high and upper middle-income households (7.6 million households in rural and 10 million households in urban areas), increased regional disparity (Bihar and Gujarat at 1:7), and the general tenor of the National Agricultural Policy (July, 2000), which ignores the agricultural labour and marginal farmers and may accentuate the pre-existing inequities with possibilities of social strife and disenchantment (Prasad, 2001).

The situation in the urban settings is diffused. But there is growing discontent due to the increasing belief that the current development policies do not have the capability to create the framework within which the conditions of the poor might improve. In urban India slums are growing at the rate of 5 per cent. 24 per cent to 28 per cent of the urban population in Karnataka,

Maharashtra and Delhi lives in slums as a fall out of poverty and deprivation. This provides a setting of recurring conflict between the urban poor and the Government Machinery as they are created out of 'illegal encroachment of government land'. There is high frequency of inter-community strife and conflicts. In fact violence is forced upon them as a way of living. The slum dwellers work mostly in the unorganized sector (in jobs requiring less skill and training). Their incomes are quite insufficient to enable them to lead a dignified life and enjoy basic rights.

Paradoxically, the condition of the working class in the organised sector is found to be drifting from resistance to hopelessness and less conflict in the context of the new economic policies. The new labour laws have diminished the space for class conflict in the organised sector of industrial India. There are three major events which have contributed towards the decline of the 'class power' of the organised workers in the last decade – (i) disinvestment in the public sector, (ii) retrenchment and contractualization of the private industrial establishments, and (iii) global recession in the industrial sector. An overview of the changing labour relations scenario may be presented by comparing the figures of industrial disputes in India in 1992 and 2002. It is seen that the figure has declined from 1714 to 413. There was also phenomenal decline in the number of workers involved in disputes and man days lost in the last decade. It needs further enquiry to be able to understand the implications of declining number of trade union strikes in an era of economic transition in favour of entrepreneurs.

b) On Caste Oriented Conflicts

Caste based conflicts are increasing in the context of enlargement of the capacity of two blocks-the political power of the dominant castes and political mobilisation of the Dalit castes or the Scheduled castes. It is causing conflict in the electoral arena, labour market, and civil society.

The quest for political power among the Scheduled Castes around the provisions of 'Reserved seats' in legislature has been a major feature of Indian Democracy. They achieved a significant breakthrough with the growth of coalition politics in 1969-71. The making of OBC and Dalit Vote Banks was a singular contribution of socialist politics which contributed towards a 'Silent Revolution' in the era of "Green Revolution" (Jeffrelot, 2002). At the same time there is marginal increase in the percentage of Dalits below the poverty line during the privatization-globalization regime from 44.7 per cent in 1987-88 to above 48 per cent in 1993-94, which is significantly higher than estimates for the general population (39 per cent). The literacy gap between the SCs and rest of the population has also remained more than 17 per cent between 1961 and 1991. According to the Census of 1991 more than 80 per cent rural Dalit women were found to be illiterate. They were also sufferers at the hands of the dominant castes in different parts of India. Between 1995 and 1997, a total of 90,925 cases were registered between with the police under different categories of crimes and atrocities against the Dalits. Nearly 70 per cent of all the offences were reported from the BIMARU states-Bihar, Madhya Pradesh, Rajasthan and Uttar Pradesh (see National SC/ST Commission Report, 1997-98).

Mass murders of the Dalits by dominant castes in Andhra Pradesh and Bihar has underlined the depth of conflict between the castes in rural India over the last several years. According to an estimate, the period between 1990 and 1999 witnessed 35 instances of caste-based massacres, the total number of victims being about 400. More than 350 of those killed were from among the lower castes (Frontline, 1999). In short the issue of caste-class convergence in the context of chronic poverty in an era of dominant caste democracy and liberalizationglobalisation is promoting anti-Dalit caste violence in rural areas and decline in the opportunities for the Dalits in the urban-industrial economy (see Black Paper, 1999).

According to the Sixth Report of the National Commission for Scheduled Castes and Scheduled Tribes (1999-2001), the extent of crimes and atrocities on persons belonging to Scheduled Castes is much higher than those on Scheduled Tribe. The cases of atrocities on Scheduled Castes are about 6-7 times more than STs, though the population of SCs is only twice that of STs. Uttar Pradesh (6122), Rajasthan (5623), and Madhya Pradesh (4667) have reported highest incidence of crime against Scheduled Castes. These three states account for 65.4 per cent of the total cases of-atrocities on SCs in the country during 1999. The position of registered cases of atrocities in other states was Gujarat (1781), Andhra Pradesh (1749), Karnataka (1277), Tamil Nadu (883), Bihar (820), Orissa (772), Maharashtra (605), Kerala (514), Haryana (121), Himachal Pradesh (54), Punjab (39) and Delhi (18). There had been a declining trend in crimes committed on members of SCs, STs, between 1997 and 2000. In the case of SCs, number of crimes came down from 32,997 in 1995 and 27,944 in 1997 to 23,742 in 2000; and for STs from 4644 in 1997 to 3958 in 2000. This decline deserves closer study to find out the relative roles of state, political mobilization, media and NGOs and increasing vigilance and resistance by SCs and STs.

One of the most obvious reasons for so many attacks on SC men and women is related to the refusal of the SCs to work without dignity and appropriate wages. The assertiveness of these castes for higher wages, freedom of choice of work and endeavor to achieve mobility as cultivators are among the most frequent reasons for atrocities against SCs.

c) Tribes and Conflicts

The Tribal dimension of chronic poverty is most pronounced in the context of conflicts and movements. They constitute 8 per cent of the population. 83 per cent of them live in the area between West-Bengal and Gujarat, 12 per cent in the North eastern region, 4 per cent in Nilgiri Hills and 1per cent in J&K and Himachal Pradesh. It is believed that confrontation has been the quintessence of the situation in the tribal areas after the rise of 'state' as a formal system of political and administrative authority. The ever-increasing exploitation of the tribals and elimination of their lands led to revolts and rebellion in many parts of India. 'Leave them alone' (or 'exclusion') as in the hills of North-East and 'light' administration (or 'partial exclusion') elsewhere was the response of the Imperial Regime in the face of determined resistance to their advancement and consolidation. The dawn of independence ushered in a new era of high hopes and soaring aspirations with an ebullient nation committed to the ideals of democracy, equity and social justice. The cause of weaker sections, particularly the tribal people, was accepted as a national task with clear premises and constitutional commitments. But the hopes were belied. The tribal people in fact faced regression as the personalized administration gave way to an amorphous faceless system. Influx of immigrants, alienation of their lands and underdevelopment are three major problems of the Tribal communities.

According to the Report of MPs and Experts (Bhuria Committee Report, 1995), "Notwithstanding the rhetoric of the past four decades, on account of absence of effective democratic decentralization at even district levels, demands and agitations for separate states in the country have taken root in Jharkhand, Bodoland, Uttarakhand, etc. Iniquitous policies and actions and economic imbalance have led to resentment among the deprived regions. Assertions on the basis of region, ethnicity, languages, etc. have been made. They have come to feel that without the political power of a state, they are not able to claim their rightful due"1.

In economic terms, the Scheduled Tribes (ST) have been found to receive a total household income of Rs. 19,556 and a per capita income of Rs. 3,504, which are 76 and 78 per cent respectively, of the national average. Both incidence and intensity of poverty are higher among the Scheduled Tribes in comparison with the national average. They have recorded a literacy level of about 40 per cent in comparison to an all India average of 54 per cent. Only about one-fourth of ST women are literate. Literacy levels are extremely low for STs in Bihar, Rajasthan, Uttar Pradesh, Madhya Pradesh and Orissa.

More than 87 per cent of the total population has been depending on agriculture for their livelihood, supplemented by collection and sale of minor forest products. However the percentage of cultivators has declined from 68 per cent to 54.5 per cent in 1991 and the proportion of agricultural labour is increasing correspondingly. Vast areas of tribal lands have been acquired under the Land Acquisition Act and still are being acquired for industrial and infrastructural development. Out of the total 213 lakh displaced persons (1951– 1990), 85.4 lakhs are Scheduled Tribes. They constitute about 40 per cent of the total number of displaced persons. From the total 83.8 lakh rehabilitated persons, 21.2 lakhs i.e. 39.4 per cent belong to STs. Dams (41 lakhs), mining (6.5 lakhs) and industries (3.8 lakhs) are the major causes of tribal displacements. A land mark judgement of Supreme Court in the case of Samatha vs. The State of Andhra Pradesh and others (11th July, 1997) has placed a check on this. The Supreme Court has ordered that government lands, forest lands and tribal lands in the Scheduled Areas cannot be leased out to non-tribals or to private companies for mining and industrial operations.

Social insecurity among the Scheduled Tribes, particularly the ST women, is also a cause of concern. Out of nearly 4000 cases of atrocities committed against Scheduled Tribes in 2000, there were 391 cases (9.8per cent) of rape. The incidents of atrocities on Scheduled Tribes were highest in Madhya Pradesh (1756), followed by Rajasthan (1221), Gujarat (367), Orissa (335), Andhra Pradesh (178), Maharashtra (171), Tamil Nadu (105) and Kerala (81). The direct and indirect relationships between the efforts of STs to move out of exploitative dependencies and the acts of atrocities is a relevant question for further systematic enquiry. At the same time, it may be concluded that the extreme forms of exploitation and violation of civil rights that exist in areas such as Chattishgarh and Jharkhand have turned them into places of long standing insurgency. Another reason for the rising violence in forest areas is encroachment by migrants who are taking over the land of the local people. This causes conflict over resource use.

Such a profile of tribal India makes it obvious that the tribals are the worst sufferers of resourcelessness and choicelessness as well as the most disenchanted section of the Indian population in post-colonial India. They are leading components in a variety of mobilizations in the last two decades including movements for environmental protection (Narmada Bachao), states reorganization (Jharkhand, Uttarakhand, and Chattisgarh), political separation (the separatist movements of the North-Eastern Tribals), and resistance to globalization (Kashipur). Such conflictual mobilizations have brought the issue of chronic poverty of tribal India to the attention of national media and policy analysts in recent years thereby prompting the governments to come forward with a variety of anti-poverty measures and development packages. Creation of three new provinces Jharkhand (out of Bihar), Chattisgarh (out of Madhya Pradesh) and Uttaranchal (out of Uttar Pradesh) is a major effort to address the challenge of tribal alienation and unrest. It also marks the beginning of assertiveness for tribal autonomy and dignity in the Hindi belt of India.

TWO TRAJECTORIES OF POVERTY, POLITICS AND CONFLICTS : WEST BENGAL AND BIHAR

India is a vast economic, cultural and political area with diversities. But the policy of the elimination of rural intermediaries and land reforms adopted after independence caused "reshuffling" of class relations in the countryside. The transformation initiative was a response to long peasant mobilizations during the freedom movement for addressing poverty. However, it performed a dual function – (i) elevating the richer section of the tenants into owner class which broadened the base of the proprietary classes who take active interest in agricultural development for maximizing profit, and (ii) growth of marginal farmers, 'back door' tenants and proletarianized labour due to new tenurial system. The change has promoted intense competition among the newly emerging proprietary classes. They are also contending with the demands and struggles of the rural masses which are being steadily pauperized and marginalized.

On the other hand, evolution of democracy has contributed to the metamorphosis of major caste groups including the Dalits into competing associations beyond the ascriptive principles of the caste system. There has been eruption of caste organizations with intense activities in nearly all sectors of the emerging economy and in the political processes which is a response to the imperatives of the democratic political system. The changes in the caste system have the following characteristics: (i) There is simultaneous weakening of the upper castes and strengthening of intermediary agrarian caste promoting a dominant caste coalitional complex in the political space, and (ii) The lower caste who are also major occupants of the lowest economic labels, are getting regrouped to counteract the adverse effect of new economic and political processes. This section has been offered preferential facilities ('reservations') and opportunities in elections, education and government services. It has contributed to making the lower castes vocal.

The impact of new constitutional projects for the abolition of the caste system and restructuring the class system through affirmative action in response to the modern India has been uneven and complex. It has contained and resolved some of the most prominent issues causing conflict in the society. But it has also given rise to new competition and conflicts due to realignment of political, social and economic groups. Therefore it is relevant to provide a glimpse of the paradoxical relationship between economic, social and political structures and processes in the context of poverty and social conflict by presenting the cases of West Bengal and Bihar.

West Bengal's Record

West Bengal and Bihar are neighbouring states which belonged to the Bengal Presidency in the colonial era. Their political economy was organized through zamindari system. Both had strong peasant movements, trade union activities and anti-poverty political formations. Both were sites of intense rural conflicts and urban movements in the post colonial decades. Both were ruled by the Congress Party between 1952 and 1967 and both got their first non-Congress governments in 1967. But they followed different trajectories in the last four decades since 1967 that resulted in major reforms in favour of poorer sections in West Bengal. Today, there is no major industrial or agrarian conflict in West Bengal.

First, we look at the politics and social change in West Bengal which along with Bihar and Orissa had the highest proportion of population below the poverty line. West Bengal has been plagued by high population density, industrial stagnation, rural conflict and economic decline in the 1980s. But these conditions were changed through reorientation of the government policies via social mobilization and political alliances which was steered by a left front coalition in office since 1977.

High levels of unrest in rural areas for effective implementation of agrarian reforms, radical trade union movements for better wages, cheaper food items, education, health and transport facilities and emergence of a leftist political front were the outstanding features of West Bengal since late 1960s. The movement of the small and marginal farmers accelerated after the foundation of first United Front Government in 1967. It culminated into the famous Naxalbari revolt and the birth of Naxalism (or Maoism and Marxist – Leninist Communist Party). The United Front Government was removed by the centre and the peasant protests and 'Naxalite' activists were ruthlessly suppressed under President's Rule. But within a decade, there was Left Front Government in Kolkata after sweeping out the Congress regime at the centre and the state in 1977. Agrarian reforms and organization of local governance system were given top priority by the Left Front Government. This resulted in a sustained period of conflict containment and political stability for decades after 1977. For example, the number of riots came down from 11,702 (1977) to 3,899 (2000) whereas there was no substantial change in the scene of Bihar or All-India.

How was this accomplished? There was redistribution of more than 9,13,000 acres of land amongst 19,93,660 households which covered a large proportion of the rural population of the landless and land-poor households. Decades old demands of tenants-farmers organizations for higher crop shares, security of tenures and legal status of tenancy agreements were accepted through "Operation Barga". It gave relief and strength to the vulnerable and exploited sections of rural Bengal, which accounted for 1.44 million share croppers in the state.

West Bengal is an example of generating conducive setting for poverty eradication and conflict resolution through a combination of reforming production relations and instruments of local governance. It has been achieved on the basis of political mobilization and electoral strength around 'peasant unity'. Now West Bengal is engaged in negotiating the path beyond the agrarian agenda for satisfactory progress in universalization of health care and basic education (Dreze and Sen, 1997). In other words the record of West Bengal shows positive correlation between poverty and conflict on one hand, and conflict, political change and economic reforms on the other.

The Case of Bihar

The history of rural unrest and agrarian movement in Bihar goes back to the Kol and Bhumiji insurrections of 1831-33 against the newly established colonial administration in Chota Nagpur and adjoining areas. The peasant movements in the regions to the north and south of the Ganges, from mid 19th century to the present day, have been regularly studied due to their significance for the peasants and agricultural workers of India. It proved to be the nucleus of All India Kisan Sabha as well as the Indian National Congress, Socialist movements and Communist movements in the twentieth century. But Bihar failed to institutionalize any change in the exploitative agrarian structure after independence. While the introduction of democracy with universal adult franchise, raised the expectations of poor peasantry, changeless agrarian system of Bihar soon became a victim of the dual failures – continuity of extremely exploitative relations and growing stagnation in the agrarian economy.

The stagnation in agricultural production around 5 per cent annual compound rate of growth between 1969–70 and 1983–84; which was lowest in India, not only caused depeasantization but also led to declining fortunes of the rich and middle peasants. It had widened the scope of conflict between the rich and middle peasants and the rural proletariat. The inability (as well as resistance) to pay minimum wages to the agricultural workers (most of whom belong to the Scheduled Castes) had turned them towards the new revolutionary leadership for their fight for wages. As a consequence violent clashes had become a general phenomenon in Central Bihar. According to official sources, there were 463 and 590 violent clashes in 1998 and 1999 respectively. But the list of events of mass murders due to the conflicts between various sections of peasants and agricultural workers began to grow particularly from 1990-91 onwards including Devas Diyara (1991, 15 killed), Bathanitola (1996, 22 killed), Laxamanpur Bathe (1997, 58 killed), Shankar Bigaha (1999, 22 killed), Senari (1999, 34 killed), and Miyanpur (2000, 34 killed).

It seems that the state machinery had become marginalized as most of these killings were carried out by armed groups belonging to peasant communities and the marginal and landless poor (see table 12). These Senawars had become more prominent than the electoral and other institutional forms of conflicts and competition. In short, Bihar is a case where politics has failed and there is absence of effective local governance apparatus, like Panchayats, Police Station and Block Development Offices. The larger political system has been affected by corruption at high places. It has led to criminalization of politics and politicization of crime as a cumulative consequence which is indicated in the increasing number of kidnappings in Bihar (see Table 13). The incidents of kidnapping have increased from 580 in 1972 to 2711 in 2000 – a five-fold increase in the state of Bihar whereas it was 769 and 926 in 1972 and 2000 in West Bengal. Bihar is also the state with the largest proportion of persons below the poverty line as 26 out of 37 districts are among the most backward districts in the country. Therefore, it should not be a surprise if Bihar is affected by increasingly violent settings of economy, polity and society as the state system has consistently failed to respond to poverty affected groups and social conflicts around poverty problems despite major changes in the governments between 1967 and 2002 at the provincial and central levels.

POVERTY OF POLITICS-LIMITS OF PLANNING AND RESERVATION

It may be useful to have an overview of the relationship between poverty and politics, as articulated through the two processes of planning and reservation during the last five decades of post-colonial India. Poverty in India, whether it is measured in terms of income or nutritional levels, is concentrated among certain occupational classes and social categories in both the rural and urban sectors. Most of the rural poor are found among (i) peasant cultivators with very small holdings, and (ii) agricultural workers from the Scheduled Castes and the Scheduled Tribes. The causes of poverty in urban settings are mostly underemployment in various occupations with low productivity occupations such as porterage, insecure employment and low real wages in some industries. Migrant workers are prominent amongst the urban poor. Furthermore, as none of the urban poor are producers of food and have to buy a part of their total requirements in the open market, they are extremely susceptible to rising food prices. In addition, the urban poor suffer from extremely bad conditions of housing, water supply and sanitation.

There has been a steady decline in the proportion of people below poverty line from about 55 per cent in the mid-1970s to 36 per cent in 1993-94 and to around 30 per cent in 2001, but their actual numbers have been rising. At the same time it is true that food insecurity and income poverty have been brought on the state's agenda through series of mobilizations, as well as natural calamities, in the last five decades. It also shows that poverty continues to create severe adversities in the lives of the rural people, particularly the small and marginal farmers, agricultural laborers and artisans and has a high incidence among the Scheduled Castes and Scheduled Tribes in rural as well as urban areas. It is regionally concentrated in seven states – Assam, Bihar, Orissa, Uttar Pradesh, Madhya Pradesh, Maharashtra, and West Bengal. But there are extremely poor districts in several other states as well. As a consequence, food security and poverty eradication have been the key objectives of the Indian planning strategy. A number of direct poverty alleviation programmes were introduced from 1971-72 after the massive electoral success of the Congress led by Indira Gandhi in 1971-72. Integrated Rural Development Programme (IRDP) and Training for the Rural Youth for Self Employment (TRYSEM) were two key components of the poverty related programmes in this period. Poverty was a major theme in politics and planning since 1971-72. But the crisis of implementation, non-viability of projects and slow economic growth created several weaknesses in it by the mid 1980s. It caused a shift from income generation to human development oriented schemes. It also exerted pressure for de-bureaucratization of the poverty related programmes through peoples' participation via Panchayat Raj institutions and NGOs.

With a paradigm shift in the late 1980s to the early 1990s, the issue of poverty lost its significance in the political discourse of India. This decline in importance was reflected in the Election Manifestos of major Indian political parties where the idea of growth and governance found more prominence than poverty alleviation and expenditure on employment generation. Expectations from private sector activities were a new component of the planning strategy in the era of liberalization.

Rise in the frequency of violent conflicts in the regions suffering from poverty is becoming a significant feature of the political landscape of India since the shift of political attention away from the challenge of poverty. Land reforms, removal of illiteracy and malnutrition, encouragement of shelter construction for the homeless, and social mobilization for breaking down the caste barriers which have trapped the SC and ST population in rural areas are some of the neglected themes in the national politics of India since the inauguration of the phase of rolling back of the state from the economic sphere.

At the same time it may also be highlighted that the engagement with poverty alleviation through planning has experienced four kinds of limits-economic, administrative, political and international constraints. The Anti-Poverty Programme of today's India involves 1 percent of GDP or 6 per cent of the Central Budget, 55 per cent of which is allocated for food subsidy or Public Distribution System (PDS), 35 per cent is allocated for Rural Works Programme, and around 5 per cent is provided for Self Employment Programmes. But there are severe resource problems due to the compulsions of allocating 50 per cent of the available national resources for debt servicing and 25 per cent for defence needs. The challenge is compounded by the continuing mal-functioning of local self-governance mechanisms and bureaucratic inefficiencies in the poverty affected areas. Politically, the situation has worsened due to the rise of crime politics nexus and more importance being accorded to politics of identity over politics of 'common interests'. Internationally there are growing pressures upon the Indian state for 'rolling back'. It is further complicated by the presence of hostile neighbours who are not keen on promoting regionalization in South Asia Economic Zone.

Reservation was the second most important political intervention in meeting the challenges of poverty and deprivation. But this has remained more symbolic than substantive. Let us first have a look at the constitutional provisions for safeguarding the interests of the SCs and STs. Article 17 (abolition of untouchability), Article 23 (prohibition of forced labour), Article 45 (universalization of primary education), Article 46 (promotion of educational and economic interests of SCs and STs), Article 330 and 332 (proportionate reservation of seats in the Lok Sabha and the State assemblies) and Article 335 (appointment to services and posts in Union and State services), are the most important provisions of the constitution of India in the context of protective measures for the amelioration of the conditions of the weaker sections of Indian society.

In the case of the Other Backward Classes (OBCs), there has been the use of Article 16(4) of the Constitution of India to address the problem of inadequate access to representation in the services under the state. It was activated in 1990 on the basis of the recommendations of a Second National Commission on Backward Classes (also known as Mandal Commission) with the caution of the Supreme Court that the benefit of reservations will not be extended to persons/ sections falling under the category of 'creamy layer'. This system of special treatment to underprivileged sections involves three types of preferences.

1. Reservations, which provide easier access to valued positions within important social institutions like legislature, government services and academic institutions. It is also used in land allotments, housing and other scarce resources.
2. There are expenditures of government resources on behalf of the beneficiaries like scholarships, grants, loans, legal aids etc.
3. There are special protections, such as measures to protect "untouchables" from discriminatory treatment.

Given such an institutional approach, the policies of reservations have created a symbolic power for all those who belong to the SCs (16.7 percent of the population), STs (8 per cent) and OBCs (52 per cent). It has also given recognition to the need for national reorientation for such sections of the population who are found to be trapped in a 'web of poverty' due to conjunction of social, economic and political deprivations and discrimination over a period of time. The reservation policy regime has promoted a progressive outlook in the society because it legitimizes integrative representation and redistributive mobilization. Besides, it has to be recognized that the exclusive emphasis upon 'timeless' system of reservation in jobs and legislature has bypassed the poor of these categories. There has been evolution of blocks of vested interests in such category of the beneficiaries of reservation in the past five decades.

The majority of the Scheduled Castes and Scheduled Tribes are agricultural labourers. Because of economic compulsions, their children have to go to work when they should be in schools. Children who labour, lose education and therefore employment opportunities when they are adults. Without the means of income for want of education, they in turn may continue to send their children to work. It strengthens the vicious circle of poverty and this has not been addressed by 'job reservation'.

Similarly the question of number has played a crucial role in determining the chances of receiving attention of the state and gain of vote power. It has created cleavages between the large, medium and small groups of SCs, STs and OBCs. For example, the SCs are 21 per cent of the population in Uttar Pradesh. But chamars constitute 12.7 per cent and Pasis are 3 per cent. They have created a sub-category of empowered and mobile SCs. But there are 6.5 per cent other SCs, with a total share of only 2.8 per cent in population, who remain most depressed due to numerical marginality. The rise of dominant castes among the OBCs like Jats, Yadavas, Kurmis, Lodhis, Reddys, Kammars, Vokkaliggas, Lingayats, etc. has led to marginalization of the other OBCs who are recognized as Most Backward Castes (MBCs) in the discourse of power.

In short, the impact of reservation policies is visible in the political culture where the SCs the STs and the OBCs have emerged as new corporate identities with constitutional protection for representation and empowerment. But it has not contributed towards any qualitative shift in the lives of the poorer sections of these communities, where poverty is getting perpetuated in overwhelming numbers despite decades of freedom and democracy, planning and reservations.

Liberalization, Poverty Alleviation and Conflicts

Opening the market of India to global companies and reducing the role of public sector have been two major components of the new economic policies. They are also associated with globalization of capital mobility and ethnicization of political mobilization. It was found that there was i) a boom in the private sector, ii) stable growth in agricultural sector (3.6 per cent per annum), iii) declining rate of population growth (1.6 per cent per annum), and iv) improvement in social indicators (like literacy rate, infant mortality rate, gender related indicators etc.). In the early 1990's, poverty worsened following structural adjustments, a poor harvest and a decline in food availability. There was some decline in poverty and by 1993-94 it fell below the 1987 level. States in the north and east, that have 40 per cent of India's population have lagged in reducing poverty since the late 1970's.

According to economic analysts, expenditure on social sector schemes as part of the welfare oriented programs of the Indian state has been increasing in real terms in the era of liberalization.

At the same time it has also been pointed out that it is mainly through increased expenditures of the Central government. The state governments are easing out of their constitutional commitment to sustain programmes in social sectors and it is a matter of concern. Here the social sector expenditure is defined as the total expenditure on social services and rural development. The social services include education, health and family welfare, water supply and sanitation. The rural development expenditure relates mostly to anti-poverty programmes and is presented as 'economic services' in the budget documents.

The realities of 'reforms' have created new challenges for India since: (a) So far mostly the better off sections are able to respond to market signals and the rural population has benefited less. (b) India is suffering marginalisation in a globalized world and loss of domestic market due to unfettered entry of the foreign companies under the WTO provisions. (c) The role of government in economic and social matters is shrinking which has caused apprehensions about 'the future of the protective discrimination' for the weaker sections.

These challenges are being listed as tasks during the Second Generation Reforms. It is recognized by the policy makers that "Freedom from ignorance, diseases and fear, along with freedom from want, are the best guarantors of human development. But education, health care, water and sanitation services, which can ensure these freedoms, are not accessible to all. To ensure easy accessibility, we need public action in these areas if human development has to gather momentum. Together, these facilities comprise a nation's social infrastructure that is as critical as physical infrastructure for a widely shared and inclusive development". These challenges have been integral in the making of the new approach to poverty (see Table 15). A set of new goals has been adopted in the field of education, health, and safety nets. Ensuring 100 per cent literacy in the next five, if not three years; aim for 75 per cent enrolment in higher secondary schools of good quality with encouragement to private sector to provide good schools in every Taluka; raising college enrollment to 20 per cent in the age group 20-24 years; and revitalizing the university system are the major goals in education. Healthcare policy goals include reducing the all-India infant and child mortality rate; expanding health care infrastructure to rural areas; ensuring access to clean drinking water; and encouragement to NGOs and private sector to engage in the health sector. The construction of social safety nets will be based on a) a model employment programme covering the whole country, b) Integrated child development services to reduce child mortality and poverty and c) group-based micro-credit schemes to cover the entire country. Thus, there are new tasks before India, in the context of Global Goals for moving further in the direction of construction of the welfare state after five decades of successful democratization of the political culture and decolonization of national economy.

The social sector expenditures have resulted in the decline of illiteracy from above 80 per cent in 1951 to less than 35 per cent in 2001. The longivity of the people of India has increased from less than 39 years in 1951 to above 65 years in 2001. Even the incidence of poverty has declined from over 50 per cent in 1950s to less than 30 per cent in 2001. But the new challenges are demanding a new interface between the nation-state and the modern world system at the global level and between the state and the market in Indian political economy. So far the shift of paradigm has been carefully utilized by dominant elite caste, the coastal zones of south and west, major industrial groups, and global financial firms. It has promoted consumerism among the middle classes and scams among the elite in power. At the same time a new wave of people's movements by political parties and non-party organizations has been created to demand freedom from illiteracy, hunger, diseases, environmental degradation, and unemployment. The pressure groups for social justice and political empowerment are also becoming increasingly visible and assertive. The Dalit movement, the women's movement, the movement of local people

(tribes) for control over land, forest, and water resources are some examples of it. The movement for Right to Information and pressure for Electoral Reforms are becoming significant as the citizens are getting increasingly anguished about criminalization of politics and increasing marginalisation of common people's concerns. It seems that the need of the hour is to drive India towards a system of participatory democracy through planning for decentralization of power and empowerment of the marginal sections of the masses like women, the Scheduled Castes and the Scheduled Tribes, based upon the twin goals of rapid growth and elimination of poverty for the construction of a just and prosperous social order. It is likely that the heritage of Indian National Movement, the basic values of the Constitution of India (including the Directive Principles) and the continuous widening of the social base of democracy in India in the last five decades may provide the required support in the era of liberalization and global market mediation.

It is important to take note of the roots of sluggishness in poverty reduction in the era of liberalization and address the same. The World Bank approach attempts to argue that there are five interrelated compartments of problems which are contributing to the continuity of poverty:

i) characteristics of agricultural growth in the 1990s,

ii) the slowdown of growth in the poorer states (which are predominantly agricultural),

iii) the problems of infrastructure, social services and poverty programmes (especially in the poorer states),

iv) poor incentive framework, and

v) weakness in governance.

The World Bank analysis has also given content to the eradication of poverty in India in the new century:

a) upliftment of 300 million people concentrated in poorer states,

b) raising literacy rate from 62 per cent (50 per cent for females) by enrolling over 300 million children (mostly poor) who are out of school,

c) addressing the gender based inequalities faced by women in the political, legal and economic systems,

d) reversing the decline in infrastructure spending to meet urban needs and to increase the rate and spread of urbanization.

It is arguing in favour of implementing "second phase of reforms" which involves – i) cuts in explicit and implicit subsidies together with privatization of power, ii) government rolling back from infrastructural activities in favour of private sector, iii) more spending on health and elementary education, iv) improvement in government and governance, v) completion of deregulation of goods and factor markets, and vi) provision of high quality infrastructure services. The critics of liberalization are arguing that liberalization has made the economy systematically "demand constrained". They indicate that the demand constrained nature of the Indian economy is manifested today as the combination of industrial recession and surplus stocks of foodgrains and foreign exchange. They argue that "withdrawal" by the state is the primary reason for the emergence of the demand constraint as it has created deflationary effects which are not offset by private investments. It has contributed negatively to the fields of employment and poverty. First of all employment in the organized sector has been virtually stagnant for some time; of late even rural employment expansion has begun to stagnate. According to the economic survey of 2003, there was a net 3 percent decline in rural employment in the preceding year which was a serious indicator of the crisis of employment. Secondly, the head-count ratio of rural poverty which had declined significantly during the eighties has ceased to decline over the nineties, and might have marginally increased (see Table 17). This perspective points out that it is ironical that the government is claiming the existence of large foreign exchange reserves, massive food grain stocks and markedly low inflation, as achievements, while their simultaneous presence is indicative, on the contrary, of an unprecedented crisis in the Indian economy, a crisis of shrinking demand whose other manifestations are retrenchments, closures, and lay offs in organised sector industrial units, a decimation of textile weavers leading to suicides, growing rural unemployment, and aggravation of rural poverty. The situation is more likely to deteriorate progressively (Patnaik, 2002).

Summing Up

Three conclusions come to the fore: a) there has been a decline in the role of politics in poverty alleviation in last several years, b) there are more conflicts between the poverty affected social groups and others in the rural areas in recent decades, and c) poverty related conflicts have positive and negative potential in the context of political and economic reforms.

It can also be suggested that the challenge of poverty in India has been through five phases since independence. First, there was political mobilization for indirectly bringing the poor into the state's agenda in 1950-1966 period through planning for industrialization of the economy and modernization of agriculture. Then during 1967-1979 there was direct 'focus on the poverty and poor'. It was an era of mobilization of poor and politics against poverty. Removing poverty was the essence of the political discourse in terms of the ideological context. The period 1980-89 was that of by-passing the poor and their problems. It created the context of liberalization and consumerism. 1990-99 was the period of Structural Adjustment Programmes (SAP). It was also a phase of diffused conflicts and mobilization around caste and regional disparities. But now, from 2000 onwards there is rediscovery of poverty and the poor. It is marked by rural disenchantment with globalization and increasing fault lines of poverty and related conflicts in every region of India. It is another matter that the new phase of rediscovery of poverty and poor is also an area of only marginal interest of the political parties and other major political actors (like trade unions, peasant organizations, etc.). Thus it has been a journey from politics of poverty to poverty of politics during the five decades of freedom.

It is also definite that political sociology of poverty will determine the course of liberalization in India. If there is deepening of disparities and destitution then there will be enough reasons for the political actors, particularly the political parties, and the poorer sections of the society to get their act together on the problems of persistence of poverty. It will make class-caste-tribe nexus more relevant for mobilizing the poor. In case there is remarkable decline in the ratio of poor in the second generation reforms as assumed by the protagonists of liberalization then there may be further marginalization of the voice and concerns of the chronic poor in the Indian polity.

13

Evolution of a Sociological Concept

INTRODUCTION

In social sciences it is often difficult to trace the origin of concepts. Concepts, theories and ideas are often products of collective endeavors. It would be extremely difficult to identify who used the term "globalization" for the first time. According to Malcolm Waters (1995) whose book titled *Globalization* is a fine primer, Roland Robertson was one of the early users of the term. More recently, Roland Robertson and Kathleen White edited *Globalization: Critical Concepts* in 6 volumes is a tour de force which present some of the most important essays on this subject. No matter who coined it first, at the dawn of the 21st century globalization as a concept, as a slogan, as a term is used more frequently than any other terms. In Singapore, from the inflow of foreign capital, technology, workers or "foreign talents", music, movies, popular culture, almost everything has resonance with globalization. Globalization is a heroic process, globalization is a sinister process, depending on which side of the debate one stands. Some tend to see globalization as a brakeless train crushing everything in its path, others see benefit in getting on board the train towards economic growth and modernization.

SOCIOLOGY AND GLOBALIZATION

Globalization as a concept in social science has a short history. Even in the revised version of Raymond Williams' *Key Words* (1983) there is no entry on globalization. The Harper Collins *Dictionary of Sociology* (1991) has an entry on "globalization of production" but no entry on globalization as such. The *Oxford Concise Dictionary of Sociology* (1994) has an entry on globalization together with globalization theory. It says, "Globalization theory examines the emergence of a global cultural system. It suggests that global culture is brought about by a variety of social and cultural developments...". The entry refers to the book edited by Martin Albrow and Elizabeth King (1990) *Globalization, Knowledge and Society*. The term globalization was probably first used as a book title in the Albrow and King edited book (1990) which was published drawing on the essays published in various issues of *International Sociology* the journal of International Sociological Association (1986-1990) Some of the journal articles contained globalization as a phrase in the titles in the 1980s and even earlier (see Moore, 1966, Meyer, 1980; Robertson, 1983a, 1983b, 1985). One could even claim that the first social science text that dealt with the subject of globalization was *The Communist Manifesto* (1848). One could even argue that Ibn Khaldun (1332-1406), the author of *Prolegomenon to the Universal History* was the real claimant of the credit. Globalization as a social process is old and has a much longer history. Many writers have traced the early globalizing processes in the dissemination of religion and culture, interactions of people, groups, communities through trade and commerce from the ancient times. Sociology has been traditionally defined as the study of society. And as the boundaries of society have expanded from local community, through states to global society, sociology has become the study of the global society. This is a good illustration of how ideas, knowledge and (social) sciences expand with the changes and expansion of realities.

Sociology, it is often said, deals with the social life. In fact, all social sciences deal with social life or its various aspects. It is difficult to conceptualize *social* as a category. In sociology, there are two meanings of social. Social used in the sense of Wallerstein or for that matter Marx, encompasses technology, economy, politics and culture. Sociology is interested in the understanding of these broad processes, especially at their interrelatedness.

There is, however, a narrow meaning of social, which is often equated with social system, or what some people call societal. Here society is an abstract system of social relations, a web or network of social relations. Following Talcott Parsons, (and before him, Durkheim) some social scientists sought to view sociology as the *scientific* study of society. I put the stress on scientific because one of the goals of science is to define one's field narrowly so that specialized and predictable knowledge can be produced and accumulated. Sociologists with a positivistic bent of mind were quite happy with the narrow definition of sociology, hence the delimited conceptualization of society in the sense of social system. In this formulation, the field of study of economics is economic system; the field of political science is political system and so on. All social sciences could live happily in a world of segregated systems of knowledge! However, a large number of sociologists having dissatisfied with this narrow conceptualization of society, sought to view society and the scope of sociology broadly. They also found the earlier compartmentalization unnecessary, unproductive and overly abstract. All these so-called subsystems interact. Albert Hirschman called for the need of trespassing into each other's domains. The rise of macro-sociology is a clear response to the attempt to overcome a delimited view of sociology. Barrington Moore, Wallerstein, Tilly, Skocpol and others have looked at society in the broadest sense of the term, in that the inspiration came from Marx, Weber and later Braudel and other social historians. Globalization, though it means many things to many people, is one of the master processes of our time. Globalization as a field in sociology is a legatee of the macro-sociological interests and development. Globalization study addresses itself to the connectivity of broad processes of technological, economic, political, cultural interrelationships. Whether one looks at the economic, cultural or media connectivity worldwide, one has to take a much broader understanding of society and social institutions. Sociology focuses its analytical lenses on the flows and processes in society whether at the local, national or global levels. In other words, sociology has a genuine claim over the field of globalization. Some contemporary writers accuse sociology, an archetypical social science, as a prisoner of nationstate.

Anthony Giddens and Immanuel Wallertsien have both lamented that sociology has been the study of modern nation states. The definitions as well as the boundaries of society, which sociology seeks to study, often overlap with those of nation-state. Since the interest taken by sociologists such as Roland Robertson of Pittsburgh and others since the late 1970s, sociology has redefined its scope and field as the social scientific study of the global processes. Ulrich Beck has explicitly called for the development of new concepts to capture the new realities of interconnectedness, plurality, multi-locality and multiplicity. Sociology has established its claim over globalization as a field of study historically. A return to national society centered focus would be a major regressive step towards objectivist, scientistic sociology and a return to what C Wright Mills called "abstracted empiricism". Or worse, sociology might become a residual discipline busy picking up areas left unattended by other social sciences. Sociology is not the only branch of social sciences that has a claim to study society because other branches of social sciences do study aspects of society. For example, institutional economists deal with social structure and cultural values to explain economic processes and market behaviors. Political scientists such as Robert Putnam have done important sociological studies of political processes. Such fields as political sociology illustrate the cross over of political science and sociology all the time. Social sciences are tasked to analyze society in all its various aspects and constellations. The long-standing relationship between sociology and globalization, gives sociology as a discipline a unique position to study all aspects of the field of globalization, a master process in human society. This does not preclude the claims of other disciplines to the subject of globalization and it reminds us the importance of each field's autonomy to venture out and explore using its own traditions and conceptual frames. While globalization as a framework is naturally biased in favor of macro-sociological issues, questions were raised to the viability of using this framework to study social realities on the ground. This led to a rethink of macro-macro relationship. Glocalization as a concept arose to help alleviate the conceptual difficulties of macro-micro relationship. Although it would be difficult to trace the first user of the term "glocalization" in its original Japanese usage, the first time the term was used in English can be attributed to Professor Roland Robertson, a British/American sociologist, who migrated from United Kingdom to the United States where he spent most of his academic career at the University of Pittsburgh, Pennsylvania, USA. Robertson's original interests in sociology were in the areas of sociology of religion, sociological theories and cultural sociology. He also ventured into areas of comparative sociology and modernization studies. His interest and knowledge of Japanese society led him to find out the use of the term "glocalization" in Japan in Japanese language, a term the marketing experts were using by which they meant that products of Japanese origin should be localized – that is, they should be suited to local taste and interests – yet, the products are global in application and reach, hence a new term "glocalization" was coined. Robertson and other sociologists interested in the subject of global processes could not help noticing that many of the social categories and practices assume a local flavor or character despite the fact that these products were invented elsewhere. Dutch sociologist Jan Nederveen Pieterse has for some time used terms such as mélange, hybridity, syncretism to capture similar processes with regard to culture. According to Nederveen Pieterse, (2004) there are three views on the issue of globalization of cultures. The first view is the clash of cultures view expressed in terms of clash of the civilizations by writers like Samuel Huntington. The second notion is best expressed in the phrase of "McDonaldization" of the world (Ritzer, 2000). This view obviously suggests a homogenized world, a world dominated by a single culture that erases differences of local cultures. The third view is that of hybridization or synthesis. Much of human evolution of culture can be seen as exchanges, diffusion, etc. where cross-breeding, borrowing and adjusting to the local needs and so on were very common. I argue below that although glocalization belongs to the same genre or has resonance with those categories there are some important differences as well.

Evolution of the Concept Glocalization

According to the dictionary meaning, the term "glocal" and the process noun "glocalization" are "formed by telescoping global and local to make a blend" (*The Oxford Dictionary of New Words*, 1991:134 quoted in Robertson, 1995:28). The term was modeled on Japanese word *dochakuka,* which originally meant adapting farming technique to one's own local condition. In the business world the idea was adopted to refer to global localization. The word as well as the idea came from Japan (Robertson, 1995:28). According to Wordspy, glocalization means "the creation of products or services intended for the global market, but customized to suit the local cultures." Although the term glocalization has come to frequent use since the late 1980s, there were several related terms that social scientists used and continue to use. One such related word, which has been in use in social sciences and related fields for quite some time is, indigenization. Some social scientists claimed that social sciences such as sociology and political science, even psychology were products of western social experiences therefore when these fields of inquiry were transported and transplanted to non-European or non-western contexts such as Latin America, Asia or Africa there was a need for indigenization of these subjects. The idea of indigenization has created quite a controversy among social scientists because it raises fundamental questions about the applicability of social scientific ideas and concepts. However, indigenization can be seen as similar to localization. In both these concepts, there is an assumption of an original or authentic "locality" or "indigenous system". One of the consequences of globalization is that it opens up doubts about the originality and authenticity of cultures. If one takes a long-term view of globalization, "locality" or "local" itself is a consequence of globalization. There are hardly any sites or cultures that can be seen as isolated or unconnected from the global processes.

Robertson, one of the pioneers in the study of globalization, did not view globalization as a recent phenomenon nor did he see it as a consequence of modernization. The theories of modernization came under serious attack in sociology because of such assumptions as unilinearity and convergence. As our knowledge of the world increased, many writers pointed out that the cultural differences are not all that superficial and nonlinearity and mutilinieartity are better descriptions of global modernity.

Besides divergence rather than convergence seems to have been the consequence of modernization. Yet the divergent cultures and societies can be studied with the help of a globalized social science and there was no need for diverse, indigenized social sciences. Social sciences to claim scientific status could not afford to forfeit its claim to universality and universal knowledge. Social sciences must be context sensitive but not context dependent. It is in this context that Robertson conceptualized globalization in the twentieth century as "*the interpenetration of the universalization of particularization and the particularization of universalism*" (Robertson, 1992:100 emphasis in the original). Khondker (1994) building on Robertson's framework argued that globalization or glocalization should be seen as an interdependent process.

"The problem of simultaneous globalization of the local and the localization of globality can be expressed as the twin processes of *macro-localization* and *micro-globalization*. Macro-localization involves expanding the boundaries locality as well as making some local ideas, practices, institutions global. The rise of world wide religious or ethnic revivalist movements can be seen as examples of macro-localization. Microglobalization involves incorporating certain global processes into the local setting. Consider social movements such as the feminist movements or ecological movements or consider new production techniques or marketing strategies which emerge in a certain local context and over a period these practices spread far beyond that locality into a larger spatial and historical arena. Consider print industry or computer industry with a specific location of its emergence has now become a global phenomena.

Overcoming space is globalization. In this view of globalization, globalization is glocalization. This view is somewhat different from the way Giddens conceptualizes the relationship between the global and the local. Globalization, for Giddens, "is the reason for the revival of local cultural identities in different parts of the world" (Giddens, 2000:31). While in this view local is the provider of the response to the forces that are global, we argue that local itself is constituted globally. Ritzer in discussing glocalization has added another – should I say, redundant – convoluted term "grobalization" to refer to what he calls "growth imperatives [pushing] organizations and nations to expand globally and to impose themselves on the local" (2004:xiii). For Ritzer, globalization is the sum total of glocalization and "grobalization". Wong argues, following Wind (1998), that a global company does not mean that it has gone global all the way. There are companies that are part global, part regional or part local involving different domains such as portfolio, supply chain, research and development and business processes. In terms of mode of business practices, there could be independent operations, joint venture or alliances (Wong, 1998:156).

Key Propositions The main propositions of gloclaization are not too different from the main arguments of a sophisticated version of globalization. 1. Diversity is the essence of social life; 2. Globalization does not erase *all* differences; 3. Autonomy of history and culture give a sense of uniqueness to the experiences of groups of people whether we define them as cultures, societies or nations; 4. Glocalization is the notion that removes the fear from many that globalization is like a tidal wave erasing all the differences. A number of books and articles on the subject of globalization give the impression that it is a force that creates a uniform world, a world where barriers disappear and cultures become amalgamated into a global whole. The tensions and conflicts between cultures are nothing but the problems of a transitory phase. Ironically, the phase of transition has been around for a long period of time. And as we have entered the third millennia many of the age-old problems of differences of cultures and religion remain. 5. Glocalizaton does not promise a world free from conflicts and tensions but a more historically grounded understanding of the complicated – yet, pragmatic view of the world.

Globalization is not Westernization Some writers view globalization as the worldwide spread of "westernization". This view is either erroneous or contains only partial truth. From a superficial point of view, various processes outwardly seem that the world is, indeed, becoming westernized. One could see the popularity of the western music, movies, and "McDonalds" as examples of westernization. More and more countries are seeing the opening of McDonalds. More and more countries playing the top chart of the pop list of USA and Hollywood movies and US-made television serials (such as, *Friends* and *The Simpsons* are becoming ubiquitous to the extent that some writers even use the term "Americanization" to describe these processes of cultural transmission. However, a closer look will reveal that these cultural goods have different meanings in different societal and cultural contexts with uneven impact on classes and agegroups. Some of the products are consumed without any modification, others are modified and indigenized to suit the local contexts and there are exceptional situations where the intentions are completely inverted. In the past, many writers found it necessary to distinguish modernization from westernization. Modernization was believed to be a set of cultural practices and social institutional features that historically evolved in Europe and North America, commonly referred to as the West. The need to separate westernization from modernization (in the past) was motivated more by nationalism than pure intellectual reasons, because historically speaking, most of the modern cultural traits began in the West, a historical fact which was difficult to accommodate in a nationalistic political culture. The Western scholars in the nineteenth century were also guilty of making exaggerated claims of western superiority. Max Weber, a German sociologist was correct to claim that the western rationality and science had become universal but his denigration of non-western cultures did not sit well among the larger intellectual community. Many Indian sociologists took pains to delineate the differences between modernization and westernization. Similar discussions exist with regard to so-called westernization of the Ottoman Empire, modernization of Japan since the Meiji restoration of 1868 or modernization of China in the early part of the 20th century such as the May 4th Movement of 1919. In the modernization process, many of the late modernizing societies were borrowing ideas and knowledge and technology most of which were generated in the early modernized societies in Europe. The geography of the West kept shifting.

In the nineteenth century, when Germany was modernizing, the idea of the West was limited to Western Europe only (mainly Britain and France). In some post-colonial situations the demarcation was based more on political expedience than logical or intellectual merits. Good westernization came to be regarded as modernization and bad modernization was designated as westernization. The distancing from westernization can also be understood as a reaction to centuries of domination and exploitation of the colonies by the western (mainly European) powers.

However, over time a more objective consideration of history indicate that many of the traits that spread worldwide originated in certain geographical regions yet as these traits were transplanted elsewhere, they became mutated and assumed different forms in different contexts. For example, parliamentary democracy evolved in England, with roots that go back to *Magna Carta* of 1215. However, as Westminster-style parliamentary democracy was institutionalized in India, Malaysia, and other former British colonies, they mutated in light of the local milieu. Westernization as a term is not equivalent to globalization. Nevertheless, westernization can be seen as an aspect of globalization. Certain institutional features and cultural traits that originated in the west were put in place in many other geographical regions lock stock and barrel under the framework of global interconnections and diffusion or forced implantation under colonial age. Yet, over time these institutions and practices mutated and assumed new meanings.

Therefore, westernization can be seen as the beginning of the process. The cultural features borrowed or imitated themselves mutate in the source countries. Thus, westernization as a category has limited conceptual value. One can associate certain literary forms, genres, and traits as part of the cultural zone we vaguely call "the west", yet these are mere influences as one can see in artistic, literary, architectural styles.

For example, the great Indian film maker late Satyajit Ray was influenced by Hollywood films and the art of film making, but he did not want to replicate Hollywood movies in Calcutta. His movies were modern capturing local themes which he projected with a modern art form and technology. Hence it was truly global, or more appropriately, glocal. Presently, Singapore is establishing linkages with both Bollywood and Indian film industries as well seeking to play the role of an outsourced location for hi-tech Hollywood productions. Globalization, like modernization, is often a fusion. Westernization as a concept has some value if used only as a descriptive rather than analytic category. As an analytic category it is rather limited. Writers such as John Meyer have used the idea of isomorphism (a term borrowed from science, botany, in particular) which means replication of the same form yet separated from the main source. His research has shown that modern education – not western education though it was perhaps modified and institutionalized in the west – has spread worldwide and a similar set of values and practices have emerged in diverse settings. For example, college graduates command more social prestige and respect almost regardless of cultural contexts. Some cultures can give more rewards than others. Globalization shows tendencies towards isomorphism, yet some people may continue to mistake this process for westernization. In the context of Singapore, the first generation leaders always emphasized the fact that although Singapore's economic development was dependent on western technology and capital, and it was reliant on multinational corporations to foster economic growth, the state maintained a certain degree of autonomy and formulated broad social development strategy.

Glocalization and hybridization In the discussion of glocalization some writers tend to conflate it with hybridization. This may be somewhat misleading. Glocalization involves blending, mixing adapting of two or more processes one of which must be local. But one can accept a hybrid version that does not involve local. In the context of higher education in Singapore a hybridized version comprising the original British model and the US model was accepted. One could find many such examples in matters of technology and business practices where two different systems or modes are combined for better results. Glocalization to be meaningful must include at least one component that addresses the local culture, system of values and practices and so on. One of the areas in Singapore where the evidence of glocalization is quite visible is the area of mass communication and especially in the area of television programming. From televised drama, sitcoms, and even "reality shows" one finds attempts of glocalization. Although some attempts are not always successful and there are instances when one can see unabashed imitation, by and large the idea of glocalization and fusion remain appealing to many Singaporeans.

Technology and glocalization Singapore, located in Southeast Asia, has attained the developed country status or High Income Economy according to the World Bank classification. Having experienced rapid state-led economic development under a favorable global economic climate, Singapore has been pursuing the goal of creating a knowledge-based economy since 1990s. Singapore's economic growth since her emergence in 1965 as an independent state entailed heavy investment in education and development of human resource in science and technology. Singapore's advancement in areas of knowledge and high technology is dependent to a large extent on international collaboration. Two aspects of Singapore's growth are striking: linkage with global market and a highly rational approach to governance, which is often evidenced by a near-absence of corruption. These two aspects have direct bearing on the issues of technological developments in Singapore. An additional factor that one has to take into account is the cultural diversity of Singapore's population. Singapore is both a multiethnic and multi-religious society, which provides an added dimension to the context of formulation of ethical standards. Its 4 million people (in 2004) comprise 76% Chinese, 14% Malay, 7% Indian, and 3% others. As many as one quarter of Singapore's population is non-citizens which indicate Singapore's reliance on foreign human resources both at working class jobs as well as high end knowledge workers. Multicultural population-base and the varying sensitivity of various groups have influenced policies concerning biotechnology.

According to Stephen Haggard, "Singapore had already broken away from the typical policy pattern of a developing country as early as 1970. By the 1980s Singaporean policymakers were identifying the country with small European economies such as Switzerland" (Haggard, 1999:355). It has been noted by a number of writers (Rodan, 1989; Wade, 1990 and Haggard, 1999) that Singapore's economic development and social modernization did not take place following a pure free market model. Singapore state was very much involved in guiding the market forces. On the one hand Singapore has relied heavily for multinational corporations to launch economic growth but it also built a high rate of savings through central Provident Fund. Singapore's development model showed certain mixed or hybrid quality.

Soon after Singapore's independence, policymakers began to focus attention on development in sciences and technology. The strive for such development was aided in the process by close relationship with the Multinational Corporations who brought investments and employed technically qualified Singaporeans. Right from the early days of national development, Singapore was well integrated with not only the international economic system bit also with global knowledge systems. Singapore's exportoriented economic development in the 1980s was dominated by IT and computer peripherals. In the 1990s emphasis on biotechnology followed an earlier emphasis on IT. Singapore's development since her independence in 1965 can be described as a transformation from a Third World society to a First World economy. Much of that development can be attributed to Singapore's adoption of modern technology. Choices of technology were not always preceded by controversies and debates.

Both the government and the general public showed a great deal of pragmatism in the choice of technology. Although in most instances, technology was adopted without much modification, the mode of use, and so on there were imprints of adaptation and glocalization. One such area is in the area of electronic road pricing system. The technology of monitoring cars from a scanner fitted in a gantry was not a Singaporean invention, but they way that technology was used was very Singaporean. Because of the drive to catch up, Singapore has always been ahead in adopting new technology. It is in recent years having achieved the developed status; some Singaporeans are showing concern with issues of privacy and so on because some of the new technology is intrusive. Singapore's love affairs with technology is evident in the fact that Singapore ranks among the top three countries in the world in terms usage of personal computers as well as hand phones. The only country ahead of Singapore in the number of Short Messaging Service (SMS) is Hong

Kong. Whenever a new technology is invented, Singapore would be one of the first places where that technology would show up. Singaporeans have a favorable attitude towards technology. Singapore International Airlines as well as Port Authority of Singapore (PSA) remain equipped with the state of the art technology. ATM machines in Singapore were introduced in the early 1980s. Singapore's public transport system is another place where one would find a great many applications of new technology. However, all cases of adaptation technology may not be seen as examples of glocalization. In many instances, for example, computer technology in Singapore was implemented without any modifications. However as Singapore entered a new phase of research in the 1990s, namely in the area of biotechnology we fins evidence of glocalization. Biotechnological research calls for a careful consideration of and orientation towards local cultural and ethical contexts. A good deal of attention has been given to these areas in Singapore. Another area where examples of glocalization can be found in both Malaysia and Singapore is the area of architectural designs. In the post-socialist world, Singapore remains a unique society where 90% of the population lives in the houses built and then sold to the citizens. When Singapore was embarked on massive public housing program, it borrowed the so-called international style of very basic and practical designs, yet a new concept of public space – though limited to the residents of the housing blocs – evolved. These spaces known as void-decks were places for wedding, funeral or any such communal gatherings. New designs blending the western and local motifs emerged in Singapore. Although the initial architectural thrust of Singapore can be viewed as "brutalism" driven by a sheer pragmatic consideration, over the years more attention has been given to the notions of fusion and hybridity, or in other words glocalization.

Conclusions Singapore's development experience, which was underpinned by appropriate science and technology policies, provides a convincing example of the effectiveness of glocalization as a conscious development strategy. Although the strategy was not always perfect and there were lapses from time to time but on the whole Singapore has shown that cultural fusion can be an asset if properly harnessed for the objective of attaining socioeconomic growth without creating gross inequality and social dislocation. The sociological concepts of globalization in general and glocalization in particular can be of great value in understanding the dynamic social transformation in Southeast Asia, especially in Singapore and Malaysia. It is always possible to be carried away with "methodological nationalism", a position that says each country or society should be examined in light of its own context through the devices of its own homegrown methodology. Such a position would lead to intellectual closure foreclosing dialogue and understanding between societies. In the globalized world such discourses have limited value. Yet, it is important to take the local context and variables and not to fall into the trap of blind imitation or aping of western ideas and concepts. However, in the end what is needed is a set of globally valid concepts that will help us examine processes of social transformation that is inextricably connected with global transformation.

14

Theoretical Models in Political Sociology

SOCIAL CLASS THEORY

Social class analysis was the first major attempt to explain political life in terms of sociological variables, so it is reasonable to consider the class model first. This is especially true because the other two models to be considered in this chapter were developed partly as counters to the social class model. Karl Marx was the first major social theorist to base his work primarily on a class model, although many of his ideas can be traced back to one or another of the earlier writers. It is the Marxian formulation of class analysis which has had the greatest influence on political sociology and which will be dealt with here. Marx's work was not limited to political sociology; indeed, much of the genius of his work lay in his attempt to comprehend the entire course of human history. Since he concluded that the basic dynamic of history could be found in economic life, his most detailed work was in economics. But his ultimate goal was to develop a theory of social change, and his model of social change was the basis of all his work. We will begin by summarizing that theory, following closely a well-known summary that Marx himself made in the introduction to one of his works.

Marx argued that men enter into social relationships independently of their wills and that their beliefs and behaviors are largely determined by the social conditions in which they find themselves. The most important of these conditions are those which are directly related to economic production, and these relationships tend to determine other aspects of social behavior and beliefs. Only in a highly affluent, technologically advanced society could men and women choose to be free. The economic conditions which determine people's social relationships vary from epoch to epoch, as economic conditions change. However, in all previous history (excepting prehistoric tribes) there has been a polarization between oppressor and oppressed. As the oppressors become better organized and more efficient, they change the economic system to make it even more exploitative. They must do this, otherwise they themselves would be destroyed by others who would. This increase in the efficiency of exploitation is the source of progress. It brings about increases in wealth and economic productivity, as well as financing advances in science and culture. However, there is a negative side as well. Social tensions increase because the noneconomic organization of society fails to change rapidly enough to fit the new economic conditions. Classes which are no longer economically useful, such as feudal lords or small businessmen or craftsmen, fight against progress in order to defend their privileged position. When these social tensions become sufficiently acute, an era of social revolution ensues and the society is changed to a more modern form. In this way the transition was made from a feudal to a capitalist society in France with the revolution of 1789. Marx expected that when economic conditions advanced fully enough there would be a similar revolutionary period and capitalist societies would be transformed into socialist societies.

Marxist theory differs on a very basic level from sociological theories-such as functionalism-which consider social order to be self-sustaining and disorder to be unusual and undesirable. Marxist theory expects tension, conflict, and change as necessary for human progress. Conflict between social classes, in particular, is viewed by the Marxist as the basic source of social evolution. Marx viewed political life as a reflection of the class struggle. When he analyzed political struggles, he viewed each of the participating parties and leaders as representatives of social classes, and he explained their behavior as resulting from their class interests. In its basic form Marxist theory has an elegant simplicity and grandeur, similar to many religious doctrines. It can be readily understood by people who are not professional social scientists. Indeed, Marx and his comrade Friedrich Engels wrote The Communist Manifesto precisely to communicate their theory to factory workers. This simplicity is often criticized by academics who are preoccupied with the subtleties and complexities of the world and mistrust any theory which seems to be guilty of "oversimplification." Marx was not concerned with the objections of these academicians, indeed he felt that their devotion to pedantic details often served to obscure basic truths about society. While the simplicity of popular versions of Marxism may have made it appeal to some people who were seeking simple answers to complex problems, Marx himself was quite capable of doing highly insightful analyses of the details of complex situations when he felt that these were called for. Indeed, many of the points which later political critics have made, in refuting a simplistic version of "vulgar Marxism," were actually anticipated by Marx in some of his own work:

On a general level, Marxism is often criticized for placing too much emphasis on economic factors and not recognizing the complex interconnectedness of the world. This, however, does not recognize the sophistication which Marx brought to his analyses of specific historical events. Any theory draws generalizations about reality and in doing so reality must be "simplified."

More meaningful criticism goes beyond simply citing the complexity of the universe and specifies ways in which the generalizations drawn by the class theorists are inadequate. Much of this more serious criticism has been made by authors who are sympathetic with the Marxist approach. Marxist theory was developed in the nineteenth century and dealt with the social situation at that time. Marx tried to avoid making explicit predictions about the future, since he felt that our understanding of future conditions would come only after we had experienced those conditions (this is a consequence of his assumption that material conditions determine ideas). Social change has proceeded rapidly since Marx's time, however, and many of the problems with social class analysis today come from resistance on the part of some of its political supporters to modifying the model in keeping with recent changes. Perhaps the most marked change since Marx's time is the tremendous growth in the economic productivity of the developed capitalist countries. Marx anticipated this increase in productivity, but underestimated the ability of capitalists to use this wealth to buy off the working classes by giving them higher and higher wages. Marx, along with other economists of his time, based his theories on a competitive model of capitalism, and did not fully anticipate the role of monopolistic corporations. He expected that capitalists would be forced to compete with each other, and consequently to maintain their workers at a minimal level of pay. He did not anticipate the development of Keynesian economics and of effective government policies aimed at regulating the economy and avoiding crises. It is not hard to understand why Marx failed to anticipate these things. He wrote at a time, for example, when there were maximum wage laws, not minimum wage laws as there are today. The growth of the new middle class is another phenomenon which cannot be readily dealt with in classic Marxist theory.

Marxist theory is generally weak in dealing with intermediate classes or strata. Marx noted the economic decline of the craftsmen and small businessmen who made up the middle class in the early days of capitalism, and he predicted that as these groups diminished as an economic force their political role would also decline. He felt that the technological advances made under capitalism would lead to an increased polarization between a relatively unskilled factory labor force and a class of wealthy capitalists. Only in scattered references in his later work did he begin to note a new development-the growth of the new middle class. Members of this class are still part of the working class in the strict economic sense since they earn their living by selling their labor power, but their level of education permits them to earn higher wages and maintain a style of life intermediate between that of the manual working class and that of the upper class. The role of intermediate classes or strata in political life is not easily explained by economic factors. While it has often been assumed that these classes will play a moderating role, seeking compromise between the upper class and the proletariat, this is not necessarily so. Further social changes may weaken the position of the middle class making their position more equivalent to that of manual workers. The recent surplus of college-educated workers in the United States has stimulated a growth of unionism among white-collar employees in many fields. Many white-collar employees are finding that despite their professional training they are working for large, impersonal bureaucracies where their economic position can be improved only through united action. The working-class pattern that these white-collar workers are assuming, however, is not the revolutionary one that

Marx hoped for, and predicted, but a class conflict which has been legalized, regulated, and made a part of the existing social system.

Rather than being resolved through major confrontations, conflicts are regularized and accepted as part of the normal course of events. Means of dealing with them are developed which contribute to a more stable social order than one in which the dominant group simply imposes its will on the weaker. Conflicts are never ultimately re-solved in this way, but neither do they lead to revolutionary upheavals. Marx, of course, was aware of the possibilities of conflicts being handled in this way, but he felt that such solutions could only be temporary. Today, theorists in the Marxist tradition such as Marcuse are grappling with the possibility that advanced industrial societies will be able to contain indefinitely the conflicts which Marx thought would lead to revolutionary change. The great increase in international inequality is another historical change which requires modifications in classical Marxist theory. In today's world inequality is often more pronounced between countries than it is between social strata in the same country. While Marx did not deal extensively with this topic, it has been thoroughly studied by liberal writers such as Hobson, and their findings have been incorporated into Marxist theory by Lenin and others.

ELITES AND MASSES

Elite theory in political sociology was advanced in direct response to Marxism. The early elite theorists were conservatives who were opposed not only to socialism, but also to liberal democracy as expressed by any movement which attempted to give the masses of the population a greater influence on political affairs.", They argued that elites were necessary and inevitable and that any revolution which pretended to abolish elites would end up by simply replacing one elite with another. Elite theorists use two basic lines of argument. First, they argue that certain aspects of human nature make elites inevitable. Second, they argue that elites are necessary for any social organization to function effectively.

Human Nature and Elites

Elite theorists often emphasize differences in inherent abilities as a source of elites. All people are not created equal: some are stronger, more intelligent, more artistic, etc. Those who have the most of a certain kind of ability constitute a sort of elite such as the elite of chess grand masters or of concert pianists. Of course, not all abilities lead to economic wealth or political power. However, those people who have the most of the particular abilities which a society rewards become the political elite. In some societies, a talent for corruption may be a prerequisite for entering the elite. Abilities are distributed continuously; that is, there is no sharp division between the people who are at the top with respect to a given ability and those who are on the bottom. Vilfredo Pareto, who was an econometrician as well as an elite theorist, assumed that abilities were distributed on a smooth curve similar to the distribution of income. In his work on elites, however, he divided societies into two discrete groups: the elite and the mass. This cannot be explained by his analysis of abilities. There are other problems with an analysis based on differences in abilities. It is difficult to measure abilities, and even when there is some measure, it is difficult to show that those with the most ability are to be found at the top. Frequently, entire ethnic, racial, or sexual groups are absent from elite positions. If one assumes that membership in the elite is determined by ability, then one can only explain this by arguing that the excluded groups are inherently inferior. Even if there are no groups which are excluded or under-represented, it is too easy for critics of elites to point to cases where highly qualified persons are excluded from elite status, while less competent individuals with the right social background and connections maintain their status.

Elite theorists have, therefore, turned to other factors than abilities to explain the persistence and necessity of elites. Personality differences can be used as an explanation of why some people are in the elite and others are not. Conservative theorists generally assume, explicitly or implicitly, that human nature is fixed and unchanging. This assumption enables them to argue that existing social institutions, which they wish to protect, cannot be improved upon because they reflect innate human behavior. This argument often goes along with an emphasis on the irrational bases of human behavior. Of course, radical thinkers such as Marx also recognized the irrational components in the behavior of many people who supported political leaders and policies which were not in their interest. But Marx thought that irrationally would eventually be overcome and that people would learn to behave rationally.

Pareto developed an elaborate theory of social behavior based on the assumption that most behavior is determined by irrational "residues" deep within the human psyche. These residues are basic principles which underlie nonlogical thought and action. Pareto did not attempt to explain how the residues came about because he believed that they corresponded to changeless human instincts; he did, however, use his theory of residues to explain persistent common elements in nonlogical beliefs (the "derivations"). The two residues which are central to Pareto's theory of elites are the "instinct for combinations" and the "persistence of aggregates." These two residues are opposites. The first refers to the tendency to discover or establish relationships between things and ideas. This includes relationships of similarity or difference, cause and effect, magical relationships, logical relationships, analogies, and all other intellectual models of relationships. The persistence of aggregates is the tendency to resist changes in these combinations. This includes stable, traditional beliefs which are the irrational bases of social order. Change and stability depend on the relative influence of these two classes of residues. Individuals who are influenced by the instinct for combinations can be characterized as speculative, intelligent, shrewd, or resourceful (foxes in Machiavelli's analogy). Those who display the persistence of aggregates are stolid, forceful, conservative, moralistic, or traditionalistic (lions).

Usually, the governing elite is dominated by the instinct for combinations, while the masses are dominated by the persistence of aggregates. This is a stable situation, since the masses are not likely to have enough initiative to challenge the rule of the elites. If both the elite and the masses are dominated by the residue of persistence of aggregates, the society will be stagnant; the elite will probably rule through force since it will lack the cleverness necessary to rule through more subtle means. Too much instinct for combinations among the masses on the other hand leads to instability, especially if the elite has "degenerated" into humanitarianism and fails to use force to maintain order. It is important for elites to be open to a certain amount of upward mobility from the masses so that those among the masses who are born with a high degree of instinct for combinations will be able to rise to the top. Today, this process is called "co-optation." If this "circulation of elites," with a certain number of the least effective elite members moving down as well, fails to take place, there may be a revolution as the elite loses its vitality and gets replaced by a group of those who had been kept out.

Social Organization and Elites

There is also a sociological argument that elites are necessary for a large social organization to function. To a degree this has even been accepted by Marxists. Marx accepted the necessity of a "dictatorship of the proletariat" after the Communists had taken power in order to suppress those who would attempt to restore their privileged position in the old society. V. I. Lenin, who led the first communist movement to actually win state power, did so on the basis of his theory that only an elitist party of professional revolutionaries, with strict discipline and control by a small central committee, could be efficient enough to win power from the capitalists. Marx, however, argued that once socialism had been established in conditions of affluence, coercion would no longer be necessary and everyone could share in the administration of common affairs. Exactly how this would be done was never specified, however, and the history of the Soviet Union after the Communist Party took power certainly provided ammunition for the argument that a revolution which intended to abolish elites would simply replace one elite with another. This might be explained as resulting from the avowedly elitist organizational structure which the party needed in order to take power. Elitist tendencies can also be found, however, even in political parties which are deeply committed to democratic ideals and which operate in a society that allows opposition political parties to function freely. Robert Michels made an extensive study of oligarchical tendencies in political parties, basing most of his analysis on the history of the German Social Democratic party, a working class party strongly committed to democratic ideas. He felt that by showing the prevalence of oligarchical rule in an avowedly democratic organization he was making a critical test of elitist theory. Michels thought that there were three basic causes of oligarchical tendencies—organizational necessities, characteristics of the leaders, and characteristics of the masses.

A complex organization requires highly trained and experienced leaders. An organization engaged in conflict with other groups needs to be able to make quick decisions and to command the organization's resources in carrying out those decisions. These organizational demands encourage the development of a professionalized, stable leadership group. These leaders find their job situation quite rewarding, both in salary and in working conditions. This is especially true in labor organizations since the gap in living standards, working conditions, and prestige is great between the leaders and the rank and file. Leaders are likely to perceive an improvement in their own living condition as representative of a general improvement in society, and consequently to become more conservative. In the German socialist party prominent leaders were usually elected members of parliament, where they relied on the support of many voters who were not party members. This enabled them to be relatively independent of the party organization and members; they had more to offer the party than the party had to offer them. The masses tend to be relatively apathetic as long as the organization is producing reasonable benefits for them. Often, they have deferential attitudes toward the leadership; but even if they were unhappy with their leaders, it would be too much trouble to do anything about it. These processes create what Michels called the "iron law of oligarchy," a tendency for small ruling elites to emerge and persist in complex organizations.

This same point was made by Max Weber in his highly influential theory of bureaucratization. Weber felt that bureaucratic administrations could not be abolished by any kind of socialist or anarchist revolution since if they did so the society would cease to operate. He did see possibilities for change, however, largely through the mechanism of a charismatic leader. A charismatic leader emerges during periods of crisis or social breakdown when things aren't working right and people look for a solution which is outside the normal routine of social life. They seek a leader with outstanding personal qualities in whom they can place their trust. While Weber was an intense German nationalist during World War I, he was also a liberal and did not live long enough to see Adolph Hitler become the terrible incarnation of his concept of the charismatic leader. Robert Michels did live long enough to leave the socialist movement and seek salvation from Benito Mussolini. Pareto, also, was sympathetic to the fascist movement, and his works were used as part of the theoretical underpinnings of fascism. Elite theory, with its emphasis on strength and leadership, has a natural affinity with fascism just as social class theory has an affinity with socialism and pluralist theory with liberal democracy.

Not all elite theorists, however, moved into totalitarianism; one of the most prominent, Gaetano Mosca, was able to reconcile his theory of elites with a belief in a limited form of liberal democracy. The critical differences between political systems, in Mosca's view, depend largely on the organization of two strata within the elite-those at the very top and a larger group of people who are not part of the ruling clique at the moment but nevertheless have considerable power and resources. Less capable families drop out of the top group, and more capable members of the second group rise to the top. This sort of mobility, which Pareto called the "circulation of the elites" is healthy up to a point. If all could compete equally for the position at the top, however, the struggle for power would use too much social energy for too little social benefit. Indeed, it may be necessary for families to be in an elite position for several generations for them to develop the virtues needed for leadership in their children. This line of argument has been applied to more modern events by Karl Mannheim. Mannheim argued that one of the reasons for the growth of fascism in Europe was the weakness of the elites. There was an increase in the number of elite groups due to the increasing complexity of society. This means that the elites became less exclusive and no one was really able to influence events in the societies. The elites were not sufficiently insulated from the masses and were not able to cultivate cultural and intellectual differences. The anti-intellectualism of the masses became popular in elite circles, the quality of intellectual and artistic work declined, while intellectuals became so numerous that their social prestige declined. After fleeing Germany,

Mannheim was impressed by the British social system which maintained a stable elite through its aristocratic traditions, while still recruiting an adequate amount of fresh blood. Too much democracy could lead to dictatorship, and a dictatorship which rules over a relatively literate and sophisticated population must be an authoritarian one since it cannot rely on the passivity and ignorance of the large majority of the population. England was Mosca's ideal also, and it is easy to see how someone who feared the success of a totalitarian movement based on support from frustrated, uneducated masses might feel that a stable, aristocratic elite on the English model could best provide some stability to society.

PRESSURE GROUPS AND POLITICS

Just as social class theory is congruent with socialism and elite theory with fascism, pluralism is the theory of modern liberal democracy. Pluralists are generally pleased with contemporary American political institutions and feel that America can serve as an example of the good society. While pluralism lacks much of the intellectual force of Marxism or of the classical elite theories, it is of great importance because of its dominant position in American political science and especially in mass education. Pluralism is what is taught to most American school children about the political system. The pluralist model of politics was developed largely by political scientists, although it is essentially based on certain sociological principles. More recently, it has been defended by some prominent sociologists as well. Pluralist theory does not make use of the whole range of sociological thinking; it passes over theories of social class or of bureaucratization and turns instead to the sociology of small groups. What the pluralists have done is to take basic ideas from the study of small person-to-person groups and attempt to generalize them to the societal level. This is, on the face of it, a surprising idea and one which few sociologists of small groups would attempt.

The most comprehensive modern statement of pluralist theory is The Governmental Process by David Truman. Truman's book is largely based on, and mimics the title of, Arthur Bentley's The Process of Government. Bentley and Truman start with the assumption that the group is the basic unit of political life. This means that politics cannot be explained by reference to feelings, attitudes, or ideas since these result from group life. Nor can politics be explained by the study of leaders, since these leaders reflect group interests and their behavior cannot be understood except from the perspective of group analysis. Since groups are so basic, Truman begins with a review of basic principles of group life taken largely from introductory sociology and social psychology texts. Groups are the basic unit of social analysis because of the uniformities of behavior which characterize group members. These uniformities result from the relationships, or interactions, between members of the group.

All of this is elementary social psychology; the distinctiveness of the pressure-groups approach lies in its attempt to generalize from a sociological theory of small groups to a theory of politics on a societal level. Truman does this by referring to "institutionalized groups," which are stable and maintain themselves in relative equilibrium for long periods of time. These groups cannot always maintain themselves in equilibrium without making claims on other groups. When they make these claims, they are defined as "interest groups." The interests which these groups defend are shared attitudes, and forms of behavior which are implied by the attitudes. Thus, it is possible to identify potential interest groups, where large numbers of people share common attitudes even though they are not organized into an interest group. They may become organized if their interests are threatened.

One of the most important types of interest groups is the "association," which is defined in an unusual way. The association is a group which results from "tangent relations," or from the fact that individuals can be members of more than one group. Associations are formed when a "considerable number" of people have similar tangent relations. The purpose of the association is to regulate the relationships of tangent groups. Examples of associations include the Parent-Teachers Associations, where the school and the family groups are tangentially related through the child. Also included would be executives of two automobile companies who are tangentially related through their employees who belong to the same union. They both interact with the same labor leaders. It would be hard to argue, however, that there would be no association of automobile manufacturers if their employees were not unionized or belonged to different unions. It could be argued, of course, that automobile executives are tangentially related in other ways, since tangency is defined very loosely, "... tangency between groups may exist not only through an individual, but through a third group by which the tangent groups are similarly affected or through a common technique." Given this broad definition, it would be difficult to cite two groups which do not have "tangent relations." The vagueness of this key concept results from the difficulty, never adequately resolved, of bridging the gap between small groups and societal structures.

When Truman begins discussing actual interest groups and associations in American politics, he is forced to put them into categories. This is difficult for him to justify on a theoretical basis since to use a category such as "business groups" presumes a community of interest which may not exist. Business groups may spend as much time fighting each other as they do dealing with other groups. And, of course, individuals may belong to diverse groups with conflicting aims. However, when all the dangers of classification have been pointed out, it is still necessary to talk in terms of types of interest groups if one is to say anything intelligible about American political life, and Truman ends up with essentially economic categories. Most of his discussion centers on labor organizations, trade associations, and agricultural groups. The others are lumped together as "other organizational beginnings," including professional' associations, "cause" organizations, veterans' and women's groups. Thus, when Truman expands the group perspective to the national scene, he is forced to fall back on categories which are closer to Marxism than to social psychology.

Pluralist theory does not place much emphasis on the nature of the government itself or of the men, and occasionally women, who control it. The theory asserts that government is a differentiated, representative group which performs governing functions for the rest of society. Thus, the government has relatively little freedom of action; it is more often in a position of reacting to initiatives and pressures from other groups. Truman has a chapter on "The Ordeal of the Executive," and places emphasis on the President's role in "... effecting a continuous adjustment of the diverse interests within the nation....". The constitutional powers of the President are limited, and he cannot be effective unless he has the support of Congress and of department heads. He wins this loyalty by catering to the group interest and affiliations of these leaders. Truman cites many incidents to show the limits of the President's control even over agencies and departments over which he has formal control. The chief source of limitations on his power in the examples cited is the Congress, which controls these agencies both through statute and through appropriations. Congress, of course, acts under the influence of groups. Pluralist theorists do not directly deny the elitist argument a relatively small group of people at the center actually carry out day-to-day processes of governing in a society or within a smaller group.

Some pluralists prefer to avoid the term "elite" and refer to the "active minority" (Truman) or "homo politicos" (Dahl). But they do recognize the importance of leadership groups, especially within pressure groups. Arnold Rose, the leading defender of pluralism within sociology, recognized the necessity of using terms like "elite" and "leaders" and admitted that there is a small active core in any group. However, pluralists do not accept the strict dichotomy between "elite" and "mass"; instead they argue that there is a gradation from highly active to relatively inactive members in any group. And again, they emphasize limitations placed on the elite's freedom of action. Interest-group leaders must satisfy their constituents that they are doing a reasonable job, and they must conform to limitations on what they can do. They may resort to internal propaganda in attempts to influence their members, but the effectiveness of this is limited unless they "deliver the goods" to their supporters. If the membership becomes incensed because of some change in government policy, or because of a change in social conditions, they may compel the leaders to take militant action.

Rose claimed that power could not be readily transferred from one area of society to another: political power is distinct from economic power, power over school systems is not power over foreign policy. In opposition to this, elite and social-class analysts emphasize the extent to which the same people exercise power in all sectors of society: the same men sit on corporate boards of directors, boards of trustees of universities, and on key councils which advise the President on foreign affairs. The extent to which power is unified in the persons of powerful individuals is a key question of fact which is argued by exponents of the opposing theoretical models. However, the lack of comparative benchmarks lends an air of unreality to much of the debate. For there is clearly some pluralism and some concentration of power in every political system, and society can be judged relatively pluralist or relatively elitist only against some standard. If the only standard which exists is the ideal of a completely egalitarian society, then any system will appear to have a concentration of power. On the other hand, if one adopts as a countermodel a society where power is vested in a tiny, monolithic, conspiratorial clique, almost any society will appear pluralistic.

Pluralism is the most comprehensive of the three major models in political sociology. Indeed, almost any social cleavage can be included in the pluralist model. But a model is useful only when it narrows down the field of study and specifies which factors are crucial to an analysis. Pluralist theory complements elite theory by drawing attention to the secondary levels of leadership, and to how the diversity which exists on this level reflects broad social divisions. However, when pluralists descend from the broad theoretical level to deal in specifics, they often fall back on social classes as a key source of "pluralism" in society. Any society will appear pluralistic if one goes no further than to refer to the multiplicity of groups which exist without any attempt to classify them or to estimate their relative degrees of power. The very generality of the pluralist model strongly limits its usefulness in doing this. The critical question is not whether a society is elitist or pluralist, but what are the important social divisions and how do they relate to the exercise of power?

CONCLUSIONS

The three theoretical models which have been discussed in this chapter are all reasonably persuasive; there have been and still are learned defenders of each of them. Each has weaknesses which make it susceptible to serious criticism, but there is usually a way to respond to this criticism by making modifications in the model without abandoning its most central assumptions.

During the 1960's the political climate changed radically as a result of the black revolt and American intervention in Vietnam. The dominance of pluralism came under strong attack as it became clear to more and more people that power was concentrated in elite groups which were not always responsive to the pressures of groups seeking social change. Young social scientists who were in college during the peak of the youth movements of the 1960's saw pluralism as an apologia for the status quo, and began to seek other explanations for the ills of the system. Today, the dominance of pluralism has been broken. The argument which Truman and other pluralists made that elites have little effect on political decision-making did not survive the Vietnam era. During the 1950's studying the elite in the United States was considered vaguely subversive although studies of elites in the socialist or Third World countries were quite respectable. By the late 1960's even the pluralists were talking of the "pluralism of elites" and conceding that many groups were excluded from effective participation in decision-making. While pluralism has lost its dominant position, no other theoretical model has assumed a similar degree of acceptance.

Marxism enjoyed a considerable renaissance in the 1970s, but it has not proven its adequacy to deal with the political conflicts of the late 1960's and early 1970's. Marx's economic theory focused largely on the conflict between workers and owners, and his theory of the evolution of the capitalist system over long periods of time emphasized the polarization of class conflict into these two groups. Many political issues such as the black revolt, the youth movement, the environmental crisis, and the women's movement were not predicted by those who were using Marxist models of thought any more than they were by pluralists. Long-term changes in class systems do generally reflect economic changes; but at a detailed level, and at a specific point in time, it is necessary to consider many aspects of social inequality which cannot be immediately reduced to their economic origins.

The study of elites has been generally accepted as an essential part of political sociology, and debate has focused on more empirical questions such as the nature, composition, and behavior of elites. Class analysis is generally accepted, also, although there remain many differences about the origins of and the necessity for class inequality. Pluralism has lost most of its claim to being adequate as a portrayal of contemporary American society (and it never claimed to be an explanation of most other societies), but much of the empirical work done by pluralists is increasingly appreciated by people whose understanding of the larger system is different. The basic ethical and philosophical values which underlie many of the differences have not, of course, been resolved. The socialist assumption that human nature can be improved cannot be reconciled with a conservative belief that it is innately determined. The liberal belief that political institutions should limit themselves to mediating disputes between existing interest groups cannot be reconciled with a radical desire to use political power to redistribute wealth and fundamentally reorganize society. But on the more mundane level of social research, the three perspectives can often be effectively combined.

15

Developing a Sociological Consciousness

THE SOCIOLOGICAL PERSPECTIVE

Sociology is the scientific study of social interaction and social organization.

- ***New Levels of Reality.*** The sociological perspective encourages us to examine aspects of our social environment in ways that delve beneath the surface. As we look beyond the outer appearances of our social world, we encounter new levels of reality.
- ***The Sociological Imagination.*** The essence of the **sociological imagination** is the ability to see our private experiences and personal difficulties as entwined with the structural arrangements of our society and the times in which we live.
- ***Microsociology and Macrosociology.*** **Microsociology** is the detailed study of what people say, do, and think moment by moment as they go about their daily lives. **Macrosociology** focuses upon large-scale and long-term social processes of organizations, institutions, and broad social patterns.

The Development of Sociology

- ***Auguste Comte: The Founder of Sociology.*** Auguste Comte is commonly credited as being the founder of sociology. He emphasized that the study of society must be scientific, and he urged sociologists to employ systematic observation, experimentation, and comparative historical analysis as their methods. He divided the study of society into **social statics** and **social dynamics.**
- ***Harriet Martineau: Feminist and Methodologist.*** Harriet Martineau wrote the first book on social research methods and was among the first to do systematic, scientifically based, social research. Her comparative analysis of slavery and the position of women in the Western world paved the way for feminist scholarship and the further pursuit of

gender equality.

- ***Herbert Spencer and Social Darwinism.*** Herbert Spencer depicted society as a system, a whole made up of interrelated parts. He also set forth an evolutionary theory of historical development. **Social Darwinism** is Spencer's application of evolutionary notions and the concept of survival of the fittest to the social world.
- ***Karl Marx: The Role of Class Conflict.*** Karl Marx focused his search for the basic principles of history on the economic environments in which societies develop. He believed that society is divided into those who own the means of producing wealth and those who do not, giving rise to **class conflict. Dialectical materialism** is Marx's theory that development depends on the clash of contradictions and the creation of new, more advanced structures out of these clashes.
- ***Émile Durkheim: Social Integration and Social Facts.*** Émile Durkheim was especially concerned with social solidarity, distinguishing between mechanical and organic solidarity. He contended that the distinctive subject matter of sociology should be the study of **social facts.**
- ***Max Weber: Subjectivity and Social Organization.*** Max Weber said that a critical aspect of the sociological enterprise is the study of the intentions, values, beliefs, and attitudes that underlie people's behavior. He used the word ***Verstehen*** in describing his approach and contributed his notions of the ideal type and a **value-free sociology.**
- ***American Sociology.*** In the United States, sociology and the modern university system arose together. The first department of sociology was established at the University of Chicago in 1893, and Chicago served as a "social laboratory" at the beginning of the century. Midcentury sociologists crafted survey techniques and refined models of society. "New breed" sociologists in the 1960s and 1970s refined Marxism and established new research approaches and perspectives.
- ***Contemporary Sociology.*** Contemporary movements in sociology include critical theory, feminism, and postmodern social theory.

Theoretical Perspectives

Contemporary sociologists acknowledge three general theoretical perspectives, or ways of looking at how various social phenomena are related to one another. These are the functionalist, the conflict, and the symbolic interactionist perspectives.

- ***The Functionalist Perspective.*** The structural-functional-or, more simply, functionalist-perspective sees society as a system. Functionalists identify the structural characteristics and **functions** and **dysfunctions** of institutions, and distinguish between **manifest functions** and **latent functions.** Functionalists also typically assume that most members of a society share a consensus regarding their core beliefs and values.

- ***The Conflict Perspective.*** The conflict approach draws much of its inspiration from the work of Karl Marx and argues that the structure of society and the nature of social relationships are the result of past and ongoing conflicts.
- ***The Interactionist Perspective.*** Symbolic interactionists contend that society is possible because human beings have the ability to communicate with one another by means of symbols. They say that we act toward people, objects, and events on the basis of the meanings we impart to them. Consequently, we experience the world as **constructed reality.**

Conducting Research

- ***The Logic of Science.*** Sociology is a social science. Science assumes that every event or action results from an antecedent cause-that is, cause-and-effect relationships prevail in the universe. These causes and effects can be observed and measured, and sociologists look for **correlations** among **variables** as a way of doing so.
- ***How Do Sociologists Collect Data?*** Four major techniques of data collection are available to sociologists: experiments, surveys, observation, and archival research. In the **experiment,** researchers work with an **experimental group** and a **control group** to test the effects of an **independent variable** on a **dependent variable.** Interviewing and questionnaires constitute the primary techniques used in **surveys,** using **random** or **stratified random samples.** Observation can take the form of **participant observation** or **unobtrusive observation.** Other techniques include **archival research** and feminist methodology.
- ***Steps in the Scientific Method: A Close-up Look.*** The scientific method includes selecting a researchable problem, reviewing the literature, formulating a **hypothesis,** creating an **operational definition,** choosing a research design, collecting the data, analyzing the data, and stating conclusions.
- ***Research Ethics*** It is important that sociologists observe the ethics of their discipline in carrying out research. They have an obligation not to expose their subjects to substantial risk or personal harm in the research process and to protect the rights and dignity of their subjects.

CULTURE AND SOCIAL STRUCTURE

Components of Culture

Culture provides individuals with a set of common understandings that they employ in fashioning their actions, and makes society possible by providing a common framework of meaning.

- ***Norms.*** **Norms** are social rules that specify appropriate and inappropriate behavior in given situations. They afford a means by which we orient ourselves to other people. **Folkways, mores,** and **laws** are types of norms.
- ***Values.*** **Values** are broad ideas regarding what is desirable, correct, and good that most members of a society share. Values are so general and abstract that they do not explicitly specify which behaviors are acceptable and which are not.
- ***Symbols and Language.*** **Symbols** are acts or objects that have come to be socially accepted as standing for something else. Symbols assume many different forms, but **language** is the most important of these. Language is the chief vehicle by which people communicate ideas, information, attitudes, and emotions, and it serves as the principal means by which human beings create culture and transmit it from generation to generation.

Cultural Unity and Diversity

- ***Cultural Universals.*** **Cultural universals** are patterned and recurrent aspects of life that appear in all known societies. All people confront many of the same problems; culture represents an accumulation of solutions to the problems posed by human biology and the human situation.
- ***Cultural Integration.*** The items that form a culture tend to constitute a consistent and integrated whole. For example, societies that value universal education also usually have norms and laws about schools, organize education into a collective activity, and create symbols and share meanings about the value of education and educational organizations.
- ***Ethnocentrism.*** The cultural ways of our own society become so deeply ingrained that we have difficulty conceiving of alternative ways of life. We judge the behavior of other groups by the standards of our own culture, a phenomenon sociologists term **ethnocentrism.**
- ***Cultural Relativism.*** In studying other cultures, we must examine behavior in the light of the values, beliefs, and motives of each culture, an approach termed **cultural relativism.**
- ***Subcultures and Countercultures.***

Cultural diversity may be found within a society in the form of **subcultures.** When the norms, values, and lifestyles of a subculture are at odds with those of the larger society, it is a **counterculture.**

Social Structure

People's relationships are characterized by social ordering. Sociologists apply the term **social structure** to this social ordering-the interweaving of people's interactions and relationships in recurrent and stable patterns.

- ***Statuses.*** **Status** represents a position within a group or society. It is by means of statuses that we locate one another in various social structures. Some are assigned to us—**ascribed statuses;** others we secure on the basis of individual choice and competition—**achieved statuses.**
- ***Roles.*** A status carries with it a set of culturally defined **rights** and **duties,** what sociologists term a **role.** A role is the expected behavior we associate with a status. **Role performance** is the actual behavior of the person who occupies a status. **Role conflict** arises when individuals are confronted with conflicting expectations stemming from their occupancy of two or more statuses. **Role strain** arises when individuals find the expectations of a single role incompatible.
- ***Groups.*** Statuses and roles are building blocks for more comprehensive social structures, including **groups** of two or more people. Roles link us within social relationships. When these relationships are sustained across time, we frequently attribute group properties to them. Sociologists distinguish groups from **aggregates** and **categories.**
- ***Institutions.*** **Institutions** are the principal social structures used to organize, direct, and execute the essential tasks of social living. Each institution is built around a standardized solution to a set of problems and encompasses the notions of both cultural patterns and social structure.
- ***Societies.*** **Societies** represent the most comprehensive and complex type of social structure in today's world. By virtue of their common culture, the members of a society typically possess similar values and norms and a common language. One particular approach for classifying societies is based on the way people derive their livelihood: hunting and gathering societies, horticultural societies, agrarian societies, industrial societies, and postindustrial societies. Another approach rests on the distinction between traditional and modern types.

Socialization

Socialization is the process of social interaction by which people acquire those behaviors essential for effective participation in society, the process of becoming a social being. It is essential for the renewal of culture and the perpetuation of society. The individual and society are mutually dependent on socialization.

- ***Nature and Nurture.*** Human socialization presupposes that an adequate genetic endowment and an adequate environment are available. Hereditary and environmental factors interact with and affect each other.
- ***Theories of Socialization.*** Theories of socialization include functionalist and conflict theory perspectives as well as three microlevel approaches. Social learning theory emphasizes **conditioning** and **observational learning.** Cognitive developmental theory argues that

socialization proceeds differently in the sensorimotor, preoperational, concrete operational, and formal operations stages. Symbolic interactionists say **reflexive behavior** facilitates the development of the self.

- ***Agents of Socialization.*** One of the most important early agents of socialization is the family. As children grow, peers and schools become important agents of socialization. The mass media, especially television, also serve as agents of socialization.
- ***Social Communication.*** If they are to adapt to their social environment, human beings must be able to communicate. **Communication** refers to the process by which people transmit information, ideas, attitudes, and mental states to one another. It includes the verbal and nonverbal processes (**body language, paralanguage, proxemics,** touch, and artifacts) by which we send and receive messages.
- ***Definition of the Situation.*** An important part of socialization is learning what constitutes reality-the basic schemes we use to make sense of and understand the social and physical world. **Definition of the situation** is the interpretation or meaning we give to our immediate circumstances. Our definitions influence our construction of reality, an insight captured by the **Thomas theorem.**

The Self and Socialization

The formation of the **self**-the set of concepts we use in defining who we are-is a central part of the socialization process. The self emerges in the course of interaction with other people and represents the ideas we have regarding our attributes, capacities, and behavior. It typically includes an **egocentric bias.**

- ***Charles Horton Cooley: The Looking-Glass Self.*** Charles Horton Cooley's notion that our consciousness arises in a social context is exemplified by his concept of the **looking-glass self**—a process by which we imaginatively assume the stance of other people and view ourselves as we believe they see us. **Self-image** is differentiated from **self-conception. Self-esteem** is governed by **reflected appraisals, social comparisons,** and self-attribution. **Personal efficacy** is another aspect of self-evaluation.
- ***George Herbert Mead: The Generalized Other.*** George Herbert Mead contended that we gain a sense of selfhood by acting toward ourselves in much the same fashion that we act toward others. According to Mead, children typically pass through three stages in developing a full sense of selfhood: the play stage, in which the child plays roles modeled on a **significant other;** the game stage; and the **generalized other** stage.
- ***Erving Goffman: Impression Management.*** Erving Goffman pointed out that only by influencing other people's ideas of us can we hope to predict or control what happens to us. Consequently, we have a stake in presenting ourselves to others in ways that will lead them to view us in a favorable light, a process Goffman calls **impression management.** Goffman introduced the **dramaturgical approach.**

Socialization across the Life Course

Socialization is a continuing, lifelong process. All societies have to deal with the **life course** that begins with conception and continues through old age and ultimately death. **Role socialization** involves **anticipatory socialization,** altering roles, and exiting from roles.

- ***Childhood.*** Though societies differ in their definitions of childhood, they all begin the socialization process as soon as possible. Children display people-oriented responses at very early ages and develop very quickly in other ways. The "social capital" contained within a family's environment is of vital consequence in channeling and shaping children's futures.
- ***Adolescence.*** In much of the world, adolescence is not a socially distinct period in the human life span. Children in many countries are socialized to assume adult responsibilities by age 13 and even younger, sometimes by way of **puberty rites.** Adolescence is not necessarily a turbulent period, nor does a sharp generation gap separate American adolescents from their parents.
- ***Young Adulthood.*** The developmental and socialization tasks confronting young adults revolve about the core tasks of work and love. Individuals are strongly influenced by age norms and tend to set their personal watches by a **social clock.** Some social scientists have looked for stages through which young adults typically pass. Others believe that unexpected events play a more important role in development. People locate themselves during the life course not only in terms of social timetables but also in terms of **life events.**
- ***Middle Adulthood.*** Middle adulthood is a somewhat nebulous period. The core tasks remain much the same as they were in young adulthood. Increasingly, work is coming to be defined for both men and women as a badge of membership in the larger society. Although economic considerations predominate, people also work as a means to structure their time, interact with other people, escape from boredom, and sustain a positive self-image.
- ***Later Adulthood.*** The last years of one's life may be filled with more dramatic changes than any previous stage. Retiring, losing one's spouse, becoming disabled, moving to a nursing home or other care facility, and preparing for death all require individuals to change and adapt. Societies differ in the prestige and dignity they accord the aged.
- ***Death.*** A diagnosis of impending death requires that an individual adjust to a new definition of self. Changes in medical technology and social conditions have made death a different experience from that of earlier times. Americans are grappling with the issue of **euthanasia,** and the **hospice** movement has arisen to provide a more humane approach to the dying experience.

SOCIAL GROUPS AND FORMAL ORGANIZATIONS

Group Relationships

Groups—two or more people who share a feeling of unity and who are bound together in relatively stable patterns of social interaction—are products of social definitions—sets of shared ideas. As such they constitute constructed realities.

- ***Primary Groups and Secondary Groups.*** **Primary groups** involve two or more people who enjoy direct, intimate, cohesive relationships and are fundamental to both us and society. **Expressive ties** predominate in primary groups. **Secondary groups** entail two or more people who are involved in impersonal, touch-and-go relationships. **Instrumental ties** predominate in secondary groups.
- ***In-Groups and Out-Groups.*** The concepts of **in-group** and **out-group** highlight the importance of boundaries—social demarcation lines that tell us where interaction begins and ends. Boundaries prevent outsiders from entering a group's sphere, and they keep insiders within the group's sphere.
- ***Reference Groups.*** **Reference groups** provide the models we use for appraising and shaping our attitudes, feelings, and actions. A reference group may or may not be our membership group. A reference group provides both normative and comparative functions.

Group Dynamics

The dynamic qualities of groups make them a significant force in human life and important to sociologists.

- ***Group Size.*** The size of a group influences the nature of our interaction. Emotions and feelings tend to assume a larger part in **dyads** than in larger groups. The addition of a third member to a group—forming a **triad**—fundamentally alters a social situation. In this arrangement one person may be placed in the role of an outsider.
- ***Leadership.*** In group settings some members usually exert more influence than others. We call these individuals **leaders.** Two types of leadership roles tend to evolve in small groups: a **task specialist** and a **social-emotional specialist.** Leaders may follow an authoritarian style, a democratic style, or a laissez-faire style.
- ***Social Loafing.*** When individuals work in groups, they work less hard than they do when working individually, a process termed **social loafing.**
- ***Social Dilemmas.*** A **social dilemma** is a situation in which members of a group are faced with a conflict between maximizing their personal interests and maximizing the collective welfare.
- ***Groupthink.*** In group settings individuals may become victims of **groupthink.** Group members may share an illusion of invulnerability that leads to overconfidence and a greater willingness to take risks.

- ***Conformity.*** Groups bring powerful pressures to bear that produce **conformity** among their members. Although such pressures influence our behavior, we often are unaware of them.

Formal Organizations

For many tasks within modern societies, people require groups they can deliberately create for the achievement of specific goals. These groups are **formal organizations.**

- ***Types of Formal Organization.*** Amitai Etzioni classified organizations on the basis of people's reasons for entering them: **voluntary, coercive,** and **utilitarian.**
- ***Bureaucracy: A Functional Approach to Organizations.*** Small organizations can often function reasonably well on the basis of face-to-face interaction. Larger organizations must establish formal operating and administrative procedures. This requirement is met by a **bureaucracy.**
- ***Characteristics of Bureaucracies.*** Max Weber approached bureaucracy as an ideal type with these characteristics: Each office has clearly defined duties; all offices are organized in a hierarchy of authority; all activities are governed by a system of rules; all offices have qualifications; incumbents do not own their positions; employment by the organization is defined as a career; and administrative decisions are recorded in written documents.
- ***Problems of Bureaucracy.*** Bureaucracies have disadvantages and limitations. These include the principle of **trained incapacity, Parkinson's law,** and the **iron law of oligarchy.** If formal organization is to operate smoothly, it requires **informal organization** for interpreting, translating, and supporting its goals and practices.
- ***Conflict and Interactionist Perspectives.*** In recent years sociologists from differing perspectives—particularly the conflict, symbolic interactionist, and ethnomethodological approaches—have looked at the ways by which organizational reality is generated through the actions of people and groups of people.
- ***Humanizing Bureaucracies.*** Among programs that make large organizations more humane are those that allow employee participation, flextime, small work groups, and employee ownership.

DEVIANCE AND CRIME

The Nature of Deviance

In all societies the behavior of some people at times goes beyond that permitted by the norms. Social life is characterized not only by conformity but by **deviance,** behavior that a considerable number of people view as reprehensible and beyond the limits of tolerance.

- ***Social Properties of Deviance.*** Deviance is not a property inherent in certain forms of behavior; it is a property conferred upon particular behaviors by social definitions.

Definitions as to which acts are deviant vary greatly from time to time, place to place, and group to group. We typically find that norms are not so much a point or a line but a zone. Deviant acts also can be redefined, as has happened in recent years in the United States. Most societies can absorb a good deal of deviance without serious consequences, but persistent and widespread deviance can be dysfunctional. But deviance may also be functional by promoting social solidarity, clarifying norms, strengthening group allegiances, and providing a catalyst for change.

- ***Social Control and Deviance.*** Societies seek to ensure that their members conform with basic norms by means of **social control.** Three main types of social control processes operate within social life: (1) those that lead us to internalize our society's normative expectations **(internalization),** (2) those that structure our world of social experience, and (3) those that employ various formal and informal social sanctions.

Theories of Deviance

Other disciplines are concerned with deviance, particularly biology and psychology. Sociologists focus on five main theories.

- ***Anomie Theory.*** Émile Durkheim contributed to our understanding of deviance with his idea of **anomie.** Robert K. Merton built on Durkheim's ideas of anomie and social cohesion. According to his theory of structural strain, deviance derives from societal stresses.
- ***Cultural Transmission Theory.*** A number of sociologists have emphasized the similarities between the way deviant behavior is acquired and the way in which other behavior is acquired-the cultural transmission theory. Edwin H. Sutherland elaborated on this notion in his theory of **differential association.** He said that individuals become deviant to the extent to which they participate in settings where deviant ideas, motivations, and techniques are viewed favorably.
- ***Conflict Theory.*** Conflict theorists ask, "Which group will be able to translate its values into the rules of a society and make these rules stick?" and "Who reaps the lion's share of benefits from particular social arrangements?" Marxist sociologists see crime as a product of capitalist laws.
- ***Labeling Theory.*** Labeling theorists study the processes whereby some individuals come to be tagged as deviants, begin to think of themselves as deviants, and enter deviant careers. Labeling theorists differentiate between **primary deviance** and **secondary deviance.**
- ***Control Theory.*** Control theory attempts to explain not why people deviate but why people do *not* deviate. Travis Hirschi argued that young people are more likely to conform if their bond to society is strong. This bond has four parts: attachment, involvement, commitment, and belief.

Crime and the Criminal Justice System

Crime is an act of deviance that is prohibited by law. The distinguishing property of crime is that people who violate the law are liable to be arrested, tried, pronounced guilty, and deprived of their lives, liberty, or property. It is the state that defines crime by the laws it promulgates, administers, and enforces.

- ***Forms of Crime.*** An infinite variety of acts can be crimes. Federal agencies keep records on **index crimes**—violent crimes against people and crimes against property. Juvenile crime is crime committed by youth under the age of 18. **Organized crime** is carried out by large-scale bureaucratic organizations that provide illegal goods and services in public demand. **White-collar crime** is crime committed by relatively affluent persons, often in the course of business activities. Crime can be committed by corporations and by governments. In **victimless crime** no one involved is considered a victim.
- ***Measuring Crime.*** Statistics on crime are among the most unsatisfactory of all social data. A large proportion of the crimes that are committed go undetected; others are detected but not reported; and still others are reported but not officially recorded.
- ***Drugs and Crime.*** Drugs and crime are related both directly—selling, using, and possessing illegal drugs all are crimes—and indirectly—drug involvement often leads to other sorts of crimes. Drug problems can be dealt with by recognizing that addiction is a brain disease. Other approaches include continued prohibition, depenalization, or legalization.
- ***Women and Crime.*** A growing percentage of youth and adults in the criminal population is female. One-quarter of the youth arrested in the United States are girls; overall, one in five arrests are female. Girls are more likely than boys to be arrested for such offenses as running away from home.
- ***The Criminal Justice System.*** The **criminal justice system** is made up of the reactive agencies of the state that include the police, the courts, and prisons. Of every 100 felonies committed within the United States, only 36 are reported to the police. Of that 36, only 7 or 8 are cleared by arrest. Of those 7 who are arrested, only 5 are prosecuted and convicted. Only 1 is sent to prison.
- ***The Purposes of Imprisonment.***

There have been four traditional purposes of imprisonment: punishment, rehabilitation, deterrence, and selective confinement.

SOCIAL STRATIFICATION

Patterns of Social Stratification

Social stratification depends upon, but is not the same thing as, **social differentiation**—the process by which a society becomes increasingly specialized over time.

- ***Open and Closed Systems.*** Where people can change their status with relative ease, sociologists refer to the arrangement as an **open system.** A **closed system** is one in which people have great difficulty in changing their status.
- ***Dimensions of Stratification.*** Sociologists typically take a multidimensional view of stratification, identifying three components: economic standing **(wealth and income), prestige,** and **power.**

The American Class System

Inequality follows relatively consistent and stable patterns that persist through time. We often refer to advantaged and disadvantaged groups in the United States as the upper class, middle class, and lower class.

- ***Is There Inequality in American Society?*** Since the early 1970s income inequality in the United States has been increasing and is now at its highest level in 50 years. In 1999 the top 20 percent of the population received nearly half of the income. Inequality in wealth is even greater.
- ***Identifying Social Classes.*** Three primary methods are employed by sociologists for identifying social classes: the **objective method,** the **self-placement method,** and the **reputational method.**
- ***The Significance of Social Classes.*** Social class largely determines people's **life chances** and **style of life** and influences patterns of behavior, including voting and sexual behavior.
- ***Poverty in the United States.*** Children and the elderly account for nearly half of all Americans living in poverty. Three theories predominate regarding poverty: the **culture of poverty** theory, poverty as *situational,* and poverty as a *structural* feature of capitalist societies.

Social Mobility

In many societies individuals or groups can move from one level (stratum) to another in the stratification system, a process called **social mobility.**

- ***Forms of Social Mobility.*** Social mobility takes a number of forms. It may be **vertical** or **horizontal** and **intergenerational** or **intragenerational.** When sociologists talk about social mobility, they usually mean intergenerational occupational mobility.
- ***Social Mobility and Status Attainment.*** More Americans are upwardly mobile than downwardly mobile across generations. Sociologists study the course of an individual's occupational status over the life cycle by looking at the **socioeconomic life cycle.** Education has the greatest influence on occupational attainment for white men. The processes of status attainment are different for women and blacks than for white males. Critics of status attainment research contend that it has a functionalist bias and that the **dual labor market** operates to sort people into **core** or **periphery** sector jobs.

- ***What Is Happening to the American Dream?*** Controversy surrounds the issue of whether the American middle class is an endangered species. Although "equal opportunity" does not apply to all Americans, depending on race, gender, and ethnicity, in real dollars most Americans are better off than their parents.

Explanations of Social Stratification

The question of why social inequality and division should characterize the human condition has provided a central focus of sociology.

- ***The Functionalist Theory of Stratification.*** The functionalist theory of social inequality holds that stratification exists because it is beneficial for society. Society must concern itself with human motivation because the duties associated with the various statuses are not all equally pleasant to the human organism, important to social survival, and in need of the same abilities and talents.
- ***The Conflict Theory of Stratification.*** The conflict theory of social inequality holds that stratification exists because it benefits individuals and groups who have the power to dominate and exploit others. Marx contended that the capitalist drive to realize surplus value is the foundation of modern class struggle.
- ***A Synthesis of Perspectives.*** Both functionalist and conflict theories have merit, but each is better than the other in answering different questions. A number of sociologists, including Gerhard E. Lenski, have looked for ways of integrating the two perspectives.

Inequalities of Race and Ethnicity

Some U.S. racial and ethnic groups continue to be the victims of prejudice and discrimination. Sociologists address these questions: Where do race and ethnicity come from? Why and how are they associated with the distribution of society's rewards? How and why do racial and ethnic stratification change?

Racial and Ethnic Stratification

Stratification represents institutionalized inequality in the distribution of social rewards and burdens. In this chapter we examined a system of stratification based on race and/or ethnicity.

- ***Races.*** The use of the concept of race for sociologists is as a social construct; a **race** is a group of people who see themselves—and are seen by others—as having hereditary traits that set them apart. An important concept based on race is **racism,** the belief that some racial groups are naturally superior and others are inferior.
- ***Ethnic Groups.*** Groups that we identify chiefly on cultural grounds—language, folk practices, dress, gestures, mannerisms, or religion—are called **ethnic groups.** Ethnic groups often have a sense of peoplehood, and to one degree or another many of them deem themselves to be a nation.

- ***Minority Groups.*** Racial and ethnic groups are often minority groups. Five properties characterize a minority. The critical characteristic that distinguishes minority groups from other groups is that they lack power.
- ***The Potential for Conflict and Separation.*** Although racial and ethnic stratification is similar to other systems of stratification in its essential features, there is one overriding difference. Racial and ethnic groups have the potential to carve their own independent nation from the existing state. The question is whether the racial or ethnic segments of the society will be willing to participate within the existing nation-state arrangement.

Prejudice and Discrimination

- ***Prejudice.*** **Prejudice** refers to attitudes of aversion and hostility toward the members of a group simply because they belong to it and hence are presumed to have the objectionable qualities ascribed to it. A new form of prejudice against African Americans that appears among affluent, suburban whites has been labeled **symbolic racism** by sociologists.
- ***Discrimination.*** **Discrimination** is action, what people actually do in their daily activities, and involves the arbitrary denial of privilege, prestige, and power to members of a minority group. Since World War II whites have shifted from more blatant forms of discrimination to more subtle forms.
- ***Institutional Discrimination.*** In their daily operation, the institutions of society may function in such a way that they produce unequal outcomes for different groups. This is called **institutional discrimination. Gatekeeping** and **environmental racism** are mechanisms by which institutional discrimination occurs.

Patterns of Intergroup Relations: Assimilation and Pluralism

In multiethnic societies, ethnic groups may either lose their distinctiveness through a process of assimilation or retain their identity and integrity through **pluralism.**

- ***Assimilation.*** **Assimilation** refers to those processes whereby groups with distinctive identities become culturally and socially fused. Two views toward assimilation have dominated within the United States, the "melting pot" view and the Anglo-conformity view.
- ***Pluralism.*** In U.S. society, Jews, African Americans, Chinese Americans, and numerous other groups have retained their identities and distinctiveness for many years, an example of **pluralism,** a situation in which diverse groups coexist and boundaries between them are maintained. In *equalitarian pluralism,* ethnic group members participate freely and equally in political and economic institutions. In *inequalitarian pluralism,* economic and political participation of minority groups is severely limited by the dominant group and may even entail **genocide.**

Racial and Ethnic Groups in the United States

The United States is undergoing a transition from a predominately white society rooted in Western European culture to a global society composed of diverse racial and ethnic groups. By the year 2050 today's minorities will comprise a much larger proportion of the U.S. population than they do today.

- ***African Americans.*** African Americans remain disadvantaged. The expected lifetime earnings of African-American men are significantly lower than those of white men, and housing segregation remains substantial. The full integration of African Americans is unlikely in the foreseeable future, primarily because of continuing social and economic barriers and low rates of interracial marriage.
- ***Hispanics.*** The nation's Hispanic population is not a consolidated minority. Hispanic groups have different histories, distinct concentrations in different areas of the United States, and substantially different demographic and socioeconomic characteristics. Hispanics are twice as likely as blacks and whites to drop out of school and typically earn less than non-Hispanics.
- ***Native Americans.*** Native-American peoples vary substantially in their history, lifestyles, kin systems, language, political arrangements, religion, economy, current circumstances, and identities. They are the most severely disadvantaged of any population within the United States. Forty-one percent of those on reservations live below the poverty level, and unemployment among males 20 to 64 years old is about 60 percent.
- ***Asian Americans.*** The average family income of Chinese, Japanese, and Korean Americans in the second and subsequent generations is almost one-and-a-half times higher than that of non-Hispanic whites. But Asian Americans are a varied group, with considerable contrasts and diversity. The earnings of Laotians, Cambodians, and Vietnamese are generally low, especially among recent refugees who typically have come from rural areas and who possess few marketable skills.
- ***White Ethnics.*** Most white Americans, including those of northwestern European background, know and identify with their ethnic ancestry, but white ethnicity is neither deep nor stable. "Symbolic ethnicity" is an ethnicity that contributes to individual identity and perhaps to family communion, but does not create or sustain strong ethnic group ties.

Sociological Perspectives on Inequalities of Race and Ethnicity

- ***The Functionalist Perspective.*** Functionalists say that ethnic differentiation reduces consensus, increases the chances of conflict, and threatens the equilibrium of a society, but it also promotes group formation and cohesion, functions as a safety valve through *scapegoating,* and helps maintain a democratic order.

- ***The Conflict Perspective.*** Conflict theorists contend that prejudice and discrimination can best be understood in terms of tension or conflict among competing groups. At least three different conflict theories exist, and they are related to ethnocentrism, Marxism, and the **split labor market.**
- ***The Interactionist Perspective.*** Interactionists say that the world we experience is **socially constructed.** In this view, ethnic groups are seen as products of social interaction. Ethnicity arises when communication channels between groups are limited and the different groups develop different systems of meanings.

The Future of Ethnic and Minority Group Relations

Ethnic status for Americans with African-, Hispanic-, Asian-, and Native-American roots is not "symbolic," is not a matter of choice, and remains heavily ascriptive.

- ***Intergroup Relations.*** Functionalists believe that there are long-run social trends that are eliminating ascription and other irrational features from modern, industrial, socially differentiated, societies. The conflict perspective, on the other hand, predicts that ethnic stratification will remain as long as it is in the interests of powerful dominant groups to keep it in place. Interactionists would predict that as long as segregation and isolation of minority groups persist, ethnocentrism will continue and probably worsen.
- ***Ethnicity.*** If ethnic stratification persists, then ethnicity will persist as well; if it diminishes significantly, perhaps ethnicity for all groups will become increasingly "symbolic."

GENDER INEQUALITY

Gender Stratification

Men and women differ in their access to privilege, prestige, and power. The distribution problem of who gets what, when, and how has traditionally been answered in favor of males. **Sex** is a biologically determined characteristic; **gender** is a socially constructed characteristic. All societies use anatomical differences to assign **gender roles. Gender identities** are the conceptions we have of ourselves as being male or female.

- ***Sexism and Patriarchy.*** Sexism operates at both an individual level and an institutional level. The most pervasive form of institutional sexism is **patriarchy.** Women exhibit four of the five properties associated with a *minority group.*
- ***Gender Inequality around the World.*** No nation treats its women as well as its men. Women in many countries suffer discrimination and abuse, yet women around the world do considerably better than U.S. women in some areas.
- ***Gender Inequality in the United States.*** U.S. women do most of the household work and childrearing. Despite increasing involvement in the paid workforce, women continue to be excluded from top jobs and to earn less than men. Sexual harassment remains a

common workplace hazard for women, and somewhere between 10 and 25 percent of women have been raped. Men still dominate U.S. political life.

Sources of Gender Roles

Gender roles can be seen as arising from biological development or cultural contributions.

- ***Gender Roles and Biology.*** The biological aspects of gender consist of the physical differences between men and women, but the role biology plays in producing behavioral differences between men and women is shrouded in controversy.
- ***Gender Roles and Culture.*** Gender roles probably represent the earliest division of labor among humans. Various societies have specific social definitions of approprate behavior for males and females.
- ***Gender Roles and Identity.*** Gender identities are the concepts we have of ourselves as being male or female. Theories of the acquisition of gender identities include Freudian, cultural transmission, and cognitive-development. Differences in self-construal may explain gender differences in the United States.

Sociological Perspectives on Gender Stratification

The major sociological perspectives offer interpretations of gender stratification that resemble and parallel their positions on class and racial or ethnic stratification.

- ***The Functionalist Perspective.*** Functionalists suggest that families are organized along instrumental-expressive lines, with men specializing in instrumental tasks and women in expressive tasks.
- ***The Conflict Perspective.*** Conflict theorists contend that a sexual division of labor is a social vehicle devised by men to ensure themselves of privilege, prestige, and power in their relationships with women.
- ***The Interactionist Perspective.*** Interactionists argue that gender inequality persists because of the way we define men and women and their appropriate roles in society. Language helps perpetuate inequality.
- ***The Feminist Perspective.*** Feminism is not a single theory but an evolving set of theoretical perspectives. Feminists argue that women are disadvantaged because society is patriarchal; the assignment of group differences is socially costly and repressive. Everyday interactions between men and women recreate and support the gender system.

POLITICAL AND ECONOMIC POWER

Power, Authority, and the State

Power determines which individuals and groups will be able to translate their preferences into the reality of day-to-day social organization.

- ***The State.*** The **state** rests on **force** and consists of people who exercise an effective monopoly in the use of physical coercion within a given territory.
- ***Sociological Perspectives on the State.*** Functionalists say the state performs four functions: enforcement of norms, overall social planning and direction, arbitration of conflicting interests, and protection of a society's members and interests against outside groups. Conflict theorists say the state is a vehicle by which one or more groups impose their values and stratification system upon other groups and depict it as an instrument of violence and oppression.
- ***Legitimacy and Authority.*** Sociologists distinguish between power that is legitimate and power that is illegitimate. Legitimate power is **authority.** Sociologist Max Weber suggested that power may be legitimated by **traditional, legal-rational,** and/or **charismatic** means.

Political Power

Politics refers to the processes by which people and groups acquire and exercise power. **Political power** is power that is organized and wielded by the state.

- ***Types of Government.*** **Government** can take the form of **totalitarianism, authoritarianism,** or **democracy,** which is promoted by a strong **civil society.**
- ***Political Power in the United States.*** A constitutional system of government defines and prescribes the boundaries within which political power is pursued in the United States. Central to American political processes are **political parties,** popular electoral participation, **interest-group** lobbying (including **political action committees**), and the **mass media.**
- ***Models of Power in the United States.*** Marxist theory holds that political processes are affected by class interests and conflict. The elitist model depicts major decisions as being made by a power elite. The pluralist perspective says that no one group really runs the government.

Economic Power

Modern economic systems provide a different answer to the question of how economic activity is organized—by the market or by the plan—and to the question of who owns the means of production—individuals or the state.

- ***Comparative Economic Systems.*** **Capitalist economies** rely heavily on free markets and privately held property, and **socialist economies** rely primarily on state planning and publicly held property. Most nations are characterized by mixed economies that include elements of both.
- ***Transition from a Command to a Market Economy.*** Eastern Europe, the former Soviet Union, and China are undergoing a transition from a command to a market economy, with marketization and privatization proceeding slowly and resulting in a high level of social uncertainty.

The Power of Corporations

The government is an important participant in the U.S. economy, but the primary productive role is played by private business.

- ***The Power of National Corporations.*** Large corporations exercise enormous power in American life and constitute **oligopolies.** The decisions made by their executives have implications and ramifications that reach throughout the nation.
- ***The Power of Multinational Corporations in the Global Economy.*** The rise of **multinational corporations** and the growing internationalization of the world economy, including **core regions** and **periphery regions,** have given economic power a new dimension. Such firms rival nations in wealth and frequently operate as private governments pursuing their worldwide interests by well-developed foreign policies.
- ***The Control of Corporations.*** Some social scientists say that a managerial revolution has separated ownership and effective control in corporate life, but others point to the institutional constraints, such as **corporate interlocks,** that operate on corporate decision makers.

The Sociology of Work

Power extends into the workplace, determining whether work will be available, how work will be organized, and the manner in which work will be remunerated.

- ***Changes in the Work Experience.*** The work experience of Americans has undergone significant change over the past 160 years; the proportion working on farms has declined, while the proportion employed in service industries has risen. Work in nonindustrialized societies is very different than work in industrialized societies.
- ***The Significance of Work.*** People work for many reasons in addition to "self-interest," and work has many social meanings, especially those that define a person's position in the social structure.
- ***Satisfaction and Alienation in Work.*** Individuals in occupations that combine high economic, occupational, and educational prestige typically show the greatest satisfaction with their work and the strongest job attachment. When individuals fail to find their work satisfying and fulfilling, they may experience **alienation.** Marx and Durkheim had differing conceptions of alienation.

The Family

The way in which we define the family determines the kinds of **family** we will consider to be normal or deviant and what rights and obligations we will recognize as legally and socially binding.

- ***Forms of the Family.*** In the **nuclear family arrangement,** spouses and their offspring constitute the core relationship. In the **extended family arrangement,** kin provide the core relationship. Most Americans will belong to a **family of orientation** and a **family of procreation.** Descent and inheritance can be **patrilineal, matrilineal,** or **bilineal,** and couples may take a **patrilocal, matrilocal,** or **neolocal** residence. Most societies are **patriarchal,** with some industrialized nations becoming more **egalitarian;** none are known that are truly **matriarchal.**

- ***Forms of Marriage.*** **Marriage** refers to a socially approved sexual union undertaken with some idea of permanence. Two types of marital regulations define the "right" spouse: **endogamy** and **exogamy. Incest taboos** are rules that prohibit sexual intercourse with close blood relatives. Societies further structure marriage relationships in one of four ways: **monogamy, polygyny, polyandry,** and **group marriage.**
- ***Patterns of Courtship.*** Societies "control" love through child and arranged marriage, social isolation of young people, close supervision of couples, and peer and parental pressures. A variety of factors operate in the selection of a mate: **homogamy,** physical attractiveness (the **matching hypothesis**), and **complementary needs. Exchange theory** provides a unifying link among these factors.

Marriage and the Family in the United States

Some see the nuclear family as the source of many modern woes, others as the last bastion of morality in an increasingly decadent world.

- ***Life within Marriage.*** Most adult Americans hope to establish an intimate relationship with another person and make the relationship work. However, increasing numbers of Americans no longer view marriage as a permanent institution but as something that can be ended and reentered.
- ***Parenthood.*** Nuclear families that are not disrupted by divorce, desertion, or death typically pass through a series of changes and realignments across time, what sociologists call the **family life course.** Altered expectations and requirements are imposed on a husband and wife as children are born and grow up.
- ***Two-Income Families.*** More than 60 percent of all mothers with children under age six are in the paid workforce. Such women also do more of the housework and child care than men. Research findings about the effect of working mothers on children are varied. In one-fifth of such couples the woman is the chief breadwinner.
- ***Beyond the Traditional Nuclear Family.*** Americans have a variety of **lifestyles,** the overall pattern of living that people evolve to meet their biological, social, and emotional needs. Among the lifestyles Americans find themselves adopting are singlehood, single parenthood, cohabitation, and relationships based on **homosexuality.**

Challenges for American Families and American Society

Some family problems stay in the family; others spill over into society.

- ***Family Violence, Child Abuse, and Incest.*** Family violence, child abuse, and incest are more common than most people think. The sexual abuse of children often leads to behavior problems, learning difficulties, sexual promiscuity, runaway behavior, drug and alcohol abuse, and suicidal behavior.
- ***Child Care.*** Most child psychologists agree that high-quality day care and preschools provide acceptable child care arrangements. The United States is one of the few industrialized nations that have no comprehensive day care program and the quality of child care available is often poor.
- ***Divorce.*** Divorce exacts a considerable emotional and physical toll from all family members. Children raised by single parents are more likely to drop out of high school, to use drugs, to have teen births, to have illegitimate children, and to be poorer than children raised in two-parent homes. More than half the adults who remarry undergo a second divorce.
- ***Care for the Elderly.*** Social scientists call middle-aged adults the "sandwich generation" because they find themselves with responsibilities for their own teenage and college-age children and for their elderly parents. Grown children still bear the primary responsibility for their aged parents.

Sociological Perspectives on the Family

- ***The Functionalist Perspective.*** Functionalists identify a number of functions families typically perform: reproduction; socialization; care, protection, and emotional support; assignment of status; and regulation of sexual behavior through the **norm of legitimacy.**
- ***The Conflict Perspective.*** Conflict theorists have seen the family as a social arrangement benefiting men more than women. Some conflict sociologists say that intimate relationships inevitably involve antagonism as well as love.
- ***The Interactionist Perspective.*** Symbolic interactionists emphasize that families reinforce and rejuvenate their bonds through the symbolic mechanism of rituals such as family meals and holidays.

RELIGION, EDUCATION, AND MEDICINE

Religion

- ***What Is Religion?*** **Religion** has to do with those socially shared and organized ways of thinking, feeling, and acting that concern ultimate meanings and assume the existence of the supernatural or "beyond." Religion is centered in beliefs and practices that are related to **sacred** as opposed to **profane** things and often involves **rituals.**

- ***A Global View: Varieties of Religious Behavior.*** Religious behavior is so varied that sociologists attempt to categorize it. One scheme distinguishes between simple supernaturalism, **animism, theism,** and a system of abstract ideals.
- ***Religious Organizations.*** Sociologists distinguish between four ideal types of religious organization: **churches, denominations, sects,** and **cults.** Whereas churches and denominations exist in a state of accommodation with the larger society, sects and cults find themselves at odds with established social arrangements and practices.
- ***Religion and Secular Change: The Protestant Ethic.*** Max Weber studied several world religions to see how a religious **ethic** can affect people's behavior and claimed that religion could be a source of social change. Specifically, he linked the rise of capitalism to the **Protestant ethic,** particularly Calvinism and **asceticism.**
- ***Adapting Tradition: Religion in Contemporary Life.*** The **secularization thesis** states that profane considerations gain ascendancy over sacred considerations in the course of social evolution, but little evidence supports the notion that secularization is occurring in the United States.
- ***Fundamentalism and Evangelicalism.*** Fundamentalist and evangelical groups are on the rise in the United States and elsewhere in the world. Fundamentalism opposes modernity and reaffirms traditional authority, accepting the Bible as the literal word of God. Evangelicals profess a personal relationship with Jesus Christ.
- ***State-Church Issues.*** The First Amendment to the U.S. Constitution has provided the foundation for the principle of the separation of church and state. The basic tenet of **civil religion** is that the United States is a nation under God with a divine mission.
- ***The Functionalist Perspective.*** Functionalist theorists look to the contributions religion makes to societal survival and are interested in **totemism.** According to Émile Durkheim, religion is the symbolization of society.
- ***The Conflict Perspective.*** Some conflict theorists depict religion as a weapon in the service of ruling elites who use it to hold in check the explosive tensions produced by social inequality and injustice. Other conflict theorists see religion as an active force shaping the contours of social life.

Education

Social scientists view **learning** as a relatively permanent change in behavior or capability that results from experience. **Education** is one aspect of the many-sided process of socialization by which people acquire behaviors essential for effective participation in society.

- ***The Bureaucratic Structure of Schools.*** As schools grew larger they had to standardize and routinize many of their operations and establish formal operating and administrative procedures.

- ***The Effectiveness of Schools.*** Successful schools foster expectations that order will prevail and that learning is a serious matter. Cross-cultural research suggests that teachers in some other countries spend more time developing concepts rather than simply stating them.
- ***Alternatives to Traditional Public Schools.*** Parents are increasingly choosing to educate their children in ways other than in traditional public schools. Alternatives include charter schools, religious schools, nonreligious private schools, and home schooling.
- ***The Availability of Higher Education.*** College and university student populations are highly skewed in terms of race, ethnicity, and family income. Only 20 percent of the nation's undergraduates are young people between 18 and 22 years of age who are pursuing a parent-financed education.
- ***The Functionalist Perspective.*** Viewed from the functionalist perspective, a specialized educational agency is needed to transmit the ways of thinking, feeling, and acting mandated by a rapidly changing urban and technologically based society.
- ***The Conflict Perspective.*** Conflict theorists see schools as agencies that reproduce and legitimate the current social order, citing **credentialism** as one factor and the **correspondence principle** as another. By reproducing and legitimating the existing social order, the educational institution benefits some individuals and groups at the expense of others.
- ***The Interactionist Perspective.*** Symbolic interactionists see classrooms as "little worlds" teeming with behavior. They see U.S. schools primarily benefiting advantaged youngsters and alienating disadvantaged youngsters through the **hidden curriculum** and **educational self—fulfilling prophecies.**

Medicine

The functions now carried out by the institution of **medicine** were once embedded in the activities of the family and religious institutions.

- ***The U.S. Health Care Delivery System.*** In recent decades the medical care industry has grown appreciably larger, consuming about 15 percent of the nation's gross domestic product. Hospitals, physicians, and nurses comprise central roles in the health care delivery system.
- ***Rising Health Care Costs: Is Managed Care the Answer?*** Soaring health care costs have led to new arrangements for financing it. Managed care arrangements are part of many traditional insurance plans. They also form the basis for health maintenance and preferred provider organizations.
- ***Alternatives to the U.S. Health Care System: A Global Perspective.*** Health care is managed differently in different countries. In China health care is provided at essentially

no charge for most citizens. In Great Britain 90 percent of the funding for its National Health Service comes from general taxation. In Kenya a national health service employs physicians and owns hospitals, but health care is also available from other sources. Canada's system provides medically necessary physician and hospital services to all citizens.

- ***The Functionalist Perspective.*** Functionalists note that **health** is essential to the preservation of the human species and organized social life. One way societies contain the negative effects of health problems and **disease** is through institutionalizing illness in a **sick role.**
- ***The Conflict Perspective.*** Conflict theorists note that some people achieve better health than others because they have access to those resources that contribute to good health and recovery should they become ill.
- ***The Interactionist Perspective.*** Interactionist theorists view sickness as a condition to which we attach socially devised meanings. For example, an increasing number of behaviors that earlier generations defined as immoral or sinful are coming to be seen as forms of sickness-the **medicalization of deviance.**

Population and the Environment

Human populations must achieve a working relationship with their *environment.* Sociologists have applied theories of *ecology* to the study of human communities, including use of the concept of *ecosystem,* with populations as their unit of study.

Population Demography is the science dealing with the size, distribution, composition, and changes in population.

- ***Elements in Population Change.*** All population change within a society can be reduced to three factors: the birth rate, the death rate, and the migration rate into or out of the society. Demographers look at **crude birth rate, general fertility rate, age-specific fertility, fecundity, zero population growth, crude death rate, age-specific death rates,** and **infant mortality rate.** Migration affects population, and demographers measure the **net migration rate.** Movement may take the form of **international migration** or **internal migration.** Births, deaths, and migration affect the **growth rate.**
- ***Population Composition.*** Sociologists are also interested in the composition of a population, particularly in the sex ratio and age composition. A **population pyramid** is a useful tool for analyzing population change and discerning population trends.
- ***Malthus and Marx: Two Views of Population Growth.*** Thomas Malthus held that population increases more quickly than food supply. Karl Marx insisted that an excess of population is related to the availability of employment opportunities, not to a fixed supply of food. Neo-Malthusians are those who agree with many of Malthus's ideas but who favor contraception for population control.

- ***Demographic Transition.*** *Demographic transition theory* holds that the process of modernization is associated with three stages in population change: high potential growth, transitional growth, and population stability.
- ***Population Policies.*** Fertility reduction policies are based on family planning, a developmentalist strategy, or a societalist perspective.
- ***The Effects of Crowding.*** Population buildup has bad effects on deer, rats, and a variety of other organisms; the impact of crowding on human behavior is more complex and does not invariably result in pathology. Social scientists distinguish between **density** and **crowding.**

The Urban Environment

The **city** is one of the most striking features of our modern era, basic to many of the characteristics of modern society.

- ***The Origin and Evolution of Cities.*** Preindustrial cities were primarily small affairs. Urbanization has proceeded rapidly during the past 180 years, resulting in industrial-urban centers, metropolitan cities, **megalopolises,** and global cities.
- ***Patterns of City Growth.*** Sociologists provide a number of models of city growth: the **concentric circle model,** the **sector model,** and the **multiple nuclei model.**
- ***Ecological Processes: Segregation and Gentrification.*** The structural patterning of cities derives from a number of underlying ecological processes. One process by which **natural areas** are formed is **segregation. Invasion** and **succession** are also critical ecological processes. **Urban gentrification** is the return of middle-class professionals to older urban neighborhoods.
- ***Urban Crisis: Cities in Decline.*** Urban decline in many American cities has been both descriptive and functional.
- ***Sprawling Urban Growth: The Rise of "Edge" Cities.*** "Outer cities,""minicities," or "edge cities" have been made possible by beltways and expressways, and the development of a service-based economy in which telecommunications allow service-sector firms to locate anywhere.

The Ecological Environment

Humans have transformed one-third to one-half of the earth's land surface and use more than half of all the world's accessible surface fresh water; some 25 percent of the world's bird species have been driven to extinction, and forested areas have decreased by a third since the rise of agriculture.

- ***Human-Environment Interactions: A Closer Look.*** Sociologists are interested in the relationships between population size, politics and economics, environment, and technology. While humans can overexploit natural resources, they can also protect and restore them.

- ***The Functionalist Perspective.*** Functionalist theorists see the ecosystem as exhibiting a tendency toward equilibrium in which its components maintain a delicately balanced relationship.
- ***The Conflict Perspective.*** Some conflict theorists say that the basic issue is not one of how much is available but which individuals and groups will secure a disproportionate share of what is available.
- ***The Interactionist Perspective.*** Symbolic interactionists focus on "people behaviors" related to environmental issues. Interests include the gap between people's attitudes and actions and the difference between public and expert perceptions of risk.
- ***Entering the New Millennium.*** In 1997, Jane Lubchenko, the president of the American Association for the Advancement of Science, called upon scientists to look at the environment as the most important issue of the future. Economist Julian Simon, in contrast, felt that the free market will result in life improving indefinitely. Others see that we have made progress in solving some environmental problems and could continue to do so. Historical analysis shows that the earth's human inhabitants have changed their view of nature as a usable resource to nature as a life-sustaining global ecosystem.

SOCIAL CHANGE

A World of Change

Sociologists refer to fundamental alterations in the patterns of culture, structure, and social behavior over time as **social change.** It is a process by which society becomes something different while remaining in some respects the same.

- ***Sources of Social Change.*** Many factors interact to generate changes in people's behavior and in the culture and structure of their society, including the physical environment, population, clashes over resources and values, supporting values and norms, innovation (**discoveries** and **inventions**), **diffusion,** and the mass media.
- ***Perspectives on Social Change.*** Evolutionary theorists, particularly those with a unilinear focus, depict history as divided into sequential stages characterized by an underlying trend. Cyclical theorists look to the course of a civilization or society, searching for generalizations regarding their stages of growth and decline. Functionalist theorists see society as a system that tends toward equilibrium, with **cultural lag** an important factor in social change. Conflict theorists hold that tensions between competing groups are the basic source of social change.
- ***Social Change in the United States.*** Computers have consequences for the use and manipulation of social power. They alter the manner in which people relate to one another, and they have implications for individual privacy, the confidentiality of communications and personal data, and employment.

- ***Social Change in Developing Nations.*** The **modernization** approach sees development as entailing a pattern of convergence as societies become increasingly urban, industry comes to overshadow agriculture, and other changes occur. According to **world system** and dependency analysis, an unequal exchange takes place between core and periphery nations, with development in core nations occurring at the cost of underdevelopment in periphery nations.

Collective Behavior

Collective behavior is not organized in terms of established norms and institutionalized lines of action.

- ***Varieties of Collective Behavior.*** Collective behavior comes in many forms, including **rumors, fashions** and **fads** (which can turn into **crazes**), **mass hysteria, panic,** and **crowds.** Types of crowds include the **acting crowd,** the **casual crowd,** the **conventional crowd,** and the **expressive crowd.** These crowd types share three characteristics: suggestibility, **deindividualization,** and invulnerability.
- ***Preconditions for Collective Behavior.*** One framework for examining collective behavior is based on the **value-added** model popular among economists and specifies six determinants of collective behavior.
- ***Explanations of Crowd Behavior.*** Sociologists offer three approaches to crowd behavior: **contagion theory, convergence theory,** and **emergent-norm theory.**

Social Movements

Social movements are vehicles whereby people collectively seek to influence the course of human events through formal organizations.

- ***Causes of Social Movements.*** Some sociologists seek the roots of social movements in social and economic deprivation; others look to the resources and organizations aggrieved persons can muster as providing the key to an understanding of social movements.
- ***Types of Social Movements.*** An **ideology** is critical to a social movement. Common forms of social movements include **revolutionary, reform, resistance,** and **expressive movements.**
- ***Social Revolution.*** **Social revolutions** are most likely to occur when: (1) a good deal of political power is concentrated in the state, (2) the military is no longer a reliable tool for suppressing domestic disorders, (3) political crises weaken the existing regime, and (4) a substantial segment of the population mobilizes in uprisings.
- ***Terrorism.*** Although what constitutes **terrorism** is a matter of social definition, sociologists have come to see terrorism as a new mode of warfare with far-reaching implications.

16

Secularism and Sociology

INTRODUCTION

"The crying evil in the east is not religion – they have religion enough – but it is bread that the suffering millions of burning Indians cry out for. It is an insult to a starving man to teach him metaphysics." said Swami Vivekananda. And it is the metaphysics of secularism that the Indian polity uses to solve the problem of communal tensions. The Blacks Law Dictionary defines 'secular' as not sacred, not ecclesiastical, and concerned with the affairs of the world. Religion is necessary. It is socially useful because it constitutes a moral force and an element of sociability. This religion must be a positive religion, that is to say, a religion based on the reference to revelation, a tradition that is associated with the church and not a religion that promotes religious disharmony leading to communal violence. The need for secularism is, supposedly, a self contained argument.

The term 'secular' is a Christian term that finds its original meaning in the Christian context. *Saeculum*, which is the ordinary Latin word for century or age, takes on a different connotation when applied to the age of separation of State from religion. This meant that the regulation of life would be distinguished from the confessional in the church. This strategy proved to be important because it helped in a peaceful coexistence of different faiths. It also allowed for a convergence of religions toward a common commitment. The secularism of today is built on the original distinction but also involves a transformation of it. Secularism today ensures that religion will exist only in the individual's private sphere. The State upholds no religion and pursues no religious goals. This is known as the 'common ground' approach wherein a common ground is set for all religions. Unfortunately this model, though ideal, has its weakness in the fact that or widening band of contradictory religious and metaphysical commitments arise leading to tension. One of the problems with secularism is that it challenges the independent ethic of the majority community which believes that because of the mere fact that they are the majority of the nation they have the prescriptive right of superiority.

People with communalist tendencies are also suspicious of religious believers who profess secularism since they consider them as either lukewarm supporters of the religions that they follow or as potential traitors to it and religious belonging finds itself threatened by a mere "concept".

Although secularism may be a western concept it has been transported and transformed in the eastern context with colonialism. In eastern nations where religions are numerous and harmony is alien the western concept of secularism forms what is called an 'overlapping consensus'. This is where the will of the majority is imposed on the minority and their consent is gained by a mere strength in numbers. Here the independent ethic is subdued so as to enable the political ethic to achieve its aims of human rights, sovereignty, freedom and equality. And since not many nations can plausibly claim that their citizens coincide in any real sense with a single ethnic or religious group there is a need for a subjugation of the independent ethic of the majority in the interest of the greater common good.

What we live in today is a society of transformation wherein social identity and social space depends on the will of the majority. There has been a transformation from hierarchical societies to horizontal societies with the enactment of laws that propounded equality and justice for all. One of the most striking developments in independent India is the successful emergence of a secular State encompassing the bulk of the world's Hindus. That is to state that we have emerged from the hierarchical colonial system into a system that stands for equality under the law. However there appears to be a disagreement as to what a secular State implies. The many theories that have been propounded in this regard are as follows

- The implication of aloofness from religion
- Impartiality towards religion
- Corrective oversight of religion
- Equal indulgence of all religions.

There is, however, a consensus on the fact that public life is not guided by religious doctrines and that every religion enjoys freedom and respect. The concept of secularism enunciated in the Constitution and upheld by the Supreme Court has been left unpracticed by the people although it propounds 'equality' and 'justice' for all. It is left unpracticed since for any democracy to function their needs to be a relatively strong commitment on the part of their citizens in terms of identity, beliefs and unity. In other words the modern democratic State needs a healthy degree of patriotism, a strong sense of identification with the polity and the willingness to make sacrifices for the public common good. Although as a nation we came to have unity in diversity what is evident from our flawed practices of secularism is that we have diversity in unity. Secularism has remained a thorny issue as people are unwilling to sacrifice their micro level commitments and ideologies for the greater common good and secularism without a strong common allegiance is likely to fail as it so obviously has.

In attempting to draw a historical perspective to the concept of secularism Partha Chatterjee traces the equality before law to 1858 when the crown assumed power and instituted uniform codes of civil and criminal Law. However the State did not bring personal law into the spectrum of uniformity since it did not want to intervene in matters close to the heart of religious doctrine and practice. The rise of nationalism also led to the refusal on the part of the Indian elite to let the colonial power intervene in areas which were regarded as crucial to the cultural identity of the nation. This has often been mistaken as the 'nonintervention of State in matters of religion', when in reality it was the apprehension on the part of the colonial state to intervene into matters of religion which they knew would have adverse socio-political effects on colonial rule. There were however overwhelming tides of social reform which after independence led to a sudden spate of new legislations on religious and social matters. This reformist agenda was carried out most comprehensively during the making of the Constitution. During discussions when objections were raised that in seeking changes in personal law, the State was intervening in the right to religious freedom B. R. Ambedkar's reply was simply that "The religious conceptions in this country are so vast that they cover every aspect of life from birth to death. There is nothing which is not religion and if personal law is to be saved I am assured that social matters will come to a standstill. " What is obvious from the statement is his belief that secular principles laid down in the Constitution are amendable for the greater common good.

Another associated problem with secularism in the Constitution of India is that it has been progressively linked with toleration. Toleration is the willing acceptance of something of which one disapproves but secularism is the willing acceptance of all religions. The term toleration presupposes disapproval and if India states is that it is a tolerant nation there is a natural presupposition of disapproval of certain religions that exist in India. However if we were to state that we were secular we would then remove the negative connotation to the term toleration.

But tolerance itself can exist only when the people of a nation see themselves as made up of equal members, bounded by common enterprise and working toward a common goal can any common ideology that is based on equality succeed. Until then the more complicated ideology of secularism will remain the hegemony of the majority which is forced upon the minority. The minority groups slowly come to feel that their way of seeing things is different from that of the majority; they feel that they aren't understood and consequently being unwilling to accommodate this difference they feel systematically unheard. Religious tension or any communal tension for that matter can be traced to this basic dichotomy. Secularism may be the need and necessity of democratic life in religiously diverse societies but as long as splinter communalist groups with sectarian ideologies like Hindu chauvinists and Muslim fundamentalists exist and as long as they are in a position to influence popular consciousness for political power secularism will remain an idealistic concept.

The question that asked before and is asked again is "Whether there exists a dichotomy between the secular principles laid down in the Constitution of India and practice of the same principles by the legislature, the courts and in actual practice vis-a-vis society?".What needs to be understood is how the utopia of secularism as envisaged in the Preamble and interpreted by the courts differs from the distopia in the contemporary scenario.

However the difference exists in the fact that the question is raised here so as to argumentatively point out the dichotomy between the secular principles laid down in the Constitution of India and in the reality situation, the reasons for the same and to provide a probable theoretical solution. The term that is carefully used here is 'theoretical', since actual practice rarely reflects idealistic concepts and more so when idealistic concepts are unclear and incompatible in socio culturally diverse eastern nations where religious affinities oft negate national unity.

CHAPTER I-SECULARISM IN THE CONSTITUTION OF INDIA

In Europe secularism gained legitimacy from the confrontation between science and theology and the emergence of a utilitarian philosophy. The belief in religious interpretations of the universe began with Nicholas Copernicus' theory that negated the geo-centric nature of the universe that was propounded by the church. Later in the Victorian age Darwin obliterated the theory of genesis with his *Origin of the Species.* Secularism began essentially as an anti theocratic ideology. With Bentham and the utilitarian philosophy of the "greatest good for the greatest number" discrimination based on religion was no longer a practicable philosophy nor was the intervention of the church in the state. In India the experience of inculcation of secular principles in the Constitution was a different experience altogether.

The Need for Secularism in the Constitution of India

Secularism is the equality of all religions or equal respect for all religions but the Constitution of India which is the ultimate legal political and social document is not explicitly secular and does not require us to be so. The framers of the Constitution stood for a secular India.It is common knowledge that Nehru had no firm or marked belief in or commitment to religion, while in strong contrast, Gandhi's personal life was imbued with his attachment to religion Gandhi's writings were prolific and his views pronounced on many matters. Gandhi's notions on religion and State are best expressed in Hind Swaraj, which was first written in Gujarati in 1909 and translated in 1910. This utopian concept of *Ramrajya* imagined return to a perfect system of division of labour practising reciprocity and not competition. He claimed that "India cannot cease to be one nation, because people belonging to different religions live in it... In no part of the world are one nationality and one religion synonymous terms; nor ever been so in India." Gandhi had his unswerving purpose or winning independence for India and the constitution of united nation, and in a society where multiple religions were observed, this nation making project entailed a separation of religion and State. He proclaimed "I swear by my religion, I will diaper it. But it is my personal affair. The State has nothing to do with it. The State will look after your secular welfare, health, communication, foreign relations, currency and so on, but not my religion. That is everybody's personal concern. "

It was in affirmation of the separation that Nehru wrote in 1945 "I'm convinced that the future government will not associate itself with any religious faith but equal freedom to all religious functions." During the Constitutional Assembly debates, Nehru held that the establishment of the secular State in this sense was a matter of faith; and act of faith above all for the majority community because they will have to demand straight that they can behave towards other minorities in a generous, fair and just manner. Nehru, Gandhi and some other Congress leaders maintained that the essential features of their position was that there shall be no State discrimination on the grounds of religion or religious affiliation against any person professing any particular form of religious faith, and that there should not be any State patronage of any religion or extension of patronage to any one religion to the exclusion of, or in preference to, others.

In current Indian political circles the Nehruvian conception of secular policies, espoused by many Indian supporters of liberal democracy, does not mean the rejection of the transcendental values of religion or that society should be religious; on the contrary, there is acceptance that all religions are meaningful and that they should have valid place in the life of the nation. However, religion is not competent in defining nationality or citizenship. The State should be neutral as between the country's many religions and tolerant of all.

Sarvepalli Radhakrishnan gives a qualification to the Indian specifications of secular politics. He stated that "When India is said to be a secular State of, it does not mean we reject the reality of an unseen spirit of the relevance of religion to life or that we exalt irreligion. It does not mean that secularism itself becomes a positive religion or that the State assumes divine prerogatives. Though faith in the Supreme is the basic principle of the Indian tradition, the Indian state will not identify itself with or be controlled by any particular religion. The holds that no one religion should be accorded special privileges in national life or international relations for that would be a violation of the basic principles of democracy and contrary to the basic interests of religion and government.. No person should suffer any form of disability or discrimination because of his religion but all alike should be free to share to the fullest degree in the common life. This is the basic principle involved in the separation of church and State."

During the debates in the Constituent Assembly, Prime Minister Nehru declared that secularism was an ideal to be achieved and that establishment of a secular State was an act of faith. He explained his vision thus:

"By secular State, as I understand, the State is not going to make any discrimination whatsoever on the ground of religion or community against any person professing any particular form of religious faith. This means in essence that no particular religion in the State will receive any State patronage whatsoever. The State is not going to establish, patronize or endow any particular religion to the exclusion of or in preference to others and that no citizen in the State will have any preferential treatment or will be discriminated against simply on the ground that he professed a particular form of religion.. At the same time we must be very careful to see that in this land of ours we do not deny to anybody the right not only to profess or practise but also propagate any particular religion."

SECULARISM AS ENUNCIATED IN THE CONSTITUTION OF INDIA

For the first 25 years of the existence of the Indian Constitution the word secular did not feature anywhere and it was only after the **44th Constitutional Amendment Act** of 1978 that the word secular was introduced into the Preamble. The Amendment Act of 1978 sought to define secular in the following words: secular means a republic in which there is equal respect for all religions however this definition of secular is contrary to the popularly accepted western notions.

The term religion has not been defined in the Constitution of India, but the Supreme Court has given it an expansive content. The guarantee under Article 25, subject to certain exceptions confers a fundamental right on every person not merely to entertain such religious beliefs as are allowed to him by his judgment or conscience, but also to exert his beliefs and ideas in such overt and outward acts and practices as are sanctioned and enjoined by his religion, and further to propagate and disseminate his religious beliefs, ideas and views for the benefit and edification of others.

The state is empowered under Article 25 (2) (a) to regulate secular activities associated with religious practices.

"We, the People of India, are having solemnly resolved to constitute India into a SOVEREIGN SOCIALIST **SECULAR** DEMOCRATIC REPUBLIC..."

Thus does the Preamble of the Constitution of India now explicitly state that we are a secular state. Three principles are usually mentioned as being the essential characteristics of a secular State.

1. The first is the principle of liberty which requires that the State permit the practice of any religion, within the principles set by certain other basic rights which the State is also required to protect.
2. The second is the principle of equality which requires that the State is not give preference to one religion over another.
3. The third principle is that of neutrality which is best described as the requirement that the States not give preference to the religious over the non religious.

This leads, in combination with the liberty and equality principles, what is known in American constitutional law as the wall of separation doctrine meaning that the State does not involve itself with religious affairs or organisations. To understand secular practice in India we must see whether three principles have been invoked and more importantly whether they have been followed. The principle of equality which implies the right to freedom of religion has been incorporated in the Constitution which gives to every citizen quite specifically the right to profess practice and propagate religion and also certain collective rights of religion however the State retains the right to regulate any activity that may be associated with religious practice so as to provide for social welfare and reform. The principle of liberty exists only for the protection of the universal basic right of equality has guaranteed by Article 14 of the Constitution of India. Article 14 has been interpreted by the courts as being one that prohibits the state from discriminating against any citizen on the basis only of religion and Article 15 of the Constitution explicitly states as much. The principle of the secular State being the separation of State and religion has also been recognised by the Constitution which declares that there should be no official State religion, no religious instruction in State schools and no taxes to support any particular religion.

The Indian Constitution spelt out in several articles the main provisions regarding the secular state even before the term secularism was first introduced into it in 1976. First it guarantees freedom of religion to individuals as well as to religions, to any religious denomination or any section thereof. Second it guarantees equality of citizenship that is no discrimination on grounds of religion and quality of opportunity in public employment. No discrimination in educational institutions and no communal electorates.

Third, it provides for the separation of the state and religion. That is, no special taxes for the promotion of religion, and no religious instruction in state educational institutions. It is clear that the intention of the constitution is neither to oppose religion nor to promote a rationalization of culture, but merely to maintain the neutrality and impartiality of the state in matters of religion.

However some critics believe that the concept of secularism in the Constitution is contradictory at the very outset since it has a Hindu majoritarian tilt. Attention has been drawn by the critics of secularism to articles in the constitution such as Article 48which deals with the slaughter of cows. Article 48 states that *"Organisation of agriculture and animal husbandry.-The State shall endeavour to organise agriculture and animal husbandry on modern and scientific lines and shall, in particular, take steps for preserving and improving the breeds, and prohibiting the slaughter, of cows and calves and other milch and draught cattle."*

This raises a question as to the credibility of the secular principles in the Constitution since the prohibition of cow slaughter is obviously to accommodate the Hindu population and more so in their support. However it is contended in this regard that if the Constitution was unsecular in the first place there would not have been the need for a secular ideology. Secularism was introduced by the "right thinking" members of the constituent and not the "right" thinking members of the constituent assembly.

It is however submitted in this regard that Secularism in the Constitution of India has been a failure as far as implementation is concerned only because it is inherently incompatible with the socio-cultural scenario that is prevalent in the country. The primary reason for this is that India is a heterogeneous society that is formed out of a combination of diverse homogenous groups that live in close proximity but lack communal harmony. Any agenda can only be implemented if there is a consensus and a reconciliation to adopt the agenda. A secular agenda is a classic example of a concept that has been include into the constitution although there is not consensus for the adoption for the same. The task therefore is to create that consensus.

EARLY JUDGMENTS OF THE SUPREME COURT

From time to time the Supreme Court of India has been interpreting the concept of secularism in the Indian Constitution differently and obviously, the perceptions of secularism vary from Bench to Bench. It is further unfortunate that the distinction between tolerance and secularism never seems to have been made by the Indian judiciary and this has left the meaning of secularism in the Constitution as ambiguous as ever.

The question that is or raised in this regard to his whether the meaning of secularism in depends on the whims and caprices of the individual Judges. It is also contended that the interpretations of the courts with reference to the concept of secularism has been altered over the years so as to suit the political conditions that is prevalent in the country.

The Supreme Court expressed its views on the secular nature of the Constitution for the first time in *Sardar Taheruddin Syedna Saheb* v. *State of Bombay* wherein *Ayyangar, J.*, explained:

"Articles 25 and 26 embody the principle of religious toleration that has been the characteristic feature of Indian civilisation from the start of history. The instances and periods when this feature was absent being merely temporary aberrations. Besides, they serve to emphasise the secular nature of the Indian democracy which the founding fathers considered to be the very basis of the Constitution."

In *M.R. Balaji* v. *State of Mysore* the Supreme Court spoke of "the noble ideal of a secular welfare State set up by the Constitution". In *Kesavananda Bharati* v. *State of Kerala* the Supreme Court reiterated that secularism was a part of the basic structure of the Constitution. Enumerating the basic features of the Constitution, Sikri, C.J. named "secular character of the Constitution" as one of them. Shelat and Grover, JJ stated that "secular and federal character of the Constitution" were among the main ingredients of the basic structure enumerated therein. Jaganmohan Reddy, J., stated clearly that "Liberty of thought, expression, belief, faith and worship" could not be amended at any cost as they are part of the basic features of the Constitution and by the 42nd Amendment to the Constitution, the words "socialist" and "secular" were inserted in the preamble qualifying the words "democratic republic".

However in the case of *Ahmedabad St. Xaviers College Society* v. *State of Gujarat* the Supreme Court held, in contradiction that "Secularism in the context of our Constitution means only an attitude of live and let live developing into the attitude of live and help live." This judgment is akin to the modern concept of secularism that finds acceptance socially. In the case of *Ziyauddin Burhanuddin Bukhari* v. *Brijmohan Ram Das Mehra* the Supreme Court went on to define the concept of secularism in the realm of philosophy and in utilitarian terms. The Court set the role of the State to be neutral or impartial in extending its benefit to citizens of all castes and creeds and cast a duty on the State to ensure through its laws that disabilities are not imposed based on persons practising or professing any particular religion.

In the landmark judgment of *S.R. Bommai* v. *Union of India* the Court in no uncertain terms declared that secularism is part of the basic structure. In this case a Bench of nine Judges expounded the basic feature of secularism at great length. It was pointed out that the concept of secularism was very much embedded in our constitutional philosophy. By the 44th Amendment what was implicit was made explicit. But the complication arose in formulating a definition. And it was merely stated that secularism is based on the "principles of accommodation and tolerance". What was heartening about the judgment was that there was unanimity about secularism being a part of the basic structure. However, there are individual observations by some judges about are the essential features of the Constitution and whether they form part of the basic structure of the Constitution. Justices Sawant and Kuldip Singh mention "social pluralism and pluralist democracy" as part of the basic structure. Justice Ramaswami describes, amongst others, "socialism and social justice, religious tolerance and fraternity as essential features".

However in later cases such as *Ismael Faruqui* v. *Union of India, R.C. Podayal* and *Ram Janambhoomi case* started diluting the active, positive concept of secularism based on scientific thinking it had advocated in the *Bommai case*. An indication of this trend had been laid in Court's justification of its concept of secularism by quoting extensively from Indian scriptures. Verma, J. quoted from the *Yajur Veda, Atharva Veda* and *Rig Veda* to justify its concept of secularism: '*Sarwa Dharma Sambhava*' i.e., tolerance of all religions. It is for a fact impractical and dangerous to actually justify secularism by religious scriptures of the majority community which obviously will not find acceptance by the larger population.

THE 'HINDUTVA JUDGMENTS' AND AFTER

The confusion stood confounded with the three cases known as the 'Hindutva Judgments', the major and crucial one being *Prabhoo's case*. The opinion of *Verma, J.* indicates the shift made by the Court from its stance on secularism advocated in *S.R. Bommai*.

The Court shifted its earlier position and took a different stand on three major grounds:

1. The Court enunciated that a speech with a secular stance alleging discrimination against any particular religion and promising the removal of the imbalance cannot be treated as an appeal on the ground of religion, as its thrust is for promoting secularism.
2. The Court again seemed to have turned away from the *Bommai case* and the 'constitutional duty' of the Court to get political parties in line with secularism, advising leaders to be only "more circumspect and careful in the kind of language they use."

3. The Court equated Hinduism and Hindutva with Indianisation:

"The words 'Hinduism' or 'Hindutva' are not necessarily to be understood and construed narrowly, confined only to the strict Hindu religious practices, unrelated to the culture and ethos of the people of India, depicting the way of life of the Indian people."

In the case of *Valsamma Paul (Mrs) v Cochin University* the court seems to have gone back to the old soft stance on secularism equating it with tolerance, while stressing the need for an 'integrated Bharat'. Yet in *Bansilal* v. *State of A.P* the court seems to rely on the *S.R. Bommai* dictum that the State can regulate personal laws citing the threat to the unity and integrity of the nation. Interestingly, the Judge in another part of the judgment accepts Hinduism as the major religion and Hindus as the majority, and that the right of freedom of religion is available to Hindus also.

There unfortunately seems to be no consistency in these cases and the opinion of judges on the issue of secularism in actual practice and as it has been represented in the constitution appears to oscillate based on the social acceptance rather than rendering social justice.

The Court has clearly not moved an inch from its original perspective on secularism as enunciated in the early cases of the 1950's and 1960's. The line of thinking the Court seems to be that 'Secularism' is toleration based on tradition' in what may seem to be a mute acceptance of the hindu belief of tolerance and acceptance of other religions which intellectuals and leaders in India, especially Hindus who see secularism by and large in terms of the ancient hindu ideas of tolerance equality of all religions would be more than willing to accept. For instance, Radhakrishnan wrote in 1955 "It may appear somewhat strange that our government should be a secular one while our culture is rooted in spiritual values. Secularism here does not mean irreligion or atheism or even stress on material comforts. It proclaims that it lays stress on the universality of spiritual values which may be attained in a variety of ways." This unity of spiritual experience despite doctrinal differences is the meaning of the secular conception of the state although it is not generally understood. It would be readily admitted that this Hindu model has made a generally positive contribution to the evolution of a tolerant and liberal culture that informs the consciousness of a vast number of people, Hindus and non Hindus in India.

However it is not surprising that this model of pluralism or secularism has proven to be inadequate to meet the needs of a modern India that is struggling to create a democratic and egalitarian society since no model of secularism can be built on the ideology of one religious group even if it is the majority community. This is especially so, since its mode of toleration has historically included absorption, subjugation and marginalization of religious minorities.

This clearly does not separate the functions of the state from that of religious practice. It is however the opinion of many that the court may have erred but it has certainly erred on the side of reason since secularism is too fundamental to be compromised.

Although this may be true from an on the surface analysis of the judgment of the judgments of the Supreme Court with regard to the concept of secularism it is clear that over the years what has been held as a "basic feature" of the constitution has been diluted. What was initially considered as a pluralistic concept has been progressively redefined on the basis of the prevalent political scenario.

The initial judgments were delivered in the Nehruvian era that believed in the politics of accommodation and this meant that secularism had to be defined in terms that suited the politics of the age that believed in the participation and representation for all. Gradually with the dilution of socialist principles with the fall of the Nehru regime and the progressive victories of communal elements in the general elections the court has followed suit and interpreted secularism to suit the politicians at the top and the vote banks at the bottom. It is further submitted in this regard that the judgments of the court may have been influenced by the party in power. Although it is not intended to cast any aspersions on the integrity of the judiciary it is certainly strange that the judgments have a significant 'Hindutva' tilt to it. It is unfortunate that communal differences on secular principles seem to have tainted the reputation of the judiciary.

SECULARISM, MODERNITY AND COMMUNAL IDEOLOGIES

Secularism is questioned on the ground that there is a need for a new philosophy. The crisis of secularism in India is that it is an alien concept that has been unwisely imposed, and is therefore the root of the problem rather than the solution. It is because there is therefore a drift from the objective of secularism that the very concept and validity of the adoption of secularism into the Indian Constitution has been questioned.

Secularism in the state and society need to be distinguished since the state, although it is bound by the constitutional and legal framework to be secular, has been unable to implement secular provisions in practice. Communalism and has therefore succeeded in eroding the foundations of our secular constitutional framework.

Prejudices based on caste and religion is so deeply embedded that they cannot be banished by mere inclusion of secular clauses in the Constitution. The state is also accused are of having neglected to promote tolerance and respect for other religions which are held to be in the essential aspects of secularism. An example of this is that although the Constitution guarantees the right of religious minorities and to have their own religious and educational institutions no positive action has been taken by the state to honour constitutional provisions.

In this regard Madan states that secularism has achieved the opposite of its intentions because it trivializes differences and the notion of unity and is thus impracticable and a "Phantom concept" in India. He claims that it is this incorporation that has caused an erosion of religion since existing differences have been replaced by artificial unity.

Ashis Nandy states and that the ideology of secularism is absurd since it merely provides mere egalitarian semantics to an alien concept which has been illogically incorporated. He claims that toleration should be derived from the faith of the citizens rather than theories of statecraft.

M N Srinivas opines that the Western connotation of secularism as a separation of the church from the state is a concept that is ethnocentric and is incapable of universalisation.

Secularism is considered as being unalterably linked with modernity. Modernity brings in its wake several important processes of change.

The most important of these are

1. Differentiation of the level of institutions, structures and functions resulting in the withdrawal of religion from such social spheres as education and marriage
2. Development of pluralism at the level of social groups including religion and world views resulting in the pluralisation and revitalization of the world
3. Rationalization as described by Max Weber which refers to the emergence of a scientific rational world view that was eventually expected to strip society of its myth, miracle, mystery and magic thus making it disenchanted
4. The development of a critical consciousness that reveals the ideologies that are hidden in the institutions and beneath the structures of religions

The end result of the same being the separation of the State from religion. Since the late 1960's because of the mushrooming proliferation of various ascriptive identities (identities that are ascribed to them) along with Hindu-Muslim communal politics all parties have reoriented their political strategies to ensure that no party can acquire any advantage on this score. All parties take into account religion caste etc so that the advantages are either evened out or shared, so that the increasing salience of ascriptive identities in the Indian democracy have been accompanied by a corresponding decrease in the electoral weightage of any single ascriptive identity in the Hindutva or the national level.

However there is widespread concern that Indian secularism is facing a serious crisis primarily for two reasons

1. Growth of communalist politics
2. Increasing belief amongst the people that secularism is a threat to their religion

In this regard Ashis Nandy is of the opinion that secularism in India has exhausted all its possibilities and is today positively harmful since it is being manipulated by the polity to perpetuate atrocities. M N Srinivas argues that there exists a grave ideological and spiritual crisis and needs a more humanistic and utilitarian concept as opposed to the ephemeral concept of secularism as laid down in the Constitution of India. It is their opinion that secularism today is being utilised for institutional greed, materialism, corruption and the culture of consumption.

HINDUISM AND 'HINDUTVA'

Communal politics has always thrived off elemental passions based on myths and folklores around a perceived stereotype oppressor existential or historical and has also had an ideology to justify its own belligerence. Communal politics in India has also broadly followed the same historical pattern. Not just communal politics in the well known religious identities but the increasing proliferation of many other relativist ascriptive identities around language caste tribe and spatial locations in India in recent times have followed much the same pattern of mass mobilisation. Hinduism may be defined as the beliefs, practices, and socio religious institutions of the Hindus. However over the years with the coming to power of the BJP and the influence of the RSS the term Hindutva has come to be mistaken for Hinduism. This unfortunate misconception has by far led to apprehensions to be cast on the secular character of our nation. The secular perceptions of Hindu communal politics especially after the Ayodhya dispute seems to have been heavily influenced by the impact of relatively recent events around which a lot of counter myths have been conjured by a section of new secular activists and a certain level of demonisation of the communal ideology and communal politics particularly its hindu version who claim that it poses a qualitatively different kind of threat to India's liberal democracy in its present tenuous stage the perception of its strengths, resilience and potentials appears to be both unreal and counter productive.

Partha Chatterjee looks at secularism and asks the basic question whether secularism is an adequate or even appropriate ground on which to meet the political challenge of Hindu majoritarianism. The author in his analysis of the Hindutva campaign states that the dogma which is propounded has undermined the character of a secular Indian state for the sake of political thrust and public appeal. The claim of the Hindu right is that the State must take action against those who do not confirm to their own version of the national culture.

The Hindu fundamentalists claim that secularism is based on the appeasement of minorities rather than equality of religions. They claim that secularism in India has undermined nationalism and has become a potent factor for disintegration of the country. The benevolent fundamentalists also provide the "ideal" solution to the problem of implementation of secular principles since they claim that Hinduism is the true religion of tolerance and therefore only a country that is based on Hinduism can be truly secular since secularism is ideally based on toleration for all religions. However the Hindu idea of tolerance does not include the three most important ingredients of secularism

1. Rejection of theocracy
2. Equality of all citizens irrespective of their faith
3. Full freedom of religion and worship

The attempt of the Hindu fundamentalists is a project Hinduism as a secular and tolerant philosophy which embraces various sects within its folds with its objective is a tolerant India. However their ideology reveals an anti secular thrust since there is an attempt to create an artificially permanent majority through the assimilation of minorities and drastically limits the scope of religious freedom. The attempt has been made to construct an Indian nationalist consciousness in terms of Hinduism in the image of a modern western state. The concept of Hindutva therefore is largely constructed in relation to the opposition of Muslims and Christians. The appeal of the Hindutva elements is based on tradition which has been altered to suit their needs. A classic example of this alteration is the politicization of Muslims as antinational. Comparisons may be drawn in this regard of the Hindutva forces to Nazi Germany. The Nazis politicized the fact that the Jews were responsible for the humiliation of Germany in the First World War and harped on the decadence of the Jewish race. The Hindutva elements do much the same when they talk of Hindu humiliation under Muslim rule and use the Muslims as scapegoats in reasoning out the ills of our country. The Muslims are held responsible for the instigation of every riot. The Muslims are always painted with the wrong colours and the justification for the same is two fold

1. The Muslims are foreigners and thus have no right to live in India unless they adopt the majoritarian hindu culture
2. The Muslim rule in India was a period of continuous oppression of the Hindus and the Muslims must repent for the same

The demolition of the Babri Masjid is an illustration of the attempts to alter "historical wrongs" and create anti Muslim sentiment. It is maintained that the Babri Masjid was constructed at the exact spot where Lord Rama was born and the temple that was erected there was destroyed by Babar and a mosque erected in its place. The mass hysteria generated by the issue culminated in the destruction of the mosque on December 6, 1992. However, the BJP does not considering the destruction of Babri Masjid as an assault on secularism since it is believed that the action has merely corrected "historical wrongs".

The entire approach of the communalist is based on total mistrust of the Muslim community and doubting their loyalty and patriotism and to the country. However it may be seen that, although the Hindutva elements have declared the Hindu State as secular, the end result would be a theocratic state with fascist tendencies wherein the minorities would be second-class citizens. A Hindu state would not only be destructive of secularism but of the basic democratic structure of our nation.

In his scathing critique of the RSS ideology and their Hindutva ideology Sitaram Yechury starts at the very root of the communalist ideologies that have been imbibed by the RSS. These ideologies that were first propagated by M S Golwalkar in his work "We or Our Nationhood Defined". Golwalkar begins his entire exercise by seeking to understand the word "swaraj". He begins by questioning what "swa" is, meaning "we". In the prologue to the book he says: "We stand for national regeneration and not for the haphazard bundle of political rights – the state."

The entire book is an elaboration of the thesis that 'we' means the Hindus and therefore swaraj means the Hindu Raj or the Hindu Rashtra. He treats secularism as virtual blasphemy and argues that "There is a general tendency to affirm that religion is an individual question and should have no place in public and political life. This tendency is based upon a misconception of religion, and has it's origin in those, who have, as a people, no religion worth the name."

In this manner he claims that no other religion is worth the name other than Hinduism and he further asserts that such a religion cannot be ignored in public or private life. The conclusion that the author arrives at is that India as it exists today is needs the ancient Hindu nation and all else does not come under the pale of what he considers to be national. He further claims that all others are either enemies or traitors to the national cause and they can become a part of the national cause only if they merge themselves with the national cause and adopt its culture.

It is held that the Hindu right wants to infuse its own principles of secularism into the constitution so that it may be consistent with its vision of Hindutva and legitimize the notion of Hinduism being a tolerant religion. Minority communalism thus stems from the desire of the minorities to preserve their distinct identity since there exists a perceived threat from the majority community. Whether minority communalism is a byproduct of the hegemonisation of majority communal ideologies is certainly debatable however there is no doubt that it is one of the major determining factors, not only of communalism but also communal violence that stems from the ascriptive identities of the minorities. A significant distinction between majority and minority communalism is that where majority communalism asks for secular state on the basis of Hindu ideology minority communalism emphasise the necessity of secularism but also desire the promotion of separate interests as a religious community without making the atrocious demand for secularism that is based on religion, which would, in essence, redefine the very nature of secularism.

An analysis of minority communities reveals communal tendencies to be most conspicuous among the Muslims. The agenda however is limited to the question of personal laws, maintenance, divorce and other typically combustible issues. It is unfortunate that this community based do not raise issues that would be of more social importance like poverty, hunger, illiteracy and unemployment. It is quite obvious that the leaders in their own self-interest seek to politicize issues of controversy the feed their ballots rather than the stomachs of the already disadvantaged minorities. In this regard Neera Chandoke opines that these communal tendencies manipulate the sentiments of the minorities for political ends.

This may be further seen from reaction to the Ayodhya dispute which focused more on the mobocratic reaction rather than pressing issues like the effects of the violence on the community. Aggressive postures were taken by organisations like the All India Babri Masjid Action Committee and Babri Masjid Movement Coordination Committee which led to furtherance of aggressive rioting.

The major issues emphasised by the Muslim fundamentalists go against the accepted ideals of secularism, which are equality, liberty and rationalism and therefore it constitutes no less a threat to the secular edifice than Hindu fundamentalism.

Hindu communalism and Muslim fundamentalism thus feed on each other. In the process both spread communal poison deeper, threatening the very fabric of our country's unity and integrity. They also act against the interests of the majority that they claim to represent. India is a secular democracy only because a majority of the population has rejected these notions of communal politics. But this is not to say that some of these sectarian ideologies do not find their way into the common consciousness as is evident from communal tension and conflict that has now become a common facet of our daily lives.

CHAPTER IV-DISCOURSE ON COMMUNAL VIOLENCE

Communalism stands for the affinity which an individual may have towards his own community which involves efforts for social and economic upliftment. However communalism in the modern context stands for the exploitation of religion for non religious purposes and has been reduced to an anti thesis of religion. Communalism is where society is divided into religious communities which are different and often opposed to each other. These antagonistic tendencies are termed as communalism. Communalism today has more to do with politics than with religion. Communalism in India is associated typically with Hindu and Muslim communities. Communalism is born out of communal parties and can be traced to several political, social as well and economic factors. Communalism is manifested through fanatical religious movements and exhibited through communal violence. Communalism is used for large scale political mobilisation and has progressive led to the disintegration of the nation. Although it is the result of a particular situation in a particular society, economy and polity, it is neither a correct diagnosis nor a solution to a social situation but an appropriation of a social crisis for political ends since it is the easy route to political power in a state of popular sovereignty opines Bipan Chandra. In general the causes of communal violence can be traced to social economic development accompanied with vote bank politics. The outbreaks of violence are rarely caused by religious dissensions and more so by the attempts of communal parties who wish to divert attention from genuine socio-economic problems by instigating communal differences. Communal violence is collective violence which is based on the discontent of a communal group which arises from the precipitation of a typically not violent campaign. Ram Ahuja mentions two theories which explain why there is a possibility for communal violence in Indian society.

Social Barriers-the minority communities suffer from anxiety and insecurity and communal violence is an offshoot of this insecurity. The insecurity that exists is due to the social barriers created by the social systems of marginalization. The reasons for the creation of social barriers are the increasing expectations of minority communities and the rising incapability to realise these expectations. The result is a perception of deprivation leading to collective effort with violence as the unfortunate consequence.

Theory of Polarization and Cluster Effect-there are three elements to this theory : Polarity, cleavage and cluster. Polarity refers to a sense of belongingness to a particular community.

Cleavage refers to the division of population into two polarities which are typically antagonistic. Cluster, refers to the habitation of a community in a common area at a given time and turn violent because of the bi polarity in identifiable clusters. The close proximity of clusters and common interest result in animosity. The potency of the violence is based on numeric, socio economic, leadership and organisational factors. The ability to control the violence depends on the expediency of the executive wings of the state.

Most communal violence even when between two distinctively identifiable ascriptive identities has involved the equally distinct interest groups and often predominantly so. Under such circumstances violence is communal only in a strictly limited sense. Mainstream secular discourse ignores the possibility of alternative policy options directed at containing communal violence within the continuing reality of multiple versions of communal politics. It refuses to squarely face the important question of whether communal violence can be eliminated from the violent polity that is socially plural in its ascriptive identities. Or on the flipside whether communal politics can be institutionally insulated from violence? Communal politics is located in this basic contradiction.

Communal violence in the post independence can be broadly divided into two era's. The first, into the era between 1950 and 1970 wherein the reasons for communal violence were mainly ascribed to partition and the influence of our "friendly" neighbours. The second era is the one that we blissfully exist in wherein we ascribe communal violence to the rise of fundamentalism. However although the characteristics of the violence in both the era's are much the same the explanations given vary so as suit mass opinion. One issue that is carefully ignored and dexterously fended off is the fact that there are secular principles with unsecular followers.

The following is a graphical representation of the number of instances of communal violence from 1954 – 1989 which shall prove as an invaluable aid in the analysis of communalism in the post independence era.

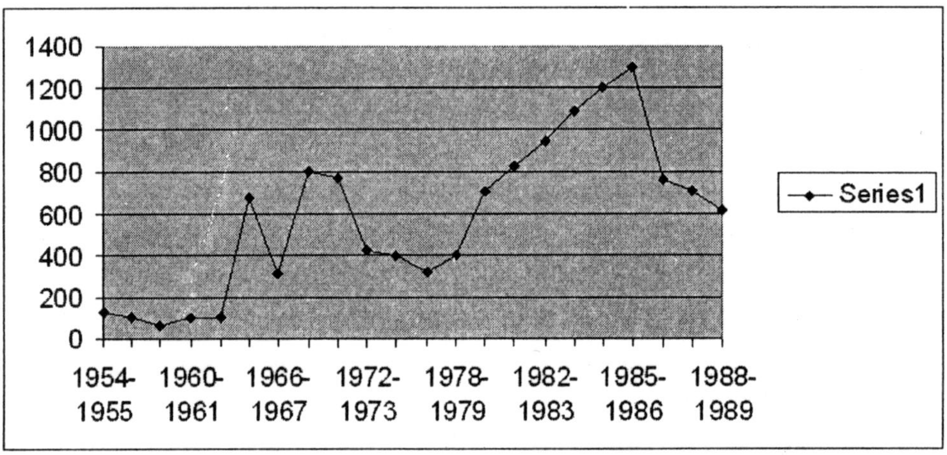

Communal Violence from Independence to the 1970's

Initial occurrences of communal violence before the term 'secular' was introduced into the Constitution were based largely on minor issues that were blown out of proportion by communal forces and then termed as communal riots.

The first major communal bombshell in the post partition era exploded in Jabalpur in 1961 and the reasons for the riot were the acute economic competition between a Hindu and a Muslim bidi manufacturer rather than ideological conflicts that emanated from religions. Economic considerations played a large part in determining the nature of the riot. This riot, although it did not have an ideological basis as is often assumed with communal conflict was so severe that Jawaharlal Nehru took up the initiative to set up a National Integration Council to promote emotional integration in the country. Nehru thought that a body like that would succeed in bringing about some measure of accommodation between Hindus and Muslims.

The next instance of communal violence in Jamshedpur and Calcutta in 1964 relatively insulated from the politics of partition erupted coinciding with the first significant dent in the congress party. In 1965, 1967 and 1968 in Hazratbal, Meerut, and Karimanj in Ahmedabad all coincided in major changes in the polity specifically the congress party. Muslim leaders however were disillusioned with the Nehruvian policy and being perturbed with the increasing communal violence formed organisations like the Majtis-e-Mushawarat so as to pool in their resources and exert some sort of influence upon the political system for realising their demands.

The Mushawarat started a debate about the plight of Muslims in post-independence India but could hardly succeed in raising the consciousness much less putting and end to communal violence especially since communal violence did not have an ideological base rather it had a socio-economic basis. In fact, after Jabalpur a chain of riots broke out in Ranchi, Jamshedpur, Aligarh and other towns brought about by the stream of Hindu refugees coming in from East Pakistan. There is a clear hypothesis that explains that these riots can be explained by what Hitler would term as 'lebensraum' or living space wherein the indigenous communities that lived in the area felt that their living space was threatened and they felt that they needed to resort to violence to retain their predominant right. These riots continued up until the Indo-Pak war in 1965. However in 1968 under the leadership of Indira Gandhi rallied the Muslim population around with her emphasis on secularism. However the Jana Sangh attempted to counter the Congress influence by engineering serious communal trouble in Gujarat and this in turn left Indira Gandhi and the nation's secular principles crippled. The Jana Sangh also succeeded in creating a strong anti-muslim sentiment by making certain claims about the identity of the Muslim community such as

1. The muslim community was alien and did not readily accept Indian culture or respect Hindu deities
2. The resistance of the Muslim community to accept a Uniform Civil Code was taken as a sign of reluctance to accept Indian culture.

The views of the Jan Sangh have found support even from Hindus who claim to be secular since it appeals to the elemental passions that the Hindu majority has lived off over the years. These communal riots were also based on a specific political agenda rather than ideological considerations.

In 1970 in the Bhivandi – Jalgaon riots occurred in which not less than 400 people died but the period after the declaration of emergency in 1975 was comparatively quieter. The primary reason for this was that both Hindu and Muslim political parties were banned. But this of course is no indication of the lack of communalistic feelings although this could probably serve as an indicator of intolerance since it is only because of repressive laws that riots were prevented.

COMMUNAL VIOLENCE IN THE 80'S AND AFTER

'Secular' principles were now explicit in the Constitution and communal violence that erupted after this point appeared more based on ideological considerations rather than political or socio-economic considerations. Communal forces now seemed to have found an enemy against which to direct their ire for political ends. It is clear from the figures that there has been a noticeable increase in communal violence after secular principles were made explicit in the Constitution. The graph rises noticeably after the mid seventies and continues to rise until the mid eighties.

The major explosion of communalistic tendencies came in 1983 as a fall out of the *Shah Bano case*. In 1983 in the Shah Bano case when the Supreme Court held that the Muslim divorcee was entitled to get maintenance from a former husband beyond the period of *iddat* under section 125 of the Criminal Procedure Code it was received by an uproar in from Muslim fundamentalists who claimed the judiciary had unnecessarily interfered with their personal law and thereby exceeded the limits of judicial power. From a purely objective standpoint the Court was right incoming to such a decision because the purpose of Section 127(3) was to avoid double benefit to the divorced Muslim woman. The order by the magistrate cancelling the award of maintenance under section 125 was to be made after being satisfied that either the divorced woman had remarried or she had received some payable to her under any customary or personal law on divorce and the Supreme Court held in this regard that the some under personal law was mere tokenism and nobody could survive on it.

The aggression against a common criminal law in the country by the Muslims was strongly resented by the Hindu community. The left parties also made it a question of strengthening secular laws in the country and opposed the Muslim orthodox view that a Muslim woman upon being divorced could not claim maintenance. Vocal Muslims received the Shah Bano decision with great hurt feeling and the more vocal voices and opposed any change in Muslim personal law and considered orthodoxy synonymous with identity. The Muslim leadership stood its ground and exerted pressure on the Rajiv Gandhi government to change the law and this led to the enactment of the Muslim Women (Protection of Rights on Divorce) Act, 1986 which exempted Muslims from the application of the Section 125 of the Criminal Procedure Code.

The Act was a blatant injustice to Muslim women it was discriminatory against them on the ground of religion and a very unprincipled compromise with the concepts of secularism and equality. The Hindu communalists took advantage of it to show how they were right in denouncing Indian secularism as pseudo secularism. Muslim women were abandoned by the so-called secular politicians and their misery was exploited by the Hindu right for furthering their and the Muslim agenda. This gave the Hindu communalists a legitimacy of sorts and took advantage of the leverage that they had in the demolition of the Babri Masjid in 1992.

The same period has also been marked by increasing recurrence of Hindu Muslim communal violence in its many variations within the generic version. More significantly depending on regional variations there have been a variety of communities have been prone to communal violence. For example in Delhi, in terms of content the Anti Sikh violence of 1984, the Mandir violence of 1990 and the Ayodhya incident show that most communal violence is not limited to muslims alone.

The relatively recent incident at Godhra also must be located in communal tension that is generated by the close proximity of two opposing religious groups. At Godhra a Muslim mob set fire to a train killing 58. More than 700 others died in the orgy of reprisals and counter-reprisals that followed. But the full, shocking truth about what really happened is linked to certain similar macro factors. The confrontation illustrates the volatile mixture of religion, history and extremist politics that plague India, a Hindu-dominated but officially secular nation. In 1947, when India achieved independence and was partitioned to create the Muslim nation of Pakistan, thousands of Hindus fleeing Pakistan settled in Godhra. Enraged that Muslims in Pakistan had evicted them, they vented their anger at Godhra's Muslims, burning their homes and businesses with truckloads of gasoline. Since then, government officials have deemed the city one of the country's most "communally sensitive" places. In 1981, Godhra was racked by the worst civil riots in its history. Curfew was clamped on the place for an entire year. When it was finally lifted, the Muslims fled the old town, building themselves crude cement villas on wasteland behind the bazaar. Again in 1992, it was wracked by riots, some started by Muslims and others by Hindus. There has since been little interaction between the groups, which regard each other with suspicion and this was exemplified in the violent attack on the Sabarmati Express that Godhra. The Hindu fundamentalists have used this incident to fuel further hatred against the Muslims. Hindu fascists had came to power in Gujarat on the basis of defamation of Muslims, claiming that they were violent, hostile to Hinduism and disloyal to India. Now, tragically, they seem dangerously close to turning this ugly fantasy into fact. Even though most Muslims in Gujarat, like their counterparts elsewhere, unequivocally condemn the killings in Godhra they are far from being accepted even by the 'secular' Hindu majority.

Communalism in India has always been a game of one upmanship with one religious group trying to upstage the other and all that they have succeeded in doing over the years is to dilute the secular principles laid down in the constitution. We have been degraded to a nation that has legitimate ideals but flawed practices that not only dilute but also stand the ideal on its head and leads to a question of credibility.

CONCLUSION

The secular discourse is often considered to be insensitive to the minorities since it imposes the will of the majority. The insensitivity of the secular discourse and the increase in the level of social violence could explain the secular party's passive endorsement of social violence by a corresponding accretion in the coercive power of the state. Contemporary secular discourse seems to be impervious to this growing phenomenon at its own cost. In its concern exclusively and manifestly with communal parties as being the cause of all communal violence has tended the larger structure of violence in the political system which enables all parties to indulge in periodic violence of its own choice. This is the reason for the lack of evolution of policy options to contain communal violence.

Secular discourse has been intellectually chained around the normative concern around an ideal society and therefore has been a failure. Secular discourse needs to be anchored around the primary nature of state and civil society. This will help in providing it with more political viability in the confrontation with communal politics and communal violence. It will also help in the correction of the secular discourse so as to tackle communal violence and adaptive to a prismatic democratic society. The amendment of the Constitution however is not an option since it could badly hurt the notions of secularism and also because since secularism forms a part of the basic structure of the Constitution it is beyond the reach of the Parliamentary power of amendment. The challenge before the government now is to ensure that Indian secularism can withstand the test of time and more importantly the tests of practicality in an unsecular democracy.

The foremost threat to secularism in India is communalism and communal violence. The inclusion of secularism in the Constitution has not served to reduce communal tension and critics claim that it has merely served to increase the tension in India. This is also evident from the statistical evidence forwarded. Secularization of the constitution has led to the desecularisation of society and a corresponding accretion of communal violence. This reason for this is uncomplicated. The middle class intelligentsia who are supposed to be the supporters and implied enforcers of secularism assume that the inclusion of secularism in the Constitution will take care of sectarian ideologies. This assumption is amateurish to say the least since the intelligentsia play a crucial role in the ideological struggle against communalism and a realization is warranted on their part to play a pivotal role in making secularism more practicable in social reality.

The measures that need to be taken by the state at this juncture to have some sort of a transformation in secularism are

1. There needs to be a link between liberal democracy as enunciated in the Constitution and the secular discourse

2. Any digression from this link is to be met with a direct confrontation of the civil society and the communal elements
3. Repression, which is counterproductive in any form or against any group, must be done away with
4. Secular discourse must shift its concern to widening the social base of democratic consciousness so as to act as a foil against communal ideologies
5. Secular discourse must seek to hegemonize values of reason, restraint and tolerance of alternative world views.

The police and the executive can play a more proactive role in promoting secularism by increased surveillance of communal groups which are known to have a violent bent of mind. They need to keep a check on tension building and keep a watch on behavioral patterns so as to discover group anxieties before they are manifested in the form of violence.

Civil Society has certain alternatives to strengthen the secular principles and these may be found in education and the media. Macaulay in his famous *Minute on Education* in 1835 states that

"We must at present do our best to form a class who may be interpreters between us and the millions whom we govern; a class of persons, Indians in blood and colour, but English in taste, in opinions, in morals and in intellect." This may be reinterpreted in the present context to inculcate secular 'liberal democratic' principles of education which preach tolerance and accommodation. Education leads to an enlightened group of individuals who are more tolerant, unaffected by superstition and understand the characteristics of religions. The education that is offered in this regard must be one that gives importance to science and rationality, promotes universal brotherhood and imbibes social values of toleration and acceptance.

The media can play a proactive role in the prevention and containment of communal ideologies and promote mass awareness. Communalism needs to be separated from State power so as to enable a more pluralistic society.

The family can play a pivotal role in legitimizing a concept such as secularism. The American sociologist Talcott Parsons believed that the two most important functions of the modern family are the primary socialization of children and the stabilization of adult personalities through marriage and the raising of children. In the present context it is worthwhile to look especially at primary socialization. Primary socialization refers to the training of children during their earliest years, whereas secondary socialization refers to later influences on the development of the child's personality and learning activities, such as his involvement with teachers and with other children at school. Primary socialization is in most societies carried out essentially within the family as part of child rearing.

Freud claimed that in the process of child rearing there are three stages. Biological, psychological and social/moral. The one which has immediate application is the social or moral stage in which one develops a conscience to adapt to the ideals of his society. A person is considered socially and emotionally mature only if his behaviour is approved of by the social group that one belongs to. The major influences that the family and the immediate social environment has in this regard are four fold i.e. hereditary influences of community oriented dislike, directional influence of paternal authority that influences perceptions, emotional or temperamental experience and association with peer groups with similar perceptions. In India however forward looking a family might be it does not attempt to sensitize the children to be more conducive to harmonious relations with people of other communities. In fact families in India enhance communal disharmony by influencing the younger ones during the process of socialisation to instinctively dislike people of another community. This is further enhanced by the associations that the family has which is typically only with people of the same religion. Therefore communal hatred is instinctively picked up by the children and they may turn out to be proactive members of communal parties by the time they reach the age of ten.

The proactive role that the family can play at this juncture are two fold. The first at the level of primary socialisation where the parent tries to inculcate and cultivate a sense of communal harmony in the children. If the parents are exposed to value education then they will inculcate in their children these secular sensibilities. The second is at the level of education and schooling. If the parents were inclined to educate their children in schools that have a more liberal outlook rather than closed sectarian ideologies the result would be a more pluralistic secular society.

Unless these measures are taken and taken in a proactive manner and more importantly taken fast, India can certainly expect a spike in the graph that had shown declining trends after the mid 80's. Although statistics are unavailable it would not be presumptuous to assume that the graph would show an increasing trend after 1992 with increasing incidence of communal violence and more importantly the rise of majoritarian politics. Be as that may it is submitted that there is a possibility of an improvement of the situation with the implementation of the aforesaid proactive measures. With all due respect to the critics of secularism who claim that it is an ideology that is impracticable it may be seen from the aforementioned arguments that the option before the state and the society is not to abandon secularism but to transcend the problems and to strengthen the secular framework if we are to live in a more pluralistic society.

CONSTITUTIONAL PROVISIONS REGARDING THE SECULAR STATE

I. Freedom of Religion

Article 25. Freedom of conscience and free profession, practice and propagation of religion.-

(1) Subject to public order, morality and health and to the other provisions of this Part, all persons are equally entitled to freedom of conscience and the right freely to profess, practise and propagate religion.

(2) Nothing in this article shall affect the operation of any existing law or prevent the State from making any law-

(a) Regulating or restricting any economic, financial, political or other secular activity which may be associated with religious practice;

(b) Providing for social welfare and reform or the throwing open of Hindu religious institutions of a public character to all classes and sections of Hindus.

Explanation I.-The wearing and carrying of kirpans shall be deemed to be included in the profession of the Sikh religion.

Explanation II.-In sub-clause (b) of clause (2), the reference to Hindus shall be construed as including a reference to persons professing the Sikh, Jain or Buddhist religion, and the reference to Hindu religious institutions shall be construed accordingly.

II. Collective Freedom of Religion

Article 26. Freedom to manage religious affairs.-Subject to public order, morality and health, every religious denomination or any section thereof shall have the right-

(a) To establish and maintain institutions for religious and charitable purposes;

(b) To manage its own affairs in matters of religion;

(c) To own and acquire movable and immovable property; and

(d) To administer such property in accordance with law.

Article 30. Right of minorities to establish and administer educational institutions.-

(1) All minorities, whether based on religion or language, shall have the right to establish and administer educational institutions of their choice.

[(1A) In making any law providing for the compulsory acquisition of any property of any educational institution established and administered by a minority, referred to in clause (1), the State shall ensure that the amount fixed by or determined under such law for the acquisition of such property is such as would not restrict or abrogate the right guaranteed under that clause.]

(2) The State shall not, in granting aid to educational institutions, discriminate against any educational institution on the ground that it is under the management of a minority, whether based on religion or language

1. Ins. by the Constitution (Forty-fourth Amendment) Act, 1978, s. 4 (w.e.f. 20-6-1979).
2. **The sub-heading "Right to Property" omitted by s. 5, ibid. (w.e.f. 20-6-1979).**

III. Citizenship

Article 15. Prohibition of discrimination on grounds of religion, race, caste, sex or place of birth.-

(1) The State shall not discriminate against any citizen on grounds only of religion, race, caste, sex, place of birth or any of them.

(2) No citizen shall, on grounds only of religion, race, caste, sex, place of birth or any of them, be subject to any disability, liability, restriction or condition with regard to-

(a) Access to shops, public restaurants, hotels and places of public entertainment; or

(b) The use of wells, tanks, bathing ghats, roads and places of public resort maintained wholly or partly out of State funds or dedicated to the use of the general public.

(3) Nothing in this article shall prevent the State from making any special provision for women and children.

(4) Nothing in this article or in clause (2) of article 29 shall prevent the State from making any special provision for the advancement of any socially and educationally backward classes of citizens or for the Scheduled Castes and the Scheduled Tribes.]

1. Added by the Constitution (First Amendment) Act, 1951, s. 2.

Article 16. Equality of opportunity in matters of public employment.-

(1) There shall be equality of opportunity for all citizens in matters relating to employment or appointment to any office under the State.

(2) No citizen shall, on grounds only of religion, race, caste, sex, descent, place of birth, residence or any of them, be ineligible for, or discriminated against in respect of, any employment or office under the State.

(3) Nothing in this article shall prevent Parliament from making any law prescribing, in regard to a class or classes of employment or appointment to an office [under the Government of, or any local or other authority within, a State or Union territory, any requirement as to residence within that State or Union territory] prior to such employment or appointment.

[(4A) Nothing in this article shall prevent the State from making any provision for reservation in matters of promotion to any class or classes of posts in the services under the State in favour of the Scheduled Castes and the Scheduled Tribes which, in the opinion of the State, are not adequately represented in the services under the State.]

[(4B) Nothing in this article shall prevent the State from considering any unfilled vacancies of a year which are reserved for being filled up in that year in accordance with any provision for reservation made under clause (4) or clause (4A) as a separate class of vacancies to be filled up in any succeeding year or years and such class of vacancies shall not be considered together with the vacancies of the year in which they are being filled up for determining the ceiling of fifty per cent. reservation on total number of vacancies of that year.]

(5) Nothing in this article shall affect the operation of any law which provides that the incumbent of an office in connection with the affairs of any religious or denominational

institution or any member of the governing body thereof shall be a person professing a particular religion or belonging to a particular denomination.

1. Subs. by the Constitution (Seventh Amendment) Act, 1956, s. 29 and Sch., for "under any State specified in the First Schedule or any local or other authority within its territory, any requirement as to residence within that State".

2. Ins. by the Constitution (Seventy-seventh Amendment) Act, 1995,s. 2.

2. Ins. by the Constitution (Eighty-first Amendment) Act, 2000, s.2 (w.e.f. 09-06-2000)

Article 29. Protection of interests of minorities.-

(2) No citizen shall be denied admission into any educational institution maintained by the State or receiving aid out of State funds on grounds only of religion, race, caste, language or any of them.

Article 325. No person to be ineligible for inclusion in, or to claim to be included in a special, electoral roll on grounds of religion, race, caste or sex.-There shall be one general electoral roll for every territorial constituency for election to either House of Parliament or to the House or either House of the Legislature of a State and no person shall be ineligible for inclusion in any such roll or claim to be included in any special electoral roll for any such constituency on grounds only of religion, race, caste, sex or any of them.

IV. SEPARATION OF STATE FROM RELIGION

Article 27. Freedom as to payment of taxes for promotion of any particular religion.- No person shall be compelled to pay any taxes, the proceeds of which are specifically appropriated in payment of expenses for the promotion or maintenance of any particular religion or religious denomination.

Article 28. Freedom as to attendance at religious instruction or religious worship in certain educational institutions.-

(1) No religious instruction shall be provided in any educational institution wholly maintained out of State funds.

(2) Nothing in clause (1) shall apply to an educational institution, which is administered by the State but has been established under any endowment or trust which requires that religious instruction shall be imparted in such institution.

(3) No person attending any educational institution recognised by the State or receiving aid out of State funds shall be required to take part in any religious instruction that may be imparted in such institution or to attend any religious worship that may be conducted in such institution or in any premises attached thereto unless such person or, if such person is a minor, his guardian has given his consent thereto.

17

Political Correctness

INTRODUCTION

As Russell Kirk wrote, one of conservatism's most important insights is that all ideologies are wrong. Ideology takes an intellectual system, a product of one or more philosophers, and says, "This system must be true." Inevitably, reality ends up contradicting the system, usually on a growing number of points. But the ideology, by its nature, cannot adjust to reality; to do so would be to abandon the system. Therefore, reality must be suppressed. If the ideology has power, it uses its power to undertake this suppression. It forbids writing or speaking certain facts. Its goal is to prevent not only expression of thoughts that contradict what "must be true," but thinking such thoughts. In the end, the result is inevitably the concentration camp, the gulag and the grave.

While some Americans have believed in ideologies, America itself never had an official, state ideology – up until now. But what happens today to Americans who suggest that there are differences among ethnic groups, or that the traditional social roles of men and women reflect their different natures, or that homosexuality is morally wrong? If they are public figures, they must grovel in the dirt in endless, canting apologies. If they are university students, they face star chamber courts and possible expulsion. If they are employees of private corporations, they may face loss of their jobs. What was their crime? Contradicting America's new state ideology of "Political Correctness." But what exactly is "Political Correctness?" Marxists have used the term for at least 80 years, as a broad synonym for "the General Line of the Party." It could be said that Political Correctness is the General Line of the Establishment in America today; certainly, no one who dares contradict it can be a member of that Establishment. But that still does not tell us what it really is. This short book, which Free Congress has decided to make available free over its website, seeks to answer that question. It does so in the only way any ideology can be understood, by looking at its historical origins, its method of analysis and several key components, including its place in higher education and its ties with the Feminist movement. Finally, it offers an annotated bibliography for those who wish to pursue the subject in greater depth.

Perhaps the most important question facing Americans today is, "Do we really want America to be an ideological state?" Because conservatives know where all ideologies lead, our answer, resoundingly, is "NO!" But if we expect to prevail and restore our country to full freedom of thought and expression, we need to know our enemy. We need to understand what Political Correctness really is. As you will soon see, if we can expose the true origins and nature of Political Correctness, we will have taken a giant step to its overthrow.

Most Americans look back on the 1950s as a good time. Our homes were safe, to the point where many people did not bother to lock their doors. Public schools were generally excellent, and their problems were things like talking in class and running in the halls. Most men treated women like ladies, and most ladies devoted their time and effort to making good homes, rearing their children well and helping their communities through volunteer work. Children grew up in two–parent households, and the mother was there to meet the child when he came home from school. Entertainment was something the whole family could enjoy.

What Happened?

If a man from America of the 1950s were suddenly introduced into America in the 2000s, he would hardly recognize it as the same country. He would be in immediate danger of getting mugged, carjacked or worse, because he would not have learned to live in constant fear. He would not know that he shouldn't go into certain parts of the city, that his car must not only be locked but equipped with an alarm, that he dare not go to sleep at night without locking the windows and bolting the doors – and setting the electronic security system.

If he brought his family with him, he and his wife would probably cheerfully pack their children off to the nearest public school. When the children came home in the afternoon and told them they had to go through a metal detector to get in the building, had been given some funny white powder by another kid and learned that homosexuality is normal and good, the parents would be uncomprehending.

In the office, the man might light up a cigarette, drop a reference to the "little lady," and say he was happy to see the firm employing some Negroes in important positions. Any of those acts would earn a swift reprimand, and together they might get him fired.

When she went into the city to shop, the wife would put on a nice suit, hat, and possibly gloves. She would not understand why people stared, and mocked. And when the whole family sat down after dinner and turned on the television, they would not understand how pornography from some sleazy, blank-fronted "Adults Only" kiosk had gotten on their set.

Were they able, our 1950s family would head back to the 1950s as fast as they could, with a gripping horror story to tell. Their story would be of a nation that had decayed and degenerated at a fantastic pace, moving in less than a half a century from the greatest country on earth to a Third World nation, overrun by crime, noise, drugs and dirt. The fall of Rome was graceful by comparison.

Why did it Happen?

Over the last forty years, America has been conquered by the same force that earlier took over Russia, China, Germany and Italy. That force is ideology. Here, as elsewhere, ideology has inflicted enormous damage on the traditional culture it came to dominate, fracturing it everywhere and sweeping much of it away. In its place came fear, and ruin. Russia will take a generation or more to recover from Communism, if it ever can.

The ideology that has taken over America goes most commonly by the name of "Political Correctness." Some people see it as a joke. It is not. It is deadly serious. It seeks to alter virtually all the rules, formal and informal, that govern relations among people and institutions. It wants to change behavior, thought, even the words we use. To a significant extent, it already has. Whoever or whatever controls language also controls thought. Who dares to speak of "ladies" now?

Just what is "Political Correctness?" "Political Correctness" is in fact cultural Marxism – Marxism translated from economic into cultural terms. The effort to translate Marxism from economics into culture did not begin with the student rebellion of the 1960s. It goes back at least to the 1920s and the writings of the Italian Communist Antonio Gramsci. In 1923, in Germany, a group of Marxists founded an institute devoted to making the translation, the Institute of Social Research (later known as the Frankfurt School). One of its founders, George Lukacs, stated its purpose as answering the question, "Who shall save us from Western Civilization?" The Frankfurt School gained profound influence in American universities after many of its leading lights fled to the United States in the 1930s to escape National Socialism in Germany.

The Frankfurt School blended Marx with Freud, and later influences (some Fascist as well as Marxist) added linguistics to create "Critical Theory" and "deconstruction." These in turn greatly influenced education theory, and through institutions of higher education gave birth to what we now call "Political Correctness." The lineage is clear, and it is traceable right back to Karl Marx.

The parallels between cultural Marxism and classical, economic Marxism are evident. Cultural Marxism, or Political Correctness, shares with classical Marxism the vision of a "classless society" i.e., a society not merely of equal opportunity, but equal condition. Since that vision contradicts human nature – because people are different, they end up unequal, regardless of the starting point – society will not accord with it unless forced. So, under both variants of Marxism, it is forced. This is the first major parallel between classical and cultural Marxism: *both are totalitarian ideologies*. The totalitarian nature of Political Correctness can be seen on campuses where "PC" has taken over the college: freedom of speech, of the press, and even of thought are all eliminated. The second major parallel is that both cultural Marxism and classical, economic Marxism have *single-factor explanations of history.* Classical Marxism argues that all of history was determined by ownership of the means of production. Cultural Marxism says that history is wholly explained by which groups – defined by sex, race and sexual normality or abnormality – have power over which other groups.

The third parallel is that both varieties of Marxism *declare certain groups virtuous and others evil a priori*, that is, without regard for the actual behavior of individuals. Classical Marxism defines workers and peasants as virtuous and the bourgeoisie (the middle class) and other owners of capital as evil. Political Correctness defines blacks, Hispanics, Feminist women, homosexuals and some additional minority groups as virtuous and white men as evil. (Political Correctness does not recognize the existence of non-Feminist women and defines blacks who reject Political Correctness as whites).

The fourth parallel is in means: *expropriation.* Economic Marxists, where they obtained power, expropriated the property of the bourgeoisie and handed it to the state, as the "representative" of the workers and the peasants. Cultural Marxists, when they gain power (including through our own government), lay penalties on white men and others who disagree with them and give privileges to the groups they favor. Affirmative action is an example.

Finally, both varieties of Marxists employ a method of analysis *designed to show the correctness of their ideology in every situation.* For classical Marxists, the analysis is economic. For cultural Marxists, the analysis is linguistic: deconstruction. Deconstruction "proves" that any "text," past or present, illustrates the oppression of blacks, women, homosexuals, etc. by reading that meaning into words of the text (regardless of their actual meaning). Both methods are, of course, phony analyses that twist the evidence to fit preordained conclusions, but they lend a "scientific" air to the ideology. These parallels are neither remarkable nor coincidental. They exist because Political Correctness is directly derived from classical Marxism, and is in fact merely a variant of Marxism. Through most of the history of Marxism, cultural Marxists were "read out" of the movement by classical, economic Marxists. Today, with economic Marxism dead, cultural Marxism has filled its shoes. The medium has changed, but the message is the same: a society of radical egalitarianism enforced by the power of the state.

Political Correctness now looms over American society like a colossus. It has taken over both political parties – recent Republican conventions were choreographed according to its dictates, while cultural conservatives were shown the door – and is enforced by many laws and government regulations. It almost totally controls the most powerful element in our culture, the entertainment industry. It dominates both public and higher education: many a college campus is a small, ivy-covered North Korea. It has even captured the clergy in many Christian churches. Anyone in the Establishment who departs from its dictates swiftly ceases to be a member of the Establishment. The remainder of this short book will explore the subject of Political Correctness further: its history, its method of analysis (deconstruction), and the means by which it has attained its influence, especially through education.

But one more question must be addressed at the outset, the most vital question: how can Americans combat Political Correctness and retake their society from the cultural Marxists?

To that end, it is not sufficient to criticize Political Correctness. It tolerates a certain amount of criticism, even gentle mocking. It does so through no genuine tolerance for other points of view, but in order to disarm its opponents, to let itself seem less menacing than it is. The cultural Marxists do not yet have total power, and they are too wise to appear totalitarian until their victory is assured.

Rather, those who would defeat cultural Marxism must defy it. They must use words it forbids, and refuse to use the words it mandates; remember, sex is better than gender. They must shout from the housetops the realities it seeks to suppress, such as the facts that violent crime is disproportionately committed by blacks and that most cases of AIDS are voluntary, i.e., acquired from immoral sexual acts. They must refuse to turn their children over to public schools.

Above all, those who would defy Political Correctness must behave according to the old rules of our culture, not the new rules the cultural Marxists lay down. Ladies should be wives and homemakers, not cops or soldiers, and men should still hold doors open for ladies. Children should not be born out of wedlock. Open homosexuals should be shunned. Jurors should not accept race as an excuse for murder.

Defiance spreads. When other Americans see one person defy Political Correctness and survive – and you still can, for now – they are emboldened. They are tempted to defy it, too, and some will. The ripples from a single act of defiance, of one instance of walking up to the clay idol and breaking off its nose, can range far. There is nothing the Politically Correct fear more than open defiance, and for good reason; it is their chief vulnerability. That should lead cultural conservatives to defy cultural Marxism at every turn.

While the hour is late, the battle is not decided. Very few Americans realize that Political Correctness is in fact Marxism in a different set of clothes. As that realization spreads, defiance will spread with it. At present, Political Correctness prospers by disguising itself. Through defiance, and through education on our own part (which should be part of every act of defiance), we can strip away its camouflage and reveal the Marxism beneath the window-dressing of "sensitivity," "tolerance" and "multiculturalism." Who dares, wins.

THE HISTORICAL ROOTS OF "POLITICAL CORRECTNESS"

America is today dominated by an alien system of beliefs, attitudes and values that we have come to know as "Political Correctness." Political Correctness seeks to impose a uniformity of thought and behavior on all Americans and is therefore totalitarian in nature. Its roots lie in a version of Marxism which seeks a radical inversion of the traditional culture in order to create a social revolution.

Social revolution has a long history, conceivably going as far back as Plato's *Republic.* But it was the French Revolution of 1789 that inspired Karl Marx to develop his theories in the nineteenth century. In the twentieth century, the success of the Bolshevik Revolution of 1917 in Russia set off a wave of optimistic expectation among the Marxist forces in Europe and America that the new proletarian world of equality was finally coming into being. Russia, as the first communist nation in the world, would lead the revolutionary forces to victory.

The Marxist revolutionary forces in Europe leaped at this opportunity. Following the end of World War I, there was a Communist "Spartacist uprising in Berlin, Germany lead by Rosa Luxemburg; the creation of a "Soviet" in Bavaria led by Kurt Eisner; and a Hungarian communist republic established by Bela Kun in 1919. At the time, there was great concern that all of Europe might fall under the banner of Bolshevism. This sense of impeding doom was given vivid life by Trotsky's Red Army invasion of Poland in 1919. However, the Red Army was defeated by Polish forces at the battle of the Vistula in 1920. The Spartacist, Bavarian Soviet and Bela Kun governments all failed to gain widespread support from the workers and after a brief time they were all overthrown. These events created a quandary for the Marxist revolutionaries in Europe. Under Marxist economic theory, the oppressed workers were supposed to be the beneficiaries of a social revolution that would place them on top of the power structure. When these revolutionary opportunities presented themselves, however, the workers did not respond. The Marxist revolutionaries did not blame their theory for these failures. They blamed the workers.

One group of Marxist intellectuals resolved their quandary by an analysis that focused on society's cultural "superstructure" rather than on the economic substructures as Marx did. The Italian Marxist Antonio Gramsci and Hungarian Marxist Georg Lukacs contributed the most to this new cultural Marxism.

Antonio Gramsci worked for the Communist International during 1923-24 in Moscow and Vienna. He was later imprisoned in one of Mussolini's jails where he wrote his famous "Prison Notebooks." Among Marxists, Gramsci is noted for his theory of cultural hegemony as the means to class dominance. In his view, a new "Communist man" had to be created before any political revolution was possible. This led to a focus on the efforts of intellectuals in the fields of education and culture. Gramsci envisioned a long march through the society's institutions, including the government, the judiciary, the military, the schools and the media. He also concluded that so long as the workers had a Christian soul, they would not respond to revolutionary appeals.

Georg Lukacs was the son a wealthy Hungarian banker. Lukacs began his political life as an agent of the Communist International. His book *History and Class Consciousness* gained him recognition as the leading Marxist theorist since Karl Marx. Lukacs believed that for a new Marxist culture to emerge, the existing culture must be destroyed. He said, "I saw the revolutionary destruction of society as the one and only solution to the cultural contradictions of the epoch," and, "Such a worldwide overturning of values cannot take place without the annihilation of the old values and the creation of new ones by the revolutionaries."

When he became Deputy Commissar for Culture in the Bolshevik Bela Kun regime in Hungary in 1919, Lukacs launched what became known as "Cultural Terrorism." As part of this terrorism he instituted a radical sex education program in Hungarian schools. Hungarian children were instructed in free love, sexual intercourse, the archaic nature of middle-class family codes, the out-datedness of monogamy, and the irrelevance of religion, which deprives man of all pleasures. Women, too, were called to rebel against the sexual mores of the time. Lukacs's campaign of "Cultural Terrorism" was a precursor to what Political Correctness would later bring to American schools. In 1923, Lukacs and other Marxist intellectuals associated with the Communist Party of Germany founded the Institute of Social Research at Frankfurt University in Frankfurt, Germany. The Institute, which became known as the Frankfurt School, was modeled after the Marx-Engels Institute in Moscow. In 1933, when Nazis came to power in Germany, the members of the Frankfurt School fled. Most came to the United States. The members of the Frankfurt School conducted numerous studies on the beliefs, attitudes and values they believed lay behind the rise of National Socialism in Germany.

The Frankfurt School's studies combined Marxist analysis with Freudian psychoanalysis to form the basis of what became known as "Critical Theory." Critical Theory was essentially destructive criticism of the main elements of Western culture, including Christianity, capitalism, authority, the family, patriarchy, hierarchy, morality, tradition, sexual restraint, loyalty, patriotism, nationalism, heredity, ethnocentrism, convention and conservatism. These criticisms were reflected in such works of the Frankfurt School as Erich Fromm's *Escape from Freedom* and *The Dogma of Christ*, Wilhelm's Reich's *The Mass Psychology of Fascism* and Theodor Adorno's *The Authoritarian Personality. The Authoritarian Personality*, published in 1950, substantially influenced American psychologists and social scientists. The book was premised on one basic idea, that the presence in a society of Christianity, capitalism and the patriarchal-authoritarian family created a character prone to racial prejudice and German fascism. *The Authoritarian Personality* became a handbook for a national campaign against any kind of prejudice or discrimination on the theory that if these evils were not eradicated, another Holocaust might occur on the American continent. This campaign, in turn, provided a basis for Political Correctness.

Critical Theory incorporated sub-theories which themselves were intended to chip away at specific elements of the existing culture, including "matriarchal theory," "androgyny theory," "personality theory," "authority theory," "family theory," "sexuality theory," "racial theory," "legal theory" and "literary theory." Put into practice, these theories were to be used to overthrow the prevailing social order and usher in social revolution based on cultural Marxism. To achieve this, the Critical Theorists of the Frankfurt School recognized that traditional beliefs and the existing social structure would have to be destroyed and then replaced. The patriarchal social structure would be replaced with matriarchy; the belief that men and women are different and properly have different roles would be replaced with androgyny; and the belief that heterosexuality is normal would be replaced with the belief that homosexuality is "normal."

As a grand scheme intended to deny the intrinsic worth of white, heterosexual males, the Critical Theorists of the Frankfurt School opened the door to the racial and sexual antagonisms of the Trotskyites. Leon Trotsky believed that oppressed blacks could be the vanguard of a communist revolution in North America. He denounced white workers who were prejudiced against blacks and instructed them to unite with the blacks in revolution. Trotsky's ideas were adopted by many of the student leaders of the 1960s counterculture movement, who attempted to elevate the black revolutionaries to positions of leadership in their movement.

The student revolutionaries were also strongly influenced by the ideas of Herbert Marcuse, another member of the Frankfurt School. Marcuse preached the "Great Refusal," a rejection of all basic Western concepts, sexual liberation and the merits of feminist and black revolutions. His primary thesis was that university students, ghetto blacks, the alienated, the asocial, and the Third World could take the place of the proletariat in the Communist revolution. In his book, *An Essay on Liberation*, Marcuse proclaimed his goals of a radical transvaluation of values; the relaxation of taboos, cultural subversion; Critical Theory; and a linguistic rebellion that would amount to a methodical reversal of meaning. As for racial conflict, Marcuse wrote that white men are guilty and that blacks are the most natural force of rebellion.

Marcuse may be the most important member of the Frankfurt School in terms of the origins of Political Correctness, because he was the critical link to the counterculture of the 1960s. His objective was clear: "One can rightfully speak of a cultural revolution, since the protest is directed toward the whole cultural establishment, including morality of existing society..." His means was liberating the powerful, primeval force of sex from its civilized restraints, a message preached in his book, *Eros and Civilization*, published in 1955. Marcuse became one of the main gurus of the 1960s adolescent sexual rebellion; he himself coined the expression, "make love, not war." With that role, the chain of Marxist influence via the Frankfurt School was completed: from Lukacs's service as Deputy Commissar for Culture in the Bolshevik Hungarian government in 1919 to American students burning the flag and taking over college administration buildings in the 1960s. Today, many of these same colleges are bastions of Political Correctness, and the former student radicals have become the faculties. One of the most important contributors to Political Correctness was Betty Friedan. Through her book *The Feminine Mystique,* Friedan became the mother of the modern feminist movement in America. Friedan was not a member of the Frankfurt School, but she was strongly influenced by it. Her work offers a useful case study of the Marxist roots of Political Correctness.

Friedan devoted almost a full chapter of *The Feminine Mystique* to Abraham Maslow's theory of self-actualization. Maslow was a social psychologist who in his early years did research on female dominance and sexuality. Maslow was a friend of Herbert Marcuse at Bandeis University and had met Erich Fromm in 1936. He was strongly impressed by Fromm's Frankfurt School ideology. He wrote an article, "The Authoritarian Character Structure," published in 1944, that reflected the personality theory of Critical Theory. Maslow was also impressed with the work of Wilhelm Reich, who was another Frankfurt School originator of personality theory.

The significance of the historical roots of Political Correctness cannot be fully appreciated unless Betty Friedan's revolution in sex roles is viewed for what it really was – a manifestation of the social revolutionary process begun by Karl Marx. Friedan's reliance on Abraham Maslow's reflection of Frankfurt School ideology is simply one indicator. Other indicators include the correspondence of Friedan's revolution in sex roles with Georg Lukacs' annihilation of old values and the creation of new ones, and with Herbert Marcuse's transvaluation of values.

But the idea of transforming a patriarchy into a matriarchy – which is what a sex-role inversion is designed to do – can be connected directed to Friedrich Engels book *The Origin of the Family, Private Property, and the Sate.* First published in 1884, this book popularized the now-accepted feminist belief that deep-rooted discrimination against the oppressed female sex was a function of patriarchy. The belief that matriarchy was the solution to patriarchy flows from Marx's comments in *The German Ideology*, published in 1845. In this work Marx advanced the idea that wives and children were the first property of the patriarchal male. The Frankfurt School's matriarchal theory (and its near-relation, androgyny theory) both originated from these sources.

When addressing the general public, advocates of Political Correctness – or cultural Marxism, to give it its true name – present their beliefs attractively. It's all just a matter of being "sensitive" to other people, they say. They use words such as "tolerance" and "diversity," asking, "Why can't we all just get along?" The reality is different. Political Correctness is not at all about "being nice," unless one thinks gulags are nice places. Political Correctness is Marxism, with all that implies: loss of freedom of expression, thought control, inversion of the traditional social order and, ultimately, a totalitarian state. If anything, the cultural Marxism created by the Frankfurt School is more horrifying than the old, economic Marxism that ruined Russia. At least the economic Marxists did not exalt sexual perversion and attempt to create a matriarchy, as the Frankfurt School and its descendants have done.

This short essay has sought to show one critical linkage, that between classical Marxism and the ingredients of the "cultural revolution" that broke out in America in the 1960s. The appendices to this paper offer a "wiring diagram" which may make the trail easier to follow, along with a more detailed look at some of the main actors. Of course, the action does not stop in the '60s; the workings of Frankfurt School are yet very much with us, especially in the field of education. That topic, and other present-day effects of Frankfurt School thinking, will be the subjects of future chapters in this book.

PROFILES

Georg Lukacs

- He began his political life as a Kremlin agent of the Communist International.
- His *History and Class-Consciousness* gained him recognition as the leading Marxist theorist since Karl Marx.
- In 1919 he became the Deputy Commissar for Culture in the Bolshevik Bela Kun Regime in Hungary. He instigated what become known as the "Cultural Terrorism."
- The Cultural Terrorism was a precursor of what was to happen in American schools.
- He launched an "explosive" sex education program. Special lectures were organized in Hungarian schools and literature was printed and distributed to instruct children about free love, the nature of sexual intercourse, the archaic nature of the bourgeois family codes, the outdatedness of monogamy and the irrelevance of religion, which deprives man of all pleasure. Children urged thus to reject and deride paternal authority and the authority of the Church, and to ignore precepts of morality, were easily and spontaneously turned into delinquents with whom only the police could cope. This call to rebellion addressed to Hungarian children was matched by a call to rebellion addressed to Hungarian women.
- In rejecting the idea that Bolshevism spelled the destruction of civilization and culture, Lukacs stated: "Such a worldwide overturning of values cannot take place without the annihilation of the old values and the creation of new ones by the revolutionaries."
- Lukacs' state of mind was expressed in his own words:
  - "All the social forces I had hated since my youth, and which I aimed in spirit to annihilate, now came together to unleash the First Global War."
  - "I saw the revolutionary destruction of society as the one and only solution to the cultural contradictions of the epoch."
  - "The question is, Who will free us from the yoke of Western Civilization?"
  - "Any political movement capable of bringing Bolshevism to the West would have to be 'Demonic'."
  - "The abandonment of the soul's uniqueness solves the problem of 'unleashing' the diabolic forces lurking in all the violence which are needed to create a revolution."
- Lukacs' state of mind was typical of those who represented the forces of Revolutionary Marxism.
- At a secret meeting in Germany in 1923, Lukacs proposed the concept of inducing "Cultural Pessimism" in order to increase the state of hopelessness and alienation in the people of the West as a necessary prerequisite for revolution. • This meeting led to the

founding of the Institute for Social Research at Frankfurt University in Germany in 1923–an organization of Marxist and Communistoriented psychologists, sociologists and other intellectuals that came to be known as the Frankfurt School, which devoted itself to implementing Georg Lukacs's program.

Antonio Gramsci

- He was an Italian Marxist on an intellectual par with Georg Lukacs who arrived by analysis at the same conclusions as Lukacs and the Frankfurt School regarding the critical importance of intellectuals in fomenting revolution in the West.
- He had traveled to the Soviet Union after the Bolshevik Revolution of 1917 and made some accurate observations that caused him to conclude that a Bolshevikstyle uprising could not be brought about by Western workers due to the nature of their Christian souls.
- Antonio Gramsci became the leader of the Italian Communist Party, which earned him a place in one of Mussolini's jails in the 1930s, where he wrote *Prison Notebooks* and other documents.
- These works became available in English to Americans.
- His advice to the intellectuals was to begin a long march through the educational and cultural institutions of the nation in order to create a new Soviet man before there could be a successful political revolution.
- This reflected his observations in the Soviet Union that its leaders could not create such a new Soviet man after the Bolshevik Revolution.
- This blueprint for mind and character change made Gramsci a hero of Revolutionary Marxism in American education and paved the way for creation of the New American Child in the schools by the education cartel.
- The essential nature of Antonio Gramsci's revolutionary strategy is reflected in Charles A. Reich's *The Greening of America*: "There is a revolution coming. It will not be like revolutions in the past. It will originate with the individual and the culture, and it will change the political structure as its final act. It will not require violence to succeed, and it cannot be successfully resisted by violence. This is revolution of the New Generation."

Wilhelm Reich

- In his 1933 book entitled *The Mass Psychology of Fascism*, he explained that the Frankfurt School departed from the Marxist sociology that set "Bourgeois" against "Proletariat." Instead, the battle would be between "reactionary" and "revolutionary" characters.
- He also wrote a book entitled *The Sexual Revolution*, which was a precursor of what was to come in the 1960s.
- His "sex-economic" sociology was an effort to harmonize Freud's psychology with Marx's economic theory.

- Reich's theory was expressed in his words: "The authoritarian family is the authoritarian state in miniature. Man's authoritarian character structure is basically produced by the embedding of sexual inhibitions and fear in the living substance of sexual impulses. Familial imperialism is ideologically reproduced in national imperialism...the authoritarian family...is a factor where reactionary ideology and reactionary structures are produced."
- Wilhelm Reich's theory, when coupled with Georg Lukacs' sex education in Hungary, can be seen as the source for the American education cartel's insistence on sex education from kindergarten onwards and its complete negation of the paternal family, external authority, and the traditional character structure.
- Reich's theory encompassed other assertions that seem to have permeated American education:
  - The organized religious mysticism of Christianity was an element of the authoritarian family that led to Fascism.
  - The patriarchal power in and outside of man was to be dethroned.
  - Revolutionary sexual politics would mean the complete collapse of authoritarian ideology.
  - Birth control was revolutionary ideology.
  - Man was fundamentally a sexual animal.
- Reich's *The Mass Psychology of Fascism* was in its ninth printing as of 1991, and is available in most college bookstores.

Erich Fromm

- Like Wilhelm Reich, Fromm was a social psychologist of the Frankfurt School who came to America in the 1930s.
- His book *Escape from Freedom*, published in 1941, is an ideological companion to Wilhelm Reich's *The Mass Psychology of Fascism.*
- Fromm asserted that early capitalism created a social order that bred a sadomasochistic and authoritarian character of which Martin Luther and Adolph Hitler were prime examples.
- He asserted that the same capitalistic social order resulted in Calvin's Theory of Predestination, which reflected the principle of the basic inequality of men that was revived in Nazi ideology.
- He asserted the authoritarian character experiences only domination or submission and "differences, whether sex or race, to him are necessarily of superiority or inferiority."
- He asserted that "Positive Freedom" implies the principle that there is no higher power than the unique individual self; that man is the center and purpose of life; that the growth

and realization of man's individuality is an end that can never be subordinated to purposes which are supposed to have a greater dignity.

- Fromm made the real meaning of this "Positive Freedom" clear in another of his many books – *The Dogma of Christ*... wherein he describes a revolutionary character such as himself as: the man who has emancipated himself from the ties of blood and soil, from his mother and father, and from special loyalties to state, race, party or religion.
- Fromm makes his revolutionary intent very clear in *The Dogma of Christ*... "We might define revolution in a psychological sense, saying that a revolution is a political movement led by people with revolutionary characters, and attracting people with revolutionary characters."

Herbert Marcuse

- Like Wilhelm Reich and Erich Fromm, Herbert Marcuse was an intellectual of the Frankfurt School who came to America in the 1930s.
- He has often been described as a Marxist philosopher, but he was in fact a fullblooded social revolutionary who contemplated the disintegration of American society just as Karl Marx and Georg Lukacs contemplated the disintegration of German society: "One can rightfully speak of a cultural revolution, since the protest is directed toward the whole cultural establishment, including the morality of existing society...there is one thing we can say with complete assurance: the traditional idea of revolution and the traditional strategy of revolution has ended. These ideas are old-fashioned...What we must undertake is a type of diffuse and dispersed disintegration of the system."
- Marcuse published *Eros and Civilization* in 1955, which became the founding document of the 1960s counterculture and brought the Frankfurt School into the colleges and universities of America.
- He asserted that the only way to escape the one-dimensionality of modern industrial society was to liberate the erotic side of man, the sensuous instinct, in rebellion against "technological rationality."
- This erotic liberation was to take the form of the "Great Refusal," a total rejection of the capitalist monster and its entire works, including technological reason and ritual-authoritarian language.
- He provided the obtuse intellectual justifications for adolescent sexual rebellion, and the slogan "Make Love, Not War."
- His theory included the belief that the Women's Liberation Movement was to be the most important component of the opposition, and potentially the most radical.
- His revolutionary efforts would blossom into a full-scale war by revolutionary Marxism against the European white male in the schools and colleges.

Theodor Adorno

- He was another Marxist revolutionary and member of the Frankfurt School who came to America in the 1930s.
- Along with others, Adorno authored *The Authoritarian Personality*, which was published in 1950.
- Adorno's book was inspired by the same kind of theoretical assertions revealed in the works of Wilhelm Reich, Erich Fromm and Herbert Marcuse based on analytical studies of German society that were begun in 1923.
- The basic theme was the same. There was such a thing as an authoritarian character that was the opposite of the desired revolutionary character. This authoritarian character was a product of capitalism, Christianity, conservatism, the patriarchal family and sexual repression. In Germany, this combination induced prejudice, anti-Semitism and fascism according to Frankfurt School theory.
- It so happened that most Americans were products of capitalism, Christianity, conservatism, the patriarchal family and sexual repression in their youth. So Theodor Adorno and other members of the Frankfurt School had a golden opportunity to execute Georg Lukacs's and Antonio Gramsci's program for creating social revolution in America instead of Germany.
- They would posit the existence of authoritarian personalities among Americans with tendencies toward prejudice, and then exploit this to force the "scientifically planned re-education" of Americans with the excuse that it was being done in order to eradicate prejudice.
- This scientifically-planned re-education would become the master plan for the transformation of America's system of fundamental values into their opposite revolutionary values in American education so that school children would become replicas of the Frankfurt School revolutionary characters and thus create the New American Child.
- This can be confirmed by noting that *The Authoritarian Personality* is the key source of the affective domain of Benjamin Bloom's *Taxonomy of Educational Objectives* of 1964, which guided the education cartel thereafter.

POLITICAL CORRECTNESS IN HIGHER EDUCATION

On a growing number of university campuses the freedom to articulate and discuss ideas– a principle that has been the cornerstone of higher education since the time of Socrates – is eroding at an alarming rate. Consider just one increasing trend: hundreds (sometimes thousands) of copies of conservative student newspapers have been either stolen or publicly burned by student radicals. In many cases these acts have taken place with the tacit support of faculty and administrators. The perpetrators are rarely disciplined.

While it would be easy to dismiss such demonstrations of intolerance as student pranks, these incidents are the surface manifestations of a more pervasive and insidious trend – a trend that has as its goal the destruction of the liberal arts tradition that has helped create and sustain Western civilization. Though some pundits have claimed that the prevalence of the ideological intolerance known as Political Correctness has been exaggerated, the opposite is closer to the truth. Political Correctness has become so deeply ingrained in American higher education that many campuses are now dominated by an atmosphere of uncertainty and apprehension. An increasing number of dedicated students and faculty members now live in fear that their intellectual pursuit of truth will offend the Grand Inquisitors of Political Correctness.

The techniques of Political Correctness are now well known: attacks on the curriculum in the name of "multiculturalism," the imposition of restrictive and vaguelyworded "speech codes" and mandatory "sensitivity training" courses for freshman that are little more than systematic efforts at ideological indoctrination. But the influence of Political Correctness has spread in other disturbing ways. Consider a few recent incidents from the university battlefield.

At Amherst College in Massachusetts, a homosexual student group covered the university's sidewalks with graffiti, including the slogan "Queer by Divine Right," which was scrawled in front of the campus chapel on Good Friday. When the *Amherst Spectator*, a conservative student newspaper, criticized these chalkings as promoting "hatred and division," student protestors publicly burned copies of the paper.

When the *Cornell Review*, another conservative student newspaper, published a parody of the course descriptions from Cornell's heavily-politicized Africana Department, campus militants blocked traffic at the center of the campus for several hours and burned stolen copies of the *Review* in a metal trash can. The militants went on to demand that the university provide "racial sensitivity" classes for incoming freshman, a campus speech code and more money for segregated minority programs such as a blacks-only dormitory.

Students who participate in ROTC programs have told friends and family that they are afraid to show up for class wearing their uniforms because their grades have been arbitrarily marked down by faculty members who are hostile to the military.

In the wake of a rash of sexual harassment charges that have been filed by extreme feminists against their alleged enemies, some professors have begun to take out insurance policies to protect themselves from the crushing financial burden of malicious and frivolous lawsuits.

A faculty questionnaire at the University of Massachusetts asks professors what "contribution to multi-culturalism" they have made. The questionnaire is then used in making decisions about tenure and promotion.

It is worth remembering that for every dramatic and well-publicized example of Political Correctness, there are innumerable instances where its influence is more subtle, but just as real.

THE ORIGINS OF POLITICAL CORRECTNESS IN HIGHER EDUCATION

While the ideology of Political Correctness is hardly restricted to our campuses, there is no doubt it originated there. The intellectual roots of this phenomenon stretch back over centuries. Ultimately, the origins of PC can be traced to the rise of modern ideology and its quest for power. In contrast to the classical and Judeo-Christian traditions, which stressed man's need to understand the moral order and conform himself to it, modern ideologies have sought to dominate and control the world. In the twentieth century these ideologies finally gained political power in Communist states. But in the West, ideology has not been able to make such a direct assault on our traditions of ordered liberty. Rather, radical intellectuals have sought to undermine the foundations of knowledge itself, concentrating their efforts on the transformation of the university.

The turning point in the academy came in the 1960s, when militant students launched a guerilla attack on the traditions of Western culture and the liberal arts. Seeing that they could not gain lasting power through demonstrations alone, many of these militants opted to remain "in the system," going on to become professors themselves. This generation of "tenured radicals" (to use Roger Kimball's phrase) has now become the establishment in the vast majority of our institutions of higher learning. As university presidents, deans, and department chairmen, they have set about hiring other ideologues in their own image and have instigated the repressive policies we know as Political Correctness. These politicized academics will be extremely difficult to dislodge from their current positions of power.

Ideology vs. Liberal Education

The stakes in this war of ideas are high, for they include the very concept of freedom itself. Americans have always understood the intimate and vital connection between liberal education and political liberty. That is why Political Correctness is nothing less than a death blow aimed at the heart of our republic.

In his seminal book, *The Idea of a University*, Cardinal John Henry Newman defined the "liberal arts" as a pursuit of knowledge for its own sake. By way of contrast, he defined the "servile arts" as those modes of study that serve only specific, immediate ends. The liberal arts are liberating, Newman argued, because they enable men to discover the underlying principles that guide us toward wisdom and virtue. Were he alive today, Newman would view Political Correctness as "servile" because its purpose is to advance a political agenda to a position of national power. Militant professors in increasing numbers are shamelessly turning their podiums into pulpits, abandoning the search for objective truth and setting about the task of indoctrinating their students.

The Devastated Curriculum

The proponents of Political Correctness have concentrated their efforts on the core of a liberal education, the curriculum. Their efforts will radically alter what new generations of

Americans will learn. In this battle the handmaiden of Political Correctness has been the "multicultural" movement. A number of critics have rightly pointed out that multiculturalism is more than an argument for courses that concentrate on groups that at one time were disadvantaged or oppressed. Rather, multiculturalism involves the systematic restructuring of the curriculum so as to hinder students from learning about the Western tradition. Since the ulterior motive behind Political Correctness is an attempt to restructure American society along egalitarian lines, it is imperative for its proponents to instill in the minds of students a thoroughgoing cultural relativism.

Perhaps the most disturbing aspect of the Politically Correct assault on the curriculum is that it has occurred at many of America's elite universities. Take, for example, the case of Stanford University, an institution that has long played a leadership role in American higher education. Stanford eliminated its long-standing Western civilization requirement in 1988 and replaced it with a multicultural program known as "Cultures, Ideas, and Values." Under this new program freshmen at Stanford can just as easily study Marxist revolutionaries in Central America as they can Plato, Shakespeare or Newton.

Stanford has also led the movement away from serious study of history. Students at Stanford, like students at all but one of the other top 50 universities in the United States, are not required to take a single course in history. Instead, they are offered a choice of courses under the heading of "American Cultures." According to one recent graduate of Stanford, it is impossible to fulfill the "American Cultures" requirement by studying Protestantism, Irish Americans, or the American West, while courses that do fulfill the requirement include "Film and Literature: US-Mexico Border Representations" and "Contemporary Ethnic Drama." Stanford students must also take courses in "World Cultures" and "Gender Studies" that include "Chicana Expressive Culture" and "Misogyny and Feminism in the Renaissance."

Because elite institutions such as Stanford set an example for the rest of American higher education, other universities eagerly adopt these devastating assaults on the curriculum. This "trickle-down" effect will have a long-lasting impact on the way future generations of Americans will be educated.

INTOLERANCE AND THE ASSAULT ON FREEDOM

The two pillars that have traditionally sustained the liberal arts are academic freedom and freedom of speech. Without the freedom to pursue the truth and to write and speak freely, authentic scholarship is impossible. But both of these fundamental freedoms have been routinely abrogated by the establishment of speech codes, "sensitivity" classes, and a general atmosphere of fear and intimidation on campus.

For example, younger professors who have not received tenure must not only be careful of what they say, but of what they publish. Ideological university administrators in the 1990s have created an environment dominated by suspicion that is far more intense than anything spawned by anti-Communist Senator Joseph McCarthy in the 1950s. The most tragic victims of this age of Political Correctness are the students. The traditional goal of a liberal arts education – acculturation, whereby students absorb the inherited wisdom of the past – has been set aside. Increasingly, a university education today seems to involve rote learning of political opinions. When all is said and done, Political Correctness substitutes smug feelings of righteousness for the traditional habits of critical thinking. One distinguished scholar recently lamented that "higher education is increasingly about acquiring attitudes and opinions that one puts on like a uniform." Because the academy is a relatively isolated world, it can allow politicized administrators to turn the campus into a laboratory for experiments in social transformation. When critics of Political Correctness have compared the atmosphere on campus to that of a totalitarian state, liberal pundits have been quick to denounce them as hysterical. Few of these pundits have any first-hand experience of daily life on campus.

The Movement for Academic Reform

Despite the institutional power of the campus radicals, forces are at work seeking to spur authentic academic reform. The academic reform movement relies on the principles of accountability, communication and a commitment to authentic scholarship. One force of academic reform is a growing demand among parents for greater accountability from colleges and universities. At a time when studies show that students are paying more and learning less than ever before, parents in increasing numbers are becoming discriminating consumers.

Another force is independent student newspapers whose journalists publicize the antics of Political Correctness on campus. In the past, campus radicals thrived in the enclosed world of the university, but their actions are no longer going undetected. The advent of conservative student newspapers on dozens of campuses has forced campus militants into the open where they are most vulnerable to the scrutiny of an exasperated public.

Two years ago, those who fund the Collegiate Network asked the Intercollegiate Studies Institute to take over the administration of their program to support and enhance responsible student journalism. The Collegiate Network contributes seed money, practical help and intellectual guidance to the 60 conservative student newspapers which provide alternative forums of discussion at many of the nations most elite (and closedminded) universities.

These alternatives papers have identified abuses at all levels of academic life and engaged in investigative journalism that has been remarkably fair and accurate. Perhaps the most well-known "scoop" came from Yale University's alternative paper, *Light & Truth*, a publication supported by the Collegiate Network. The editors of *Light & Truth* discovered that the $20 million gift of alumnus Lee Bass was not being used for its intended purpose of supporting an integrated course in Western civilization. Their report broke open the scandal, which ended when Yale returned Mr. Bass's money. The subsequent furor cost Yale a great deal more than Mr. Bass's $20 million – both in monetary terms and in the loss of confidence of many Yale donors that the current administration can be trusted.

Not all the scandals uncovered by alternative campus papers are of this magnitude, but there are innumerable abuses that can be exposed by investigative student journalism. The law school at the University of North Carolina, Chapel Hill, banned representatives of the U.S. military from setting up recruiting tables there, despite receiving federal tax dollars from the Defense Department. An article about this outrageous assault on freedom that ran in both the student-run *Carolina Review* and in the national student newspaper published by ISI, *CAMPUS*, raised a hue and cry on and off campus. North Carolina legislators took immediate action and passed a bill prohibiting taxpayer-supported schools from discriminating against the military when prospective employers come to the university.

At the University of Wisconsin, Madison, the *UWM Times*, a conservative student newspaper, revealed that a university administrator had been soliciting signatures for local Democrat candidates for public office, in direct violation of a state law forbidding university employees from engaging in political campaigning. The university chancellor, despite having issued a directive against such campaigning, refused to reprimand the administrator in question – perhaps because the chancellor himself violated both the state law and his own directive by signing one of the petitions while at work. The story was picked up by the *Milwaukee Journal-Sentinel* and the abuse was brought to an end. Now that alternative newspapers and organizations dedicated to academic reform are spreading the word, the larger communities that surround our institutions of higher education are getting more involved in serious academic reform. For example, the National Association of Scholars is encouraging university trustees to take a more active and vocal role in opposing the excesses of Political Correctness. Efforts of this type must be expanded and intensified.

In the long run, the most direct method of defeating the inquisitors of Political Correctness is simply to stand up to them. Individual acts of defiance often entail serious risks: students can face star-chamber proceedings that are humiliating and demoralizing while faculty can lose their bids to receive tenure. But every act of resistance causes a ripple, encouraging others to stand up to ideological intimidation. With the support of a significant number of parents, donors and alumni, these Davids may yet slay the Goliaths who tower over them.

The Fire of True-Learning

Perhaps the strongest force for true academic reform is that which seeks to defeat the ideological depredations of Political Correctness by winning the war of ideas. The best students have a questioning intelligence that cannot be satisfied with political slogans. When such students have access to serious scholarship they respond with enthusiasm. Even today acculturation still takes place under the mentorship of outstanding scholars at various institutions around the country. Moreover, some colleges and universities continue to swim against the ideological tides of our time. The Intercollegiate Studies Institute (ISI), in conjunction with the Templeton Foundation, has identified the best professors, departments, colleges and textbooks in American higher education today. This program, the Templeton Honor Rolls for Education in a Free Society, celebrates excellence and serves as a guide for parents and students contemplating the daunting choice of which college or university to attend. By singling out the best in higher education, the Templeton Honor Rolls also encourage donors to reward universities that preserve the traditions of the free society. Prospective college students, their parents and donors can also benefit from a comprehensive guide to 100 of the top institutions of higher learning in America published by the ISI. The guide contains substantial, essay-length treatments of all 100 institutions, including 80 elite schools that were selected on the basis of competitive admissions standards and 20 schools that ISI particularly recommends for their commitment to a liberal arts education. The ISI college guide warns students about the ideological dangers on the campuses and steers them in the direction of the best professors and departments. As best-selling author William J. Bennett wrote of this project, "All too often, Americans treat colleges and universities with a deference that prevents them from asking hard questions and demanding real results. But if there is ever to be genuine, long-lasting education reform, parents and students will have to become shrewder and better-informed consumers of education. The ISI guide is a powerful tool in this effort."

One of Edmund Burke's most famous sayings is that "the only thing necessary for the triumph of evil is for good men to do nothing." For generations, Americans have treated higher education with respect and awe – a token of their faith in the liberating power of the liberal arts. But in the face of Political Correctness, it is time for the American public to temper its respect with a critical sensibility and to undertake a more direct effort to call academia to account. It is time for good men and women to demand that American higher education live up to its best traditions and eschew the tyranny of Political Correctness.

POLITICAL CORRECTNESS: DECONSTRUCTION AND LITERATURE

Literature is, if not the most important cultural indicator, at least a significant benchmark of a society's level of civilization. Our nature and environment combine to form each individual mind, which in turn expresses itself in words. Literature, as the words society collectively holds up as exemplary, is then a starting point of sorts – a window into the culture.

Today's literary field is therefore worth examining for the insights it provides into our current cultural milieu. The contemporary American literary field is awash in "isms:" Marxism, Freudianism, feminism, and so on. Most of these are the academic cousins of what is called in the common culture "Political Correctness." Literary theorists take their particular brand of criticism and apply it to literature in an effort to find self-affirmation in a "discovered" meaning of the text. For a feminist critic, for example, no longer does Andrew Marvel's "Upon Appleton House" have the beauty of the grounds as its theme; it speaks instead of the evils of a patriarchal line of inheritance. These "cultural critics," so named because they critique literature based on the point of view of a particular culture, arose in the 1960s, but their schools of criticism only truly began to pick up steam with the arrival of the school of deconstruction in the 1970s.

The works of the father of deconstruction, Jacques Derrida, began to be translated from the French by American professor Gayatri Spivak in the mid-1970s, a time when the U.S. literary scene was ripe for its influence. The economic Marxists were alive and well on American campuses, and the cultural critics were still being fed by the radicalism of the times. Feminists, "queer theorists" and "literature-by-people of color" critics had gained a foothold in the earlier decade, but they had in their meager arsenals only a vague feeling of repression. What they lacked was philosophical backing – the courage prompted by having their own *logos*. The arrival of deconstruction from France provided that philosophy.

At that time, that generation of academics was doing what all academics do, telling the previous generation that it had it all wrong. In this case the rebellion was against the New Critics – so-called even now, decades after their prime. The New Critics specialized in finding the meaning of texts without regard to background information such as authorial intent, a process that had "the text is everything" as its guiding principle.

The new generation of critics set out to turn that principle on its head. Instead of "the text is everything," the new generation claimed that "everything is text" and turned to analyzing anything and everything in relation to the literary work. If a poet wrote a poem that included a female character, the critics would look into the poet's relationship with his mother, his wife, his sister and so on in an effort to offer up an interpretation of the work. This could have (and often did have) the positive effect of using biographic information to gain new understanding of the work; however, these new interpretations were not attempts to discern the true meaning of the work (as the New Critics had done) or even to discover the author's intended meaning (as traditional readings attempted). This new generation of critics instead became prime practitioners of what is known in literary circles as "cultural criticism." They strained to view literature from the "woman's point of view" or the "gay point of view" or the "radical minority point of view." Their attempts were not to find meaning – they were influenced too greatly by relativists for that – but to find sexism, racism or "homophobia" in the works of male, European or heterosexual authors.

Derridean deconstruction became a tool for these cultural critics. Simply stated, deconstruction is a school of thought that posits that words have no meaning. Instead, words have "traces" of meaning. The meaning of a word is continually disappearing, leaving us with only the memory, or trace, of what that meaning once was. (Similar to Heidegger's term being, Derrida often uses the crossed-out word trace in an effort to indicate a meaning that is simultaneously present and disappearing.)

A metaphor may be helpful to understand the underlying philosophy of deconstructionism. If I say the word "pen," then you think of the object there in the desk drawer. But if I throw the pen at someone, then the word "pen" begins to lose the benign meaning of a writing apparatus with ink; to use deconstructionist terms, the original understanding of the word "pen" undergoes erasure to leave only a trace. Instead the word "pen" becomes associated with a weapon, a projectile, a means of expressing (perhaps) anger. If the pen strikes someone, then the word "pen" to that person means something painful, a personal injury, impetus for striking back and so on. These meanings constantly grow and change because the human mind is always interpreting and reinterpreting. Because of this, deconstruction argues, it never fully settles on *the* stable meaning for the word "pen." Based on this linguistic argument, deconstructionists conclude that since any meanings in words are so quickly diffused, we can never really communicate at all. Words no longer have meaning.

The postmodern catch word "differance," along with terms like "erasure" and "trace," entered American scholarship through Derrrida's writings. By combining the concepts of (and the French words for) "deferment" and "difference," Derrida came up with this name for the endless deferment of meaning that takes place. Derrida claims that differance is the reason that words cannot have meanings; the mind continually understands things in different ways so that the original meaning loses its importance as the *proper* meaning-it becomes a mere trace.

Ultimately this is insufficient for today's cultural critics – they need words to mean things so that they can point to artistic works and bemoan how they illustrate or exemplify the repression of minority cultures. But other than its general philosophy, deconstruction offered something more important. It offered the techniques to "show" how all language deconstructs itself.

The deconstructionists specialized in "deconstructing" literary works – although they steadfastly insist that the works deconstruct themselves and the critic only illustrates how this happens. These techniques of deconstruction usually involve isolating the surface meaning of the literary work – the "traditionalist" meaning – and attempting to show how the work itself violates that traditional meaning. For example, they will take a love poem and pick apart the language until they find something that they can interpret as unloving. Elizabeth Barrett Browning's sonnet "How Do I Love Thee? Let Me Count The Ways," ends with the words "I shall but love thee better in death." The clever deconstructionists might combine these with Browning's earlier words, "when feeling out of bounds for the edge of beauty and ideal grace," to conclude that Mrs. Browning is actually reaching for her husband's death. "Why is she looking for the *edge* of beauty?" the deconstructionist asks. "She clearly does not want to remain in or before beauty; instead, she is seeking some way around it." The deconstructionist attributes this apparent disparity to the problem with language, "differance," and quickly concludes that the poem – like all other language – has no meaning.

Once they realized the power of this school of thought, the cultural critics embraced it readily, for here they discovered a method of attack on the traditional interpretations of literary works. They used deconstruction to remove traditional meaning and replaced it with *new* meaning.

That meaning was the Political Correctness that infests our society today. For example, after the traditional meaning of "How Do I Love Thee?" has been destabilized in the process described above, a feminist critic might come along and-in the absence of a stable traditional interpretation – declare that the poem is "really" concerned with how women in nineteenth-century England were conditioned to see themselves as secondary to men.

Since "everything is text" in the postmodern mantra, the cultural critics did not hesitate to apply their methods to music, movies, television and anything they encountered. They found that they could remove the meaning from all cultural phenomena and substitute the values of whichever group they preferred. For example, homosexual analysts could remove the truth from the Bible and instead interpret it as full of homophobic hate – God's truth was torn down, and a human political agenda was inserted.

This example is not particularly outrageous, as Derrida's stated goal in deconstructionism was to remove the idea of what he called the "transcendental signified." Standard models of linguistics operate with respect to a signifier-signified pair. The signifier is the word, and the signified is that which the word represents. When difference enters the picture, the thing signified is deferred continually until it can be deferred no longer – that is, until it reaches into the realm of metaphysics. The final meaning reached by any word is God, as He is the ultimate meaning of traditional Western thought.2 The "transcendental signified" of which Derrida is trying to rid himself and the Western world is in fact God. Derrida labels belief in God a product of deficient Western thinking, and in true Nietzchean fashion he claims that God is a construct of language rather than the other way around.

Naturally, Derrida quickly became the darling of the American university establishment. He lectured at universities along the Eastern seaboard, and grew to love that area of America. Soon America returned that affection by granting him a position in the English department of Yale University. Yale then began to draw to other deconstructionists and postmodernists; J. Hillis Miller, Geoffrey Hartman and others. Another European, Paul DeMan, also came to America and began teaching deconstruction. DeMan's history provides yet another reason why deconstructionists sought so avidly to remove meaning from language. In pre-World War II Belgium, DeMan had worked for an explicitly pro-Nazi newspaper. DeMan's detractors note that removing the meaning from language was an excellent way to dismiss his pro-Nazi writings.

Through deconstruction the cultural critics adopted a tool that turned literature, philosophy and culture into nonsense. For instance, in his own writing, in order to remain true to his own philosophy, Derrida eschews all forms of the verb "to be." In deconstructionist terms the verb "to be" implies meaning; thus, it cannot exist. Derrida therefore goes back and crosses out all "to be" verbs, making his writing all but incomprehensible. In beginning to attack the signifier-signified construction, Derrida writes "the sign is that ill-named thing, the only one, that escapes the instituting question of philosophy: 'What is…?'" At the same time Derrida is attempting to communicate his ideas about traditional linguistic models, he is forced by his own philosophy to scratch out the very words that allow him to communicate.

If Derrida were to follow the logic of his own theories he would find that the very concept of communicating his ideas by written or spoken word should be impossible. If deconstructionist theories were even remotely accurate, all verbal communication – and by extension all other forms of communication – would be impossible. As New Critic Dr. M. H. Abrams of Cornell University states, "I hope that Derrida remembers that words do mean things next time someone warns him of an oncoming bus."

Not only does the embrace of deconstruction harm logical philosophy, it also renders the creation of literature virtually impossible. If words mean nothing, then they are nothing more than sounds. True, Lewis Carroll did create a well-known poem using nonsensical but pleasant-sounding words, but how many poems like "jabberwocky" can be created before we reach the saturation point? (Some would argue that we have already reached that point.)

As university literature departments "progress," the divide widens between those who produce literature and those who analyze and teach it. While Samuel Taylor Coleridge, T.S. Eliot and an entire cadre of great authors were well-educated men, it seems that a literary education in an American university actually *hinders* one's ability to write well. As professors of literature embrace the philosophy of deconstruction they lose the ability to write beautifully because meaning is necessary for beautiful writing. As a result, a distinction has emerged within English departments between M.F.A. (Master of Fine Arts) and Ph.D. programs – to the extent that they now have distinct faculties. America's greatest hope for good literature today lies not in the universities, but in the "amateurs" writing after their nine to five work days or while the kids are at school. The intelligentsia has forgotten its literature in its haste to promote its politics.

Already there is a backlash against deconstructionism. Just as the current thriving generation of critics looked upon New Criticism as passé, so the students of today are beginning to look upon deconstruction as obsolete. Derrida still lectured up to his recent death (he spoke in Washington, D.C. as recently as 1995), but, like their forebears, today's literature students are beginning to rise up and tell their predecessors that they had it all wrong. A primary factor in this backlash is the difficulty that lies in communicating deconstructionist ideas (note that what is offered here is merely an outline, not the actual methods of deconstructing a literary work). As a result of this difficulty, today's MTV generation has stumbled upon a positive side effect of their fifteen-second attention spans: They lack the patience to wade through Derrida's nearly unintelligible syntax and decipher his terminology.

Unfortunately, that has not stopped the cultural critics from indoctrinating this new generation in feminist interpretation, Marxist philosophy and so-called "queer theory." Requirements for reading Shakespeare, Milton, Chaucer, and other dead white males are disappearing to be replaced by options to take studies in "the Roles of Women in the Renaissance" (an excuse to lament the sexism of the past) or "The Bible as Literature" (a course designed to denigrate the Bible as cleverly crafted fiction instead of God's truth).

Deconstruction has succeeded in destabilizing the traditional meanings of texts. What happens next remains to be seen, but there are indications that its influence is waning. Already we see Shakespearean plays revived in the cinema; "Much Ado About Nothing," "Hamlet," and "Romeo and Juliet" – all recently adapted for the screen – have long since been abandoned by the American academy in favor of lesser works. Jane Austen's novels, once highly touted by the intelligentsia as undiscovered works of a female author, are now derided in our universities as being too conservative because of their themes of love and marriage. The popular culture has, in a moment of taste, seen the worth of these and revived them as cinema adaptations.

But the real death knell for deconstruction will sound when the next generation of literary critics realizes that the very nature of what it does – read, think, analyze – is antithetical to deconstruction's philosophical goals. The reliable savior of the intelligentsia is the common man and his common sense. Common sense dictates that words do mean things, and as deconstruction posits otherwise it will be relegated to the margins of society. Sadly, its effects will linger on – it has given a sense of validity to cultural criticism and established a marketplace for its ideas.

The deconstructionists are already abandoning their enclave at Yale as their school of thought is eclipsed by trendier, simpler and narrower ideologues. These are the feminists, Marxists and queer theorists – none of whom are leaving their tenured offices peacefully. Instead, they have begun to recruit and train new graduate students to take their places. Applications for graduate and teaching degrees are at an all time high as these campus establishment "radicals" encourage the next generation to help them enshrine their ideology permanently in the American university system.

Radical Feminism and Political Correctness

Perhaps no aspect of Political Correctness is more prominent in American life today than feminist ideology. Is feminism, like the rest of Political Correctness, based on the cultural Marxism imported from Germany in the 1930s? While feminism's history in America certainly extends longer than sixty years, its flowering in recent decades has been interwoven with the unfolding social revolution carried forward by cultural Marxists.

Where do we see radical feminism ascendant? It is on television, where nearly every major offering has a female "power figure" and the plots and characters emphasize inferiority of the male and superiority of the female. It is in the military, where expanding opportunity for women, even in combat positions, has been accompanied by double standards and then lowered standards, as well as by a decline in enlistment of young men, while "warriors" in the services are leaving in droves. It is in government-mandated employment preferences and practices that benefit women and use "sexual harassment" charges to keep men in line. It is in colleges where women's gender studies proliferate and "affirmative action" is applied in admissions and employment. It is in other employment, public and private, where in addition to affirmative action, "sensitivity training" is given unprecedented time and attention. It is in public schools, where "self awareness" and "self-esteem" are increasingly promoted while academic learning declines. And sadly, we see that "a woman's right to choose" leads many fellow Americans, including many with stewardship of public law and culture, to believe it is "the right thing to do" to allow the most helpless to be put to death.

While it is the theme of this essay that the radical feminist movement is embraced by present day Political Correctness ideology, derived from cultural Marxism, feminism as such does have earlier roots. Feminism was conceived and birthed in America in the 1830s, in the generation experiencing the first stage of the industrial revolution. Women, who for centuries had shared the challenges of surviving in an agrarian life, were becoming part of a middle-class gentry with more time and energy to spend writing newspaper articles and novels for their "sisters." The initial stages of the feminization of American culture had started.

These feminists, radical in their time, became a staple of the idealistic Transcendentalists, who included Ralph Waldo Emerson, Henry David Thoreau and many radical Unitarian ministers of the day. They were also abolitionists, bent on destroying slavery and Southern culture as well. Spurred by the rhetoric of Harriet Beecher Stowe (author of *Uncle Tom's Cabin*), Julia Ward Howe (author of the words to

"The Battle Hymn of the Republic"), and Margaret Fuller (the first radical feminist newspaper columnist), the men and women of this idealist Transcendentalist generation propelled our nation toward Civil War.

Who were these Transcendentalist idealists, and why should we be reminded of them today? They were the precursors of today's idealistic Boomer generation. While we cannot draw a continuous link between the Transcendentalists and today's Boomers, their characteristics are very similar. We may glimpse where the elite Boomers are leading us by reviewing the history of the Transcendentalists and their causes.

The Transcendentalists supported abolition of slavery, women's rights, temperance, pacifism (but not in the anti-slavery cause), and other causes which we now observe in New Age popular culture. They developed into spiritualism (talking with the dead), Eastern mysticism and phrenology (discerning personality by the shape of one's skull). They would be right at home in today's New Age milieu. Luther George Williams points out, referring to women's groups and civil rights groups that: Freed slaves secured the vote only after the 13th, 14th and 15th Amendments (ratified in 1870), but women fared worse. They did not receive the vote until the passage of the 19th Amendment in 1920. However, the substantial political victories that these groups achieved (during the Civil War period) guaranteed that they would remain allies. Today, their political organizations dominate every aspect of society, politics and education in America – including the military.2 Indeed, the present-day radical feminist assault on VMI and the Citadel has a political parallel to the Transcendentalist activism of the Civil War period. This current assault is in part a continuation of a century-old effort to destroy Southern culture. In contrast to today's radical feminists, social feminists of the 1890s and early 20th century were of a less totalitarian character. They stood for women's suffrage but also advocated the strengthening of the family.

Today, the feminization of American culture, moving rapidly since the 1960s continues to intensify. Radical Feminists demand that women be allowed to "choose" entry to the infantry, artillery, special forces and combat engineering positions in the Army and Marine Corps. These demands follow the Feminization of combat aviation in the U.S. Navy, Air Force and Army since 1993.

The feminization of American politics was advanced in the 1996 presidential election, when parties produced "feminized" conventions featuring soft, emotional, Oprah Winfrey-type orations and sentimental film clips of the presidential candidates. Both candidates were portrayed as soft, gentle, emotion-driven creatures sufficiently in touch with their feelings that all women across America would feel "comfortable" in their care. With 60 million female votes at stake, both parties pandered to America's "feminine" side.

There is no doubt in the media that the "man of today" is expected to be a touchy feely subspecies who bows to the radical feminist agenda. He is a staple of Hollywood, the television network sitcoms and movies, and the political pundits of talk shows. The feminization is becoming so noticeable that newspapers and magazines are picking up on it. For example, the *Washington Times* and *National Review* magazines combined to tell us that "behind the breezy celebration of 'guy stuff' in today's men's magazine lurks a crisis of confidence. What does it mean to be masculine in the 90s?" It is revealed that today's men's magazines (*Esquire, GQ, Men's Health, Men's Fitness, Men's Journal, Details, Maxim, Men's Perspective)*"are all geared to a new feminized man...." Some examples? The old masculine attitude toward personal appearance is disappearing. If memory serves, our fathers' acts of personal upkeep were mostly limited to shaving and putting on a tie. According to Lowry:

[I]t's hard to imagine [them] interested in articles on 'A Flat Belly for the Beach' (Verge), or the three new men's fragrances for the fall season (GQ), or even 'The New Fall Suit' (Esquire). But somewhere along the line men became less concerned with being strong and silent, and more worried about making themselves pretty.

Indeed the feminization of American culture is nearly completed. And the last bastion of male domination, the U.S. military, is under assault. If this "feminization" trend were driven only by radical feminists seeking to pull down a perceived male-dominated hierarchy, there would be more hope that the cycles of history would move America toward a stable accommodation between men and women. But the drive is deeper, and it will not be satisfied by any accommodation. The radical feminists have embraced and been embraced by the wider and deeper movement of cultural Marxism. For dedicated Marxists, the strategy is to attack at every point where an apparent disparity leaves a potential constituency of "oppressed" persons – in this case women, who are the largest of all constituencies. Cultural Marxists, men and women, are making the most of it, and the theory developed by the Frankfurt School provides the ideology.

The Frankfurt School theorized that the authoritarian personality is a product of the patriarchal family. This idea is in turn directly connected to Engels's *The Origins of the Family, Private Property and the State,* which promotes matriarchy. Furthermore, it was Karl Marx who wrote in *The Communist Manifesto* about the radical notion of a "community of women." He also, in 1845, wrote disparagingly in his *The German Ideology* of the idea that the family was the basic unit of society.

The concept of the "authoritarian personality" is not just to be interpreted primarily as a model for the conduct of warfare against prejudice as such. It is a handbook for psychological warfare against the American male, to render him unwilling to defend traditional beliefs and values. In other words, the aim was to emasculate him. Undoubtedly the Institute for Social Research at Frankfurt University meant this, as it used the term "psychological techniques for changing personality."

The "authoritarian personality," studied in the 1940s and 1950s by American followers of the Frankfurt School, prepared the way for such psychological warfare against the male gender role. The aim was promoted by Herbert Marcuse and others under the guise of "women's liberation" and under the New Left movement in the 1960s. Evidence that psychological techniques for changing personality are intended to focus in particular on the emasculation of the American male has also been provided by Abraham Maslow, founder of "third force humanist psychology" and promoter of psychotherapeutic techniques in public school classrooms. 8 He wrote that "the next step in personal evolution is a transcendence of both masculinity and femininity to general humanness."

Cultural Marxist stalwarts apparently know exactly what they want to do and how they plan to do it. They have actually already succeeded in accomplishing much of their agenda.

How did this situation come about in American universities? Gertrude Himmelfarb has observed that it slipped past traditional academics almost unobserved until it was too late. It occurred so "quietly" that when they "looked up", postmodernism was upon them with a vengeance. "They were surrounded by such a tidal wave of faddish multicultural subjects such as radical feminism, deconstructed relativism as history and other courses" which undermine the perpetuation of Western civilization.10 Indeed, this tidal wave slipped by just as Antonio Gramsci and the Frankfurt School had envisioned – a quiet revolution that could not be resisted by force.

The Frankfurt School had devised the concept of designating the opponents of the Marxist cultural revolution as "authoritarian characters." According to available accounts:

There was a meeting of American scholars at a conference on religious and racial prejudice in 1944. Over the next five years, a Frankfurt School team under the direction of Max Horkheimer conducted in-depth social and psychological profiles of Americans under a project entitled "Studies of Prejudice." One of the results was a book entitled "The Authoritarian Personality" by Theodor Adorno, et al, that summarized one of the largest public opinion surveys ever undertaken in the United States. It was published in 1950, and conformed to the original Critical Theory in every respect. As a document which testified to the belief system of the Frankfurt School revolutionaries it was essentially anti-God, anti-Christian, anti-family, anti-nationalist, anti-patriot, anti-conservative, antihereditarian, anti-ethnocentric, anti-masculine, anti-tradition, and anti-morality. All of these are elements in critical theory.

"Cultural Marxism," as preached by the Frankfurt School alumni in the U.S., is being implemented by the elite Boomers. This has laid the foundation for and spurred the widely popular and destructive concepts of "affirmative action," "multiculturalism" and "diversity." One can't escape these terms today. They have grown from the study of anti-Semitism and discrimination by the Institute for Social Research during the 1940s and the systematic infusion of the language of "discrimination," "civil rights," 'women's rights," and other "minority rights" into American culture.

According to Raehn: Critical Theory as applied mass psychology has led to the deconstruction of gender in the American culture. Following Critical Theory, the distinction between masculinity and femininity will disappear. The traditional roles of the mothers and fathers are to be dissolved so that patriarchy will be ended. Children are not to be raised according to their biological genders and gender roles according to their biological differences. This reflects the Frankfurt School rationale for the disintegration of the traditional family.

Thus, one of the basic tenets of Critical Theory was the necessity to break down the traditional family. The Frankfurt School scholars preached:

Even a partial breakdown of parental authority in the family might tend to increase the readiness of a coming generation to accept social change.

The transformation of American culture envisioned by the cultural Marxists goes further than pursuing gender equality. Embodied in their agenda is "matriarchal theory," under which they purpose to transform American culture to be female-dominated. This is a direct throwback to Wilhelm Reich, a Frankfurt School member who considered matriarchal theory in psychoanalytic terms. In 1993, he wrote in "The Mass Psychology of Fascism" that matriarchy was the only genuine family type of "natural society."

Erich Fromm, another charter member of the Institute, was one of the most active advocates of matriarchal theory. Fromm was especially taken with the idea that all love and altruistic feelings were ultimately derived from the maternal love necessitated by the extended period of human pregnancy and postnatal care:

Love thus was not dependent on sexuality, as Freud had supposed. In fact, sex was more often tied to hatred and destruction. Masculinity and femininity were not reflections of "essential" sexual differences, as the romantics had thought. They were derived instead from differences in life functions, which were in part socially determined.

This dogma was a precedent for today's radical feminist pronouncements appearing in newspapers and in TV programs, including TV newscasts. For its promoters, male and female roles result from cultural indoctrination – an indoctrination carried out by the male patriarchy to the detriment of women.

Indeed, cultural Marxism has, in the 1990s, melded with radical feminism in the elite Boomer generation, that throwback to the dangerous Transcendentalists of the early 19th century. A cauldron of discontent is forming in our nation, a discontent which has the potential to dismantle American civilization.

Destructive criticism of primary elements of American culture inspired the 1960s counter-culture revolution. Idealistic Boomers coming of age strove to transform the prevailing culture into its opposites, in the spirit of social revolution. Now the elite Boomers are in positions of power, and they are working to destroy the nation's historic institutions. They aim to destroy as well the heritage we call "Western Civilization." Richard Bernstein has written in his book on multiculturalism, "the Marxist revolutionary process for the past several decades in America has centered on race and sex warfare rather than class warfare" as in earlier times.15 This reflects a scheme more total than economics to restructure American society. As the social revolutionaries readily proclaim, their purpose is to destroy the hegemony of white males. To accomplish this, all barriers to the introduction of more women and minorities throughout the "power structure" are to be brought down by all means available. Laws and lawsuits, intimidation, and demonizing of white males as racists and sexists are pursued through the mass media and the universities. The psycho–dynamic of the revolutionary process aim for psychic disempowerment – decapitation – of those who oppose.

Steve Forbes has emphasized: This country's founders recognized three primal values in the Declaration of Independence, and they ranked them properly: Life, liberty, and the pursuit of happiness.

Forbes observes that if the order of these fundamental human rights is switched – with happiness before liberty or liberty before life – we come to moral chaos and social anarchy.

This very condition is what Judge Robert Bork describes as "modern liberalism." He defines its characteristics as "'radical egalitarianism' (equality of outcomes rather than of opportunities) and 'radical individualism' (the drastic reduction of limit to personal gratification)."

Judge Bork also identifies radical feminism as "the most destructive and fanatical" element of this modern liberalism. He further describes radical feminism as "totalitarian in spirit."

Most Americans do not realize that they, through their institutions, are being led by social revolutionaries who think in terms of the continuing destruction of the existing social order in order to create a new one. The revolutionaries are New Age Elite Boomers. They now control the public institutions in the United States. Their "quiet" revolution, beginning with the counter-culture revolution of their youth, is nearing completion. A key, or even a dominant element because purportedly it represents that largest political and social constituency among their potential followers, is feminism. The Marxist movement in its "quiet" cultural latter-day phase is seemingly sweeping all before it. With its sway over the media, fully in the grip of feminism, it is hard to discern the stirrings of a counter-culture. Are the elite Boomers, the New Totalitarians, the most dangerous generation in America's history? William Strauss and Neil Howe suggest so, in their book *Generations: The History of America's Future – 1584 – 2069.* 19 James

Kurth writes: The United States itself has become a great power that opposes much of what was once thought of as Western Civilization, especially its cultural achievements and its social arrangements. The major American elites – those in power in politics, business, the media, and academia – now use American power, especially the "soft power" of information, communications, and popular entertainment, to displace Western Civilization not only in America but also in Europe.

Will American men, of every race, and more traditionalist women of every age and circumstances – who may well be a silent majority of their sex – rise to challenge Political Correctness? Or will American men continue in voluntary submission toward a future of peonage under a new American matriarchy? Would that be a precursor to a condition of anarchy, and an end to America's experiment with democracy? It may well be that the fate of American civilization depends on American men steadfastly resisting Politically Correct feminism. Even more, they must resourcefully oppose the wider grip of Political Correctness, the cultural Marxism for which radical feminism is only one avenue of attack.

Bibliogrpahy

Ambedkar, B.R.: *Annihilation of Caste*. Bombay: Bharat Bhushan Press, 1937.

Asthana, M.D. and Pedro, M.: *Towards Hunger Free India: Agenda and Imperatives*, New Delhi: Manohar, 2001.

Baily, F.G.: *Caste and Economic Frontier*. Bombay : Oxford University Press, 1960.

Bakshi, P. M.: *Supreme Court on Mandal Commission Caste, 1992*. New Delhi: Orient Law House, 1993.

Bayly, S.: *Caste, Society and Politics in India*. Cambridge: Cambridge University Press, 2000.

Beteille, A.: *Caste, Class and Power*. Bombay: Oxford University Press, 1963.

Beteille, A.: *Castes : Old and New*. Bombay : Asia Publishing House. 1969.

Beteille, A.: *Inequality among Men*. Bombay: Oxford University Press, 1977.

Bhalla, G.S. and Hazell, P.: *Rural Employment and Poverty*. Economic and Political Weekly, 2003.

Bird, K.: *Chronic Poverty and Understanding Intra-household Differentiation*. CPRC, Delhi, Mimeo, 2002.

Briggs, G. W.: *The Chamars*, Calcutta : Association Press, 1920.

Brown, M.M.: *Human Development Report*. New Delhi: Oxford University Press, 1999.

Chadha, G.K. and Sharma, Alakh: *Growth, Employment and Poverty: Change and Continuity in Rural India*. Delhi: Vikas Publishing House, 1997.

Chandrasekhar, C.P. and Ghosh, Jayati: *The Market That Failed: A Decade of Neoliberal Economic Reforms in India*. New Delhi: Left Word Books, 2002.

Chaudhuri, P.: *The Indian Economy: Poverty and Development*. New Delhi: Vikas Publishing House, Pvt. Ltd., 1992.

Cox, O.C.: 1948. *Caste, Class and Race*. New York: Garden City.

Dandekar, V.M.and Rath, N.: *Poverty in India*. Bombay: Indian School of Political Economy, 1971.

Dantwala, M.L.: *Poverty in India :Then and Now 1870-1970*. Bombay: Macmillan India, 1973.

Desai, A.R.: *Agrarian Struggle in India After Independence*. Delhi: Oxford University Press, 1986.

Galanter, Marc: *Competing Equalities.* Oxford University Press, 1991.

Ghurye, G.S.: *Caste and Class in India.* Bombay: Popular Book Depot, 1957.

Gupta, D.: *Social Stratification.* New Delhi: Oxford University Press, 1997.

Haq, M. : *The Poverty Curtain.* New York: Columbia University Press, 1976.

Hickey, S.: *The Politics of Chronic Poverty.* IPDM, January, Mimeo, 2002.

Isaacs, H.R.: *India's Ex-Untouchables.* New York: John Day and Company, 1965.

Kamble, N.D.: *Poverty Within Poverty.* New Delhi: Sterling Publishers Pvt. Ltd, 1979.

Ketkar, S.V. : *The History of Caste in India.* Ithaca: Taylor and Carpenter, 1909.

Kolenda, P.: *Caste in Contemporary India.* Jaipur and New Delhi: Rawat Publication, 1997.

Kurien, C.T.: *Dynamics of Rural Transformation.* New Delhi: Orient Longman, 1989.

Leach, E.R.: *Aspects of Castes in South India.* Cambridge University Press, 1962.

Myrdal, G.: *Asian Drama: An Inquiry Into the Poverty Of Nations.* New York: Pantheon, 1968.

Pal, R. M. and Bhargava, G.S.: *Human Rights of Dalits: Social Violation.* New Delhi: Gyan Publishing House, 1999.

Parikh, Kirit and Radhakrishna, S.R.: *India Development Report.* New Delhi: Oxford University Press, 2002.

Rao, C.H.H. and Hans, L.: *Economic Reform and Poverty Alleviation in India.* New Delhi: Sage Publications, 1996.

Rao, M.S.A. and Frankel, F.R.: *Dominance and State Power in Modern India.* New Delhi: Oxford University Press, 1989.

Sen. A. and Jean, D.O.: *Poverty and Famine, Hunger and Public Action in India: Economic Development and Social Opportunity.* New Delhi: Oxford University Press, 1999.

Sharma, B.D.: *Whither Tribal Areas?* New Delhi: Sahyog Pustak Kutir, 1996.

Shariff, A.: *India: Human Development report.* NCAER, New Delhi: Oxford University Press, 1999.

Srinivas, M.N.: *Caste in Modern India.* Bombay: Asia Publishing House, 1964.

Zinkin, T.: *Caste Today.* London: Oxford University Press, 1963.

Index

□□□